Strange Monsters

of the

Pacific Northwest

Michael Newton

4880 Lower Valley Road, Atglen, PA 19310 USA

Other Schiffer Books by Michael Newton:
Strange Kentucky Monsters, 978-0-7643-3440-5, $14.99
Strange Indiana Monsters, 0-7643-2608-2, $12.95
Strange California Monsters, 978-0-7643-3336-1, $14.99

Other Schiffer Books on Related Subjects:
Pacific Northwest Haunts, 978-0-7643-3436-8, $16.99
Washington's Haunted Hotspots, 978-0-7643-3277-7, $14.99
Lost Treasure Ships of the Oregon Coast, 978-0-7643-3197-8, $14.99
Haunts of Western Oregon, 978-0-7643-3224-1, $14.99

Schiffer Books are available at special discounts for bulk purchases for sales promotions or premiums. Special editions, including personalized covers, corporate imprints, and excerpts can be created in large quantities for special needs. For more information contact the publisher:

Published by Schiffer Publishing Ltd.
4880 Lower Valley Road
Atglen, PA 19310
Phone: (610) 593-1777; Fax: (610) 593-2002
E-mail: Info@schifferbooks.com

For the largest selection of fine reference books on this and related subjects, please visit our web site at:
www.schifferbooks.com
We are always looking for people to write books on new and related subjects. If you have an idea for a book please contact us at the above address.

This book may be purchased from the publisher.
Include $5.00 for shipping.
Please try your bookstore first.
You may write for a free catalog.

In Europe, Schiffer books are distributed by
Bushwood Books
6 Marksbury Ave.
Kew Gardens
Surrey TW9 4JF England
Phone: 44 (0) 20 8392 8585; Fax: 44 (0) 20 8392 9876
E-mail: info@bushwoodbooks.co.uk
Website: www.bushwoodbooks.co.uk5

Copyright © 2010 by Michael Newton
Unless otherwise noted, all photos are the property of the author.
Library of Congress Control Number: 2010940505

All rights reserved. No part of this work may be reproduced or used in any form or by any means—graphic, electronic, or mechanical, including photocopying or information storage and retrieval systems—without written permission from the publisher.
The scanning, uploading and distribution of this book or any part thereof via the Internet or via any other means without the permission of the publisher is illegal and punishable by law. Please purchase only authorized editions and do not participate in or encourage the electronic piracy of copyrighted materials.
"Schiffer," "Schiffer Publishing Ltd. & Design," and the "Design of pen and inkwell" are registered trademarks of Schiffer Publishing Ltd.

Designed by *Danielle D. Farmer*
Cover Design by *Bruce Waters*
Type set in Bard Regular/ New Baskerville BT/ Amorinda/Souvenir Lt BT

ISBN: 978-0-7643-3622-5
Printed in USA

Dedication

For Ivan Sanderson

Acknowledgments

Thanks to Jody Gripp, at the Tacoma Public Library; to Kimberly Kuhn, at the Albany Public Library; to Chief Criminal Deputy Gene Seiber, Lewis County (WA) Sheriff's Office; once again to Dinah Roseberry at Schiffer Books, for her continuing support; and to my wife Heather for her priceless assistance.

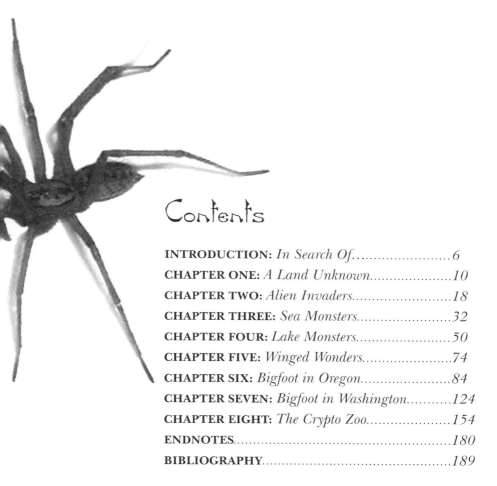

Contents

Introduction

Map of Oregon counties. *Courtesy of U.S. Census Bureau.*

Map of Washington counties. Courtesy of U.S. Census Bureau.

In Search Of ...

Nearly two hundred years ago, in 1812, French naturalist Georges Cuvier (1769-1832) declared that the great days of zoological discovery were done. With fewer than 6,000 species of animals known to science worldwide, he declared, "There is little hope of discovering new species of large quadrupeds." As for huge, unidentified creatures reported at sea, Cuvier wrote, "I hope nobody will ever seriously look for them in nature; one could as well search for the animals of Daniel or for the beast of the Apocalypse."[1]

Today, we know that Cuvier was wrong. He lived to witness the discovery of the American tapir (1819), the whale shark (1828), and three new species of whales. By 1850 the number of known living species had increased to 108,897. In 1911, it topped half a million and then doubled again by 1946. In 2007, published estimates of Earth's animal population varied from three to thirty million living species.[2]

Despite that relentless advance in knowledge, some modern Cuviers still claim that no new species of any significant size remain undiscovered today. While it is unquestionably true that most recent discoveries involve relatively small creatures, the list of twenty-first century surprises includes the world's largest known spider (*Heteropoda maxima*) in Laos, a nine-foot catfish in Thailand; three new lemurs in Madagascar; and a nine-foot spitting cobra in Kenya. Dutch zoologist Marc van Roosmalen, working in Brazil, has personally discovered six new species of monkeys, a giant peccary, a dwarf manatee, a dwarf porcupine, a black dwarf lowland tapir, and a new brocket deer.[3]

Our world, it seems, is not as well-explored as some "experts" believe.

In December 2002, spokesmen for Conservation International announced that forty-six percent of Earth's land surface — some 26.3 million square miles — still qualified as wilderness, a label applied to regions 3,800 square miles or larger, with seventy percent or more of their original vegetation intact and fewer than ten human dwellers per square mile. Two months later, in February 2003, satellite photos revealed 1,000 previously unmapped islands in the Indonesian archipelago. Of that nation's 18,000 known islands, only one-third are inhabited by humans. Whiskeytown Falls, a four hundred-foot waterfall located in northern California's Whiskeytown National Recreation Area, was not discovered until autumn of 2003.[4]

Water covers seventy-one percent of our planet, and our knowledge of what transpires beneath its surface is spotty, at best. In October 2003, Jesse Ausubel, director of the ongoing Census of Marine Life (CML), told BBC News, "Some ninety-five percent of the ocean is still unexplored biologically. We know more about the surface of the moon." During the first three years of a projected ten-year global survey, CML researchers catalogued 15,304 marine species, including five hundred previously unknown to science. Meanwhile, in June 2003, scientists aboard the research vessel *Tangaroa* reported discovery of four hundred new species during a four-week survey of the waters off northern New Zealand.[5]

While biologists celebrate the accidental discovery of previously unknown species, other researchers pursue creatures well known from legends, folklore, and eyewitness sightings, whose existence is denied by mainstream science. Since the late 1950s, that pursuit has been labeled cryptozoology, which is the study of "hidden" animals. These animals, often called cryptids, are known in popular jargon as "monsters." Some deserve that description, based on their size, ferocity, or freakish form, but others seem innocuous.

Cryptozoologists investigate rumored creatures in four broad categories. As described by author Chad Arment, the categories include:

1. Animals resembling known living species, but with physiological differences, such as pygmy elephants, blue tigers, or 100-foot anacondas.

2. Apparent members of known living species found far outside their normal geographical range, such as kangaroos or "black panthers" in North America.

3. Creatures resembling known extinct or extirpated species, such as thylacines in Australia and dinosaurs reported from Third World jungles.

4. Animals resembling no known species, either living or extinct, such as Washington's "Batsquatch."[6]

Strange Monsters of the Pacific Northwest reviews the current state of cryptozoological research in Oregon and Washington. It includes eight chapters, arranged topically. *Chapter One* surveys the region as a potential cryptid habitat, examining the likelihood that unknown creatures may share the region with its 10.3 million human occupants. *Chapter Two* provides examples of "misplaced" animals recognized by science in the Pacific Northwest — and some that are persistently ignored. *Chapter Three* details legends and sightings of monsters at sea, from prehistoric times to the present. *Chapter Four* pursues freshwater phantoms said to infest lakes and rivers. *Chapter Five* collects reports of unknown flying creatures. *Chapters Six* and *Seven* investigate the ape-like creature popularly known as Bigfoot or Sasquatch, and *Chapter Eight* concludes the tour with reports of creatures that fit no of other category — a menagerie of bizarre and "impossible" beings that appear with surprising frequency across the Pacific Northwest. Our search may prove unsettling and, for some, even frightening. If it upsets hidebound dogmatic thinking in the process, so much the better... because a world of mystery awaits us.

Chapter One

A Land Unknown

   No one knows precisely when the first specimens of *Homo sapiens* set foot in the Pacific Northwest. Sage bark sandals found near Oregon's Fort Rock Cave by archaeologist Luther Cressman in 1938, date back some 13,200 years, while human and animal bones recovered in present-day Washington are roughly the same age. Other signs of human habitation date from 9000 B.C.E. in Washington, and from 8000 B.C.E. along the lower Columbia River, as well as in Oregon's western valleys and around coastal estuaries. Archaeologists have identified 125 distinct aboriginal tribes dwelling in the Pacific Northwest before the first European explorers arrived. Major tribes included the Bannock, Cayuse, Chasta, Chinook, Kalapuya, Klamath, Lummi, Makah, Molalla, Nez Perce, Okanogan, Palouse, Quileute, Quinault, Snohomish, Spokane, Takelma, Umpqua, Wenatchee, and Yakima.[1]

The first Spanish conquistadors arrived in 1565, having crossed the vast Pacific Ocean from the Philippines. Nehalem tribal tales recount the wreck of the *San Francisco Xavier* on Oregon's coast, in 1707, but Juan Pérez was first to land officially, in 1774, exploring the coastline from Oregon northward to present-day British Columbia. Juan Francisco de la Bodega y Quadra and Bruno de Heceta were next to arrive, in the Santiago and Sonora. Heceta found the mouths of the Columbia and Quinault Rivers, but could not proceed further along inland. He claimed the land for Spain, from the Columbia to Russia's scattered outposts, farther north.[2]

British explorer James Cook was next on the scene, in 1778, surveying Oregon's coastline in a futile search for the fabled Northwest Passage. He sighted Cape Flattery, at the entrance to the Strait of Juan de Fuca, but further exploration of the straits awaited Captain Charles Barkley's arrival in 1789. Captain George Vancouver sailed from England in April 1791 and met American Captain Robert Gray off Oregon's coast a year later. Gray named the Columbia River after his ship, and lent his own name to Washington's Grays Harbor, while Vancouver navigated the Strait of Juan de Fuca on April 29 and explored Puget Sound on June 4, naming it for one of his lieutenants.[3]

Political wrangling over the Northwest had already begun, in 1789, when Spaniards seized ships owned by Englishman John Meares on Nootka Island, near present-day Vancouver Island, B.C. The "Nootka crisis" threatened war, but conflict was avoided by ratification of the Nootka Conventions, signed by diplomats of Spain and Britain between October 1790 and January 1794. While Spain did not forsake its claims in the Northwest, it permitted international trade from Nootka Island and abandoned Fort San Miguel, built on the island in 1789.[4]

"Range Enough for Elephants and Lions"

The United States, just eleven years old when the third Nootka Convention was signed, still had no territorial claims in the Pacific Northwest, but future president Thomas Jefferson followed exploration of the region while living in France, during 1785-89. King Louis XVI planned a "scientific mission" to the region in 1785, but bad weather stalled the French party in Australia during 1788, and it proceeded no farther. Meanwhile, John Ledyard, who had sailed with Captain Cook, approached Jefferson in 1786 with plans to walk across Siberia, sail for the Northwest in a Russian vessel, then hike across North America to the East Coast. That expedition failed when Empress Catherine the Great had Ledyard jailed in Siberia and deported to Poland.[5]

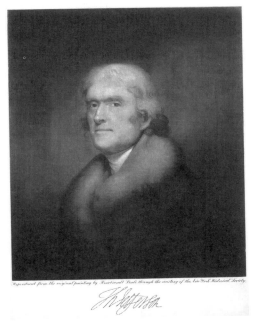

Reproduced from the original painting by Rembrandt Peale through the courtesy of the New-York Historical Society

Thomas Jefferson believed the North American interior might harbor prehistoric creatures. *Courtesy of the Library of Congress.*

Still, Jefferson maintained his interest in the far-off region. In March 1897, four years before he occupied the White House, Jefferson attended the inauguration of President John Adams in Philadelphia. While there, on March 10, he delivered a speech to the American Philosophical Society, as its newly-elected president. Jefferson's subject was the recent discovery of large fossil bones, unearthed in a West Virginia mine. The relics included part of an "arm" and "hand," including huge curved claws, which prompted Jefferson to dub the creature *Megalonyx* or "Great-Claw."[6]

Unaware that the first remains of his Megalonyx had been found near Buenos Aires, Argentina, in 1789 and identified by Georges Cuvier as the ground sloth *Megatherium* in 1796, Jefferson hypothesized that the beast might be a giant cat. "Let us say then," he suggested, "what we may safely say, that he was more than three times as large as the lion: that he stood as pre-eminently at the head of the column of clawed animals as the mammoth stood at that of the elephant, rhinoceros and hippopotamus: and that he may have been as formidable an antagonist to the mammoth as the lion to the elephant."[6]

In fact, Jefferson suggested, the cat might still survive in North America's vast wilderness. "In the present interior of our continent," he told his audience, "there is surely space and range enough for elephants and lions, if in that climate they could subsist; and for the mammoth and megalonyxes who may subsist there. Our entire ignorance of the immense country to the West and North-West, and of its contents, does not authorise (sic) us to say what it does not contain."[7]

As president, in April 1803, Jefferson executed the Louisiana Purchase, acquiring 820,000 square miles of wilderness from France at a cost of $18.29 per square mile. The new territory included all or part of fourteen present U.S. states and two Canadian provinces, but still left the Pacific Northwest up for grabs. To remedy that situation, Jefferson asked Congress for $2,500 to finance exploration of the region, explaining that "[t]he river Missouri, and Indians inhabiting it, are not as well known as rendered desirable by their connection with the Mississippi, and consequently with us.... An intelligent officer, with ten or twelve chosen men...might explore the whole line, even to the Western Ocean."[8]

Corps of Discovery

Jefferson chose twenty-eight-year-old Captain Meriwether Lewis to lead that expedition, dubbed the Corps of Discovery. On June 20, 1803, Jefferson wrote to Lewis, informing him that "the object of your mission is to explore the Missouri River, and such principal stream of it as by its course and communication with the waters of the Pacific Ocean whether the Columbia, Oregon, Colorado or any other river may offer the most direct and practicable water communication across this continent for the purposes of commerce." In broad terms, the party was ordered to study the Northwest's native tribes, flora and fauna, geology, and to evaluate any potential obstacles that the British or French inhabitants posed to further American expansion.[9]

Lewis chose thirty-two-year-old Virginian William Clark as his second-in-command, departing from Pittsburgh on August 31 with seven soldiers, a river pilot, and "three young men on trial." The Corps of Discovery grew to include thirty-three hearty souls by the time it left Camp Dubois, near modern-day Hartford, Illinois, to penetrate terra incognita on May 14, 1804. The round-trip spanned twenty-eight months, climaxing with the party's return to St. Louis on September 23, 1806. Expedition member Patrick Gass published the first account of Lewis and Clark's adventure in 1807, but another seven years elapsed before an official report was released.[10]

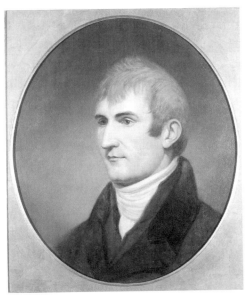

Meriwether Lewis died under suspicious circumstances after exploring the Pacific Northwest. *Courtesy of Library of Congress.*

By that time, Lewis was already dead, under circumstances best described as curious. Appointed by Jefferson to serve as governor of the Louisiana Territory, residing in St. Louis, Lewis was a fair administrator, but he angered local politicians by obstructing their land-grabs in the territory under his control. Summoned to answer their complaints, he left St. Louis for Washington, D.C. in September 1809, but never completed the journey. Stopping at an inn some seventy miles outside Nashville, Tennessee, on November 10, Lewis was found dead the next morning, his wrists slashed and body punctured by multiple gunshots. The innkeeper's wife described Lewis acting strangely during dinner, later pacing in his room and talking to himself, as if addressing a lawyer. She heard gunfire in the night, and someone calling for help, later claiming that she peered through a slit in the door and saw Lewis crawling across the floor. Nonetheless, she went to sleep and left her servants to discover him, beyond help, near sunrise. His death was ruled a suicide, with William Clark and Thomas Jefferson concurring, but Lewis's family suspected murder. Years later, a court of inquiry considered charging the innkeeper with homicide, but dropped the case for lack of solid evidence.[11]

Aside from his political quarrels in St. Louis, why would someone murder Lewis? More than a century after the fact, author Eric Penz published a novel, *Cryptid*, theorizing that Lewis was silenced by forces intent on suppressing the Corps of Discovery's most sensational find — a previously unknown species whose existence surpassed Jefferson's speculation on living mammoths and Megalonyxes, threatening the very foundation of biblical Creationism.[12]

William Clark, meanwhile, survived and prospered, first as governor of the Missouri Territory from 1813 to 1820 and then as America's Superintendent of Indian Affairs from 1822 until his death in St. Louis on September 1, 1838. If he had any guilty knowledge of his partner's "suicide," Clark took it to his grave.[13]

The Modern Northwest

American acquisition of the Pacific Northwest was a gradual process, spanning several decades. The Anglo-American Treaty of 1818 established U.S. control below the 49th parallel while Spain relinquished its claims in the Adams-Onís Treaty of 1819. Two years later, however, Russia claimed primacy through the Ukase (proclamation) of 1821 while London's Parliament simultaneously imposed the laws of Upper Canada on British subjects residing below the 49th parallel, in what it called "Columbia Country." Separate treaties with Britain and the U.S. erased Russia's claims during 1824-25, but conflict with Britain persisted until the Oregon Treaty was ratified in June 1846. Even then, local politicians schemed to make the Northwest a separate nation, until Congress formally established the Oregon Territory (including modern-day Washington, Idaho, and parts of eastern Montana and Wyoming) in August 1848. The northern half of that block became Washington Territory February 1853. Oregon attained statehood in February 1859, followed by Washington in November 1889.[14]

Lewis and Clark's expedition laid the groundwork for exploration and settlement of the Pacific Northwest, producing 140 maps, while documenting more than one hundred animal species and 176 species of plants. As finally established, Oregon spanned 98,446 square miles and ranks ninth in size among America's states, while Washington comprised 71,342 square miles and ranks eighteenth. In terms of population, by 2008 Washington ranked thirteenth among the fifty states, with 6,549,224 year-round residents (88.6 persons per square mile), while Oregon ranked twenty-seventh with 3,790,060 (35.6 per square mile).[15]

Those statistics, however, sketch a distorted picture of the Northwest's surviving wilderness. Fifty-seven percent of Oregon's population resides in Portland and its suburbs, while 49.8 percent of all Washingtonians live in or around Seattle. Adjusted to eliminate those city-dwellers, Oregon's population density drops to sixteen and a half persons per square mile. Washington's declines to forty-six per square mile.[16]

However, even those figures stop short of presenting the true picture. Within Oregon, 44,984 square miles are covered by forest, and another 2,384 square miles by water. Washington's corresponding figures include 33,228 square miles of woodlands and 4,756 square miles underwater. Between the two states, twenty national forests cover 50,120 square miles. More than a dozen major mountain ranges carve the Northwest landscape, and Washington has more glaciers than all of the other forty-seven contiguous states combined. Oregon boasts more abandoned ghost towns than any other U.S. state, and its Hells Canyon is the deepest river gorge in North America.[17]

Clearly, then, the Pacific Northwest is neither densely settled nor fully explored in comparison to other American states. While early explorers generally followed sea coasts and rivers, charting visible mountains and other obvious landmarks from a distance, modern cartographers rely primarily on aerial and satellite photography, coupled with software including computer-aided design, geographic information systems, and specialized illustration programs.[18] None of those methods reliably penetrate forests, much less lakes and rivers. And, as we saw from the example of California's Whiskeytown Falls, even major geological formations may remain undiscovered to the present day. What, then, do modern maps tell us about the animals living within a given area?

Thus far, no evidence supports Thomas Jefferson's suggestion that living mammoths may roam the Pacific Northwest, but the region has produced many other zoological mysteries. Our quest begins with well-known animals from other states and continents that surface in the region to confound ecologists and offer hope to students of cryptozoology.

Chapter Two

Alien Invaders

In 1913, while studying wildlife of the Pacific Northwest for the U.S. Department of Agriculture's Bureau of Biological Survey, Washington naturalist Theophilus Scheffer made a startling discovery. Examining a captive mountain beaver (*Aplodontia rufa*) — which, in fact, is neither a beaver nor a mountain-dweller, but the world's most primitive rodent — Scheffer spied a previously unknown flea that measured .31 inches in length. Subsequently named *Hystrichopsylla schefferi* in Scheffer's honor, the insect proved to be Earth's largest and most primitive flea, with females growing to .47 inches. The schefferi lives only on mountain beavers, a curious pairing that still intrigues entomologists.[1]

As we shall soon discover, half-inch fleas are not the Northwest's strangest creatures — and, as natives found, they do not qualify anywhere else on Earth as "alien." While fascinating (or repugnant), H. scheffeři does not figure in the quest for out-of-place exotic or invasive species: "OOPS" for short, to some researchers. Happily, for those who treasure natural anomalies, the region has no shortage of intruders.

Invertebrates

The vast majority of Earth's known animals are invertebrates: creatures without backbones. Their eleven recognized phyla include the ubiquitous insects, with 1.1 million classified species and estimates of undiscovered species ranging from six to fifty million.[2] Other common examples include worms, jellyfish, arachnids, crustaceans and mollusks.

No comprehensive census of invertebrates exists for the Pacific Northwest, but known lowland species of insects and spiders exceed 15,000, while a 1996 survey of marine invertebrates listed nearly 4,000 species offshore.[3] Official agencies, such as the Oregon and Washington Departments of Fish and Wildlife (ODFW and WDFW), generally ignore invertebrates unless a species is endangered or invaders pose a threat to the ecology.

A list published by the United States Geological Survey names 139 aquatic invertebrates introduced by humans to the Pacific Northwest. They include twenty-three annelids (segmented worms), eight bryozoans (tiny colonial animals resembling, but unrelated to, corals), eleven coelenterates (corals and jellies), thirty-nine crustaceans (including shellfish), forty-six mollusks, seven tunicates (sea squirts), two entoprocts (tentacled filter feeders), and three sponges.[4]

Of those 139 species, only six appear on the ODFW's list of "ten most unwanted invaders." Those include the quagga mussel (*Dreissena rostriformis bugensis*), the zebra mussel (*D. polymorpha*), the New Zealand mud snail (*Potomopyrgus antipodarum*), the red swamp crayfish (*Procambarus clarkii*), the rusty crayfish (*Orconectes rusticus*), and the Chinese mitten crab (*Eriocheir sinensis*).[5]

Terrestrial invertebrates that spark concern among state wildlife officers and conservationists include the gypsy moth (*Lymantria dispar*), a Eurasian species at large since 1868 in North America, where it endangers hardwood forests; the hemlock woolly adelgid (*Adelges tsugae*), a native of East Asia that imperils hemlock trees; fruit flies

Tegenaria gigantea is the Pacific Northwest's largest exotic arachnid. *Courtesy of U.S. Dept. of Fish & Wildlife.*

(*Drosophilidae spp.*), which were accidentally imported from Europe and North Africa to devour various fruit crops in colonized regions; European yellow jackets (*Vespula germanica*), whose painful stings in swarms may prove lethal; Asian long-horned beetles (*Anoplophora glabripennis*), who destroy elm, maple, poplar and willow trees; dangerously venomous brown spiders (*Family Loxoscelide*); and various species of aggressive house spiders (*Genus Tegenaria*), including a "giant" species (*T. gigantea*), whose leg span ranges from one to three inches.[6]

Both professional scientists and amateur researchers have much to learn about alien invertebrates, but they do not generally concern cryptozoologists.

Freshwater Fish

While no two sources perfectly agree, research conducted for this volume identified 140 known species of freshwater fish in the Pacific Northwest. That census includes seventy-six species found both in Oregon and Washington, forty-nine found in Oregon alone, and fifteen found only in Washington. Confusion surrounds the total number of exotic or invasive species, with Oregon's Invasive Species Council listing thirteen freshwater fish for the Beaver State, while the U.S. Geological Survey names sixty-two for the Northwest at large (forty-seven native transplants and fifteen exotics).[7]

Identified foreign invaders include the Amur goby (*Rhinogobius brunneus*), brown trout (*Salmo trutta*), cherry salmon (*Oncorhynchus masou*), common carp (*Cyprinus carpio*), giant gourami (*Osphronemus gorami*), goldfish (*Carassius auratus*), grass carp (*Ctenopharyngodon idella*), Oriental weatherfish (*Misgurnus anguillicaudatus*), tench (*Tinca tinca*), two species of sailfin catfish (*Pterygoplichthys sp.*), red-bellied pacu (*Piaractus brachypomus*) and another unidentified pacu species (*Colossoma or Piaractus sp.*), red piranha (*Pygocentrus nattereri*) and an unidentified piranha species (*Pygocentrus or Serrasalmus sp.*).[8]

Curiously, the federal list of invasive species omits one that concerns Pacific Northwest wildlife officials most: the northern snakehead (*Channa argus*), a native of East Asia confirmed as present in the U.S. since 2000.

Red piranhas have been found in Oregon waters. *Courtesy of the U.S. National Oceanic and Atmospheric Association.*

The subject of four horror films during 2003-06, snakeheads commonly reach four feet in length and weigh fifteen pounds. Their long jaws bristle with razor-sharp teeth, used to consume other fish, crustaceans and amphibians. The northern snakehead also possesses a bifurcate ventral aorta that permits it to breathe on land, as well as under water. Young members of the species may wriggle overland, though ichthyologists deny that adults are able to come ashore.[9]

Amphibians

The Pacific Northwest claims thirty-seven amphibian species, including twenty-four salamanders and thirteen frogs. Oregon has twenty-six native species, while Washington harbors twenty-seven (including two salamander species that appear nowhere else on Earth). Two frog species — the American bullfrog (*Rana catesbeiana*) and the green frog (*R. clamitans*)

— are domestic transplants, introduced by humans to the Northwest from their normal ranges in the eastern and southern United States.[10]

Of the two outsiders, only the American bullfrog is considered a significant pest. Introduced to the Northwest as a human food source in 1895, R. catesbeiana soon conquered its new environment, where it preys on smaller frogs, young turtles, fish, and snakes. Today, wildlife officials rank it among Oregon's "Ten Most Unwanted Invaders," and eradication efforts persist, including capture of adult specimens and mass-destruction of eggs skimmed from ponds. Thus far, speedy re-colonization of cleared areas has defeated all bids to extirpate the invaders.[11]

Reptiles

Wildlife officials recognize forty-four reptile species breeding in the Northwest, including twenty-one snakes, fifteen lizards, and eight turtles. Oregon claims twenty-seven native reptile species while Washington boasts twenty-five (none exclusive to the Evergreen State).[12]

The eastern snapping turtle ranks among Washington's "Ten Most Unwanted" invasive species. *Courtesy of U.S. Dept. of Fish & Wildlife.*

Humans have introduced four reptile species presently established in the wild — two lizards and two turtles. They include the plateau striped whiptail lizard (*Aspidoscelis velox*); the common wall lizard (*Podarcis muralis*), found only on Vancouver Island; the eastern snapping turtle

Nile monitors may reach seven feet in length. *Courtesy of the U.S. National Oceanic and Atmospheric Association.*

(*Chelydra serpentina serpentina*); and the red-eared slider (*Trachemys scripta elegans*). Possession of snapping turtles is banned by law in Washington, where wildlife officials rank Chelydra serpentina among the state's "Ten Most Unwanted" invaders. Females produce an average twenty to forty eggs per year, with a record count of 104, while competing with native species for food and nesting sites.[13]

A more unusual reptilian visitor to the Pacific Northwest is the Nile monitor (*Varanus niloticus*), an African lizard that boasts a record length of seven feet 11-3/4", with recorded weights above twenty-two pounds. Nile monitors dine on any smaller species they can catch, deemed potentially dangerous to humans and their domestic pets based on size and defensive demeanor. Nonetheless, they are frequently sold as exotic pets and have established breeding colonies in southern Florida. Federal authorities predict "Nile monitors that are temperate-adapted will eventually spread throughout Florida and the Gulf States, and further north along the Atlantic Coast at least as far north as Georgia and, perhaps, the Carolinas. Their presence in the United States presents a cause for serious concern."[14]

That warning might seem to exclude the Pacific Northwest, but a six-foot Nile monitor surfaced in Grants Pass, Oregon, on September 8, 2008, gracing the yard of Ryan Nelson's home. Nelson called the owners of a local exotic pet store, MB Reptiles, to capture the lizard alive. Police logically suspected that the monitor was an escaped or abandoned pet, but its presumed negligent owner remains unidentified.[15]

More surprising still are the reports of crocodilians at large in the Northwest, far from their normal range in Dixie and Third World jungles. Worldwide, the order Crocodilia includes three families of large amphibious reptiles, with twenty-five known living species. Those include thirteen crocodiles, eight caimans, two alligators, the gharial, and false gharial — none of which should normally exist in the Pacific Northwest.[16]

That said, it cannot be denied that crocodilians have surfaced repeatedly throughout the region, for over forty years. The first documented case dates from 1967, when two supposed alligators were seen chasing ducks at the south end of Lake Washington, below Mercer Island. No further details are available, and since the reptiles were not captured, they cannot be identified conclusively as American alligators (*Alligator mississippiensis*).[17]

Nineteen years later, in June 1986, two more alien reptiles bobbed up in Seattle's 259-acre Green Lake. These were captured, and proved to be caimans of uncertain species (sub-family *Caimaninae*). The larger of them measured thirty inches long. Soon afterward, a caiman of similar size eluded hunters at Kirkland's Houghton Beach, on Lake Washington. Animal Control teams stalked a three-foot specimen at Redmond's Cottage Lake in 1992, but failed to secure it.[18]

Flash-forward another nine years, to summer 2001, when residents of Willamina, Oregon, reported ducks disappearing from Willamina Pond in Huddleston Park. Soon, *Salem Statesman Journal* reporter Henry Miller got a call claiming an alligator sighting at the pond. April Wooden, co-founder of Willamina's Museum of Local History, says a city employee spied the gator by night, its eyes reflecting his flashlight beam. Fishermen weighed in with sightings while a hastily erected sign warned swimmers:

Alligators and related crocodilians occasionally surface in the Pacific Northwest. *Courtesy of U.S. Dept. of Fish & Wildlife.*

"CAUTION — Alligator in pond. If seen call 911 or City Hall." ODFW biologists baited traps with raw meat and dead fish, but caught nothing. In time, the excitement faded.[19]

Until June 16, 2005, when the action shifted to Medford, 197 miles south of Willamina. This time, the reptile at large was a verified pet — an American alligator named Usal, which escaped from owner Paul Sabin while Sabin was distracted caring for a sick Burmese python. The 42-inch gator was recaptured after three days on the loose, subsequently sent to live at a Colorado sanctuary for exotic reptiles.[20]

Five days after Usal's capture in Medford, another crocodilian appeared in Eugene, Oregon, 122 miles farther north. This time, the culprit was a four-foot caiman of undisclosed species, spotted in a local resident's driveway. Officers from the Lane County Animal Regulation Authority snared the caiman, which supervisor Mike Wellington described as "pretty dangerous." The caiman's owner, who had left town on vacation, heard the bulletin and raced home to reclaim his pet, dubbed "Tank."[21]

Three weeks later, a similar case produced criminal charges in Puyallup, Washington. WDFW officers hauled a four-foot-long caiman from a water retention pond, then traced its owner and confiscated a second caiman from his home. While Seattle's KIRO-TV reported that the first caiman had escaped captivity "about a week ago," state authorities later charged its unnamed owner with "releasing deleterious wildlife."[22]

Birds

The Pacific Northwest is rich in avian species, including 456 recognized in Oregon and 467 in Washington. Of those, two Oregon species — the California condor (*Gymnogyps californianus*) and the sharp-tailed grouse (*Tympanuchus phasianellus*) — have officially been extirpated. Both states acknowledge eight introduced species, including the chukar (*Alectoris chukar*), European starling (*Sturnus vulgaris Linnaeus*), gray partridge (*Perdix perdix*), house sparrow (*Passer domesticus*), northern bobwhite (*Colinus virginianus*), ring-necked pheasant (*Phasianus colchicus*), rock dove or rock pigeon (*Columba livia*), and wild turkey (*Meleagris gallopavo*). Washington alone identifies three more alien species breeding in the state: the California quail (*Callipepla californica*), Eurasian collared dove (*Streptopelia decaocto*), and skylark (*Alauda arvensis*).[23]

Strangely, neither "complete" list of recognized birds includes the mute swan (*Cygnus olor*), although that Eastern Hemisphere native rates a spot on the Oregon Invasive Species Council's list of "100 most dangerous invaders." Normally found throughout Europe and Asia, with occasional winter forays to North Africa, mute swans have been dispersed by humans throughout southern Africa, Australasia and North America. Present in the United States since the late nineteenth century, increasing their numbers at an average rate of ten percent each year, mute swans are deemed a threat to the environment for consuming essential submerged vegetation. The U.S. Department of the Interior rejects claims by a special interest group, "Save the Mute Swans," that the species is native to North America and thus deserves legal protection.[24]

Mammals

Oregon claims 130 species of land-dwelling mammals, while Washington acknowledges 105. Washington wildlife officials list thirty-two marine species, compared to twenty-seven for Oregon. Six of Oregon's marine species are deemed "accidental," including Baird's beaked whale (*Berardius bairdii*), the black right whale (*Eubalaena glacialis*), Cuvier's beaked whale (*Ziphius cavirostris*), the false killer whale (*Pseudorca crassidens*), the rough-toothed porpoise (*Steno bredanensis*), and Stejneger's beaked whale (*Mesoplodon stejnegeri*).[25]

On land, both states offer nearly identical lists of nine introduced mammalian species. Eight on which they agree include the black rat (*Rattus rattus*) and Norway rat (*R. norvegicus*), the house mouse (*Mus musculus*), the eastern gray squirrel (*Sciurus carolinensis*) and eastern fox squirrel (*S. niger*), the eastern cottontail rabbit (*Sylvilagus floridanus*), the nutria or coypu (*Myocastor coypus*), and the mountain goat (*Oreamnos americanus*). Slight disagreement involves reports of the common opossum (*Didelphis marsupialis*) in Washington and the closely-related Virginia opossum (*D. virginiana*) in Oregon.[26]

While neither official state roster includes them, feral hogs (*Sus scrofa*) exist in the wild throughout the Pacific Northwest. A map published by the United States Department of Agriculture notes hog sightings in northwestern Washington and scattered throughout Oregon. Oregon's Invasive Species Council acknowledged the problem in 2004, with confirmed occurrences of feral hogs in nine counties, including Coos, Crook, Curry, Jackson, Jefferson, Josephine, Klamath, Wasco, and Wheeler. In Washington, feral hogs have "made themselves at home" in Olympic National Park since April 2001. Two months later, WDFW regional wildlife manager Jack Smith issued a plea for information on hog sightings in "an area stretching from the Quinault Indian Reservation to the Wynochee River valley."[27]

Feral hogs are a problem because they breed prolifically and eat almost anything, ranging from native plants and animals to crops and garbage. They generally live in groups of twenty to fifty (called sounders), and fight viciously with long tusks that may inflict lethal damage on humans and other large animals. Feral hogs breed with domestic pigs, given the chance, and in the South that pairing has produced some giant specimens. Georgia hunters shot one, dubbed "Hogzilla," in June 2004. It measured more than seven feet in length, weighed eight hundred pounds, and sported twenty-eight-inch tusks (the North American record).[28]

No such monstrous hogs have thus far surfaced in the Pacific Northwest, but some of the other alien mammals reported are even more startling.

Consider the apparent kangaroo seen by witness William Shearer in Puyallup, Washington, sometime in 1967. Shearer described the hopping animal as calf-sized and bluish-gray in color. Kangaroos (*Macropus spp.*), of course, are native to Australia, although many — with the smaller but related wallabies from Australia and New Zealand — have been transported worldwide through the exotic pet trade. At least a dozen breeding colonies of wallabies exist in Great Britain, with numbers ranging from twelve to 120 per group. No such invasion is acknowledged in America, yet sightings of stray kangaroos nationwide date from the 1930s.[29]

Sightings of "black panthers" in North America remain officially unexplained. *Courtesy of U.S. National Oceanic and Atmospheric Association.*

More startling — and potentially frightening — is the repeated Northwest sightings of alien big cats, dubbed "ABCs" by most cryptozoologists. The first case on record, from July 1976, involves a lion (*Panthera leo*) seen by "all sorts of people" in Tacoma, Washington. Multiple witnesses described a large cat sporting "a shaggy black mane, light brown body, and a black tuft at the end of a long tail" — in short, the very textbook picture of a male Old World lion. Police turned out in force, found nothing, and eventually put the blame on "Jake," a hapless collie-shepherd mix found idling at the city dump. Thirteen years later, in August 1999, residents of Port Angeles, Washington, saw and heard a roaring "lioness." Author George Eberhart alludes to yet another lion sighting in Spokane, but he provides neither dates nor details.[30]

Next up, comes the report of a "black panther" seen by two men in Longview, Washington, during July 1987. Science recognizes no "black panthers," a term normally applied to melanistic jaguars and leopards. Debate continues as to whether melanistic cougars (*Puma concolor*) exist, explaining "panther" sightings throughout North America since 1869, but authors Loren Coleman and Mark Hall suggest a different explanation. They propose that prehistoric American lions (*P. leo atrox*), presumed extinct for some 10,000 years, may still survive in North America. While most illustrations of P. l. atrox include no mane on male specimens, Coleman and Hall hypothesize that males of the species closely resembled P. leo, and that females of the species may have black fur — thus explaining not only America's "panther" sightings, but also mysterious cases of lions and panthers seen together in various states since the 1930s.[31]

Dead and Gone?

One final group of "normal" cryptids still awaits discussion here: specifically, those species deemed extinct, or extirpated, and which may still survive. The classic case of a surprise survivor is the coelacanth (*Latimeria chalumnae*), a primitive lobe-finned fish believed extinct for sixty-five million years before a living specimen was caught off the coast of South Africa in December 1938. A second was netted at the Comoros, in 1952, and more followed, from waters surrounding Mozambique (1991) and Madagascar (1995). In 1997, a small but thriving Indonesian population was discovered, deemed a second species (*L. menadoensis*). Twenty-first century captures include specimens taken from South Africa's Simangaliso Wetland Park (2000), off the coast of Kenya (2001), from

Tanzania (2003), another from Madagascar (2004), and from Zanzibar (2007).[32] Other "extinct" and "extirpated" species surface every year, though few — if any — rate the coverage granted to coelacanths, the ultimate "living fossils."

Both Oregon and Washington acknowledge wolverines (*Gulo gulo*) within their borders. The species is listed as threatened in Oregon, with survivors found only in Deschutes, Harney, and Wheeler counties. Washington stops short of calling wolverines endangered, listing them as "state candidates" and a "federal species of concern," but no living specimen had been confirmed for eighty years prior to February 2006, when a year-old, nineteen-pound female was caught alive at Harts Pass. Researchers fitted the wolverine, whom they dubbed "Melanie," with a collar and satellite-tracking device to chart its travels — and, perhaps, to discover other specimens at large. So far, no others have been found. The search continues... [33]

Three months after Melanie surprised state wildlife officials, researchers from the University of Idaho confirmed discovery of a giant Palouse earthworm (Driloleirus americanus) in Whitman County, Washington. Named for the town where its first specimen was discovered in 1897, the D. americanus may exceed three feet in length and burrows to depths of fifteen feet. Its range extends from eastern Washington into Idaho, but its seeming disappearance in the early 1980s prompted the World Conservation Union to list the species as

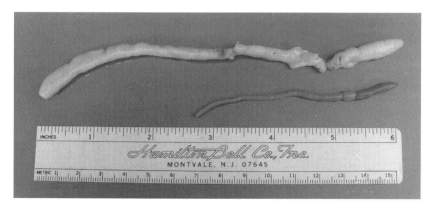

The giant Palouse earthworm is Washington's largest invertebrate. *Courtesy of U.S. Dept. of Fish & Wildlife.*

endangered in 2001. Four years later, in May 2005, Idaho graduate student Yaniria Sanchez-de Leon unearthed a six-inch specimen. Formal identification was delayed until January 2006, and university officials withheld the announcement until May.[34]

A small discovery, perhaps, but nonetheless riveting for experts in the field. As Jodi Johnson-Maynard, a soils scientist at the University of Idaho, told the *Seattle Post-Intelligencer*, "It was very exciting. Just to find something we thought, perhaps, was gone is a great thing." Ann Kennedy, a soil expert at Washington State University and member of several expeditions that sought giant earthworms in vain, agreed. "It is kind of like a Bigfoot thing," she said, "but that's OK. Lately, worms are the big thing. People used to think they were kind of icky and now they're kind of neat to talk about."[35]

What else awaits discovery in the Pacific Northwest? Our search, like the evolution of life on Earth, begins at sea.

Chapter Three

Sea Monsters

Before white interlopers found their way to the Northwest, Kwakiutl tribesmen spun tales of the pugwis, a "man-of-the-sea" or "wild man of the undersea world," variously described as an aquatic spirit in human form, a merbeing, or an ocean-going shape-shifter. Some legends describe the pugwis as benign, while others speak of killer whales (*Orcinus orca*) that swallow canoes and transform their occupants into cetaceans. Their normal habitat was Puget Sound.[4]

Long before the arrival of "white" Europeans, aboriginal tribesmen in the Pacific Northwest recorded their sightings of monsters at sea in paintings and carvings. The Manhousat people of Flores and Vancouver Islands feared the sea beast *hiyitl'iik*, while the neighboring Comox tribe spoke of *Numske lee Kwala*. Sechelt folklore records sightings of *T'chain-ko*. All were similar serpentine creatures, depicted with large heads and short legs or fins.[2]

Today we know that some marine monsters were whales, whale sharks (*Rhincodon typus*), oarfish (*Regalecus glesne*), or giant squids (genus *Architeuthis*), but others remain unidentified, with eyewitness sightings as yet unexplained.

The Pacific Northwest provides ample space for monster-watching. Oregon boasts 296 miles of coastline while Washington claims 157. Tidal shoreline (including various islands) increases the total to 3,026 miles for Washington and 1,410 for Oregon.[3] So, what is swimming offshore?

Men-of-the-Sea

Before white interlopers found their way to the Northwest, Kwakiutl tribesmen spun tales of the pugwis, a "man-of-the-sea" or "wild man of the undersea world," variously described as an aquatic spirit in human form, a merbeing, or an ocean-going shape-shifter. Some legends describe the pugwis as benign, while others speak of killer whales (*Orcinus orca*) that swallow canoes and transform their occupants into cetaceans. Their normal habitat was Puget Sound.[4]

The pugwis is depicted in various carved masks and totem poles produced for sale by modern artists, generally portrayed with a round face, prominent eyes and incisors resembling a beaver's, sometimes with gills. Most carvings pair the creature with a mundane animal — a cormorant, kingfisher, loon or seagull perched atop its head; a frog protruding from its mouth — and one by artist Tim Alfred catches the pugwis midway through its morph into a killer whale.[5]

No modern sightings of the pugwis are recorded from Puget Sound, but author Loren Coleman links it to "lizard man" sightings at British Columbia's Thetis Lake, near Colwood, in August 1972. Witness Mike Gold told police that the Thetis Lake creature was "shaped like an ordinary body, like a human being body but it had a monster face, and it was all scaly [with] a point sticking out of its head [and] great big ears. It was silver." From that, Coleman concludes that the pugwis are "a sort of cross between Sasquatch and the Creature from the Black Lagoon."[6]

Contact and Confusion

The first "sea serpent" sighting by an Anglo-European settler occurred in 1881, near Nanaimo, on British Columbia's Vancouver Island. Another three years passed before witness John Barker glimpsed a startling "sea pet" passing Tacoma, Washington, on October 27, 1884. Barker described the beast as sixty feet long and four feet thick, with "horns" on its back.[7]

According to the *Tacoma Daily Ledger* of July 3, 1893, a group of unnamed local fishermen sailed on July 1 from Tacoma to Henderson Island in Black Fish Bay. They camped near a party of anonymous surveyors, and that night beheld "a monster fish, or whatever you may call it...fully 150 feet long, and at its thickest part...about thirty feet in circumference."[8] Nor was the creature's size its strangest attribute.

As we reached the woods the "demon of the deep" sent out flashes of light that illuminated the surrounding country for miles, and his roar — which sounded like the roar of thunder — became terrific. When we reached the woods we looked around and saw the monster making off in the direction of the sound, and in an instant it disappeared beneath the waters of the bay, but for some minutes we were able to trace its course by a bright luminous light that was on the surface of the water. As the fish disappeared, total darkness surrounded us, and it took us some time to find our way back to the beach where our comrades lay. We were unable to tell the time, as the powerful electric force had stopped our watches.[9]

If its fantastic elements were not enough to brand that tale a hoax, the truth emerges when we realize that Washington State has no Black Fish Bay or Henderson Island.[10]

The next report from Washington is more intriguing. On October 26, 1895, seventeen witnesses watched an unknown creature swimming in Bellingham Bay. They estimated the length of its dark body at 150 feet, with an upraised neck twenty to thirty feet long.[11]

Eight months later, on July 8, 1896, *The New York Times* reprinted an item from the *Tacoma Daily Ledger*, describing the capture of a "sea serpent" in Hood Canal — a fifty-mile fjord with an average width of one and a half miles and average depth of 177 feet that separates the Kitsap and Olympic Peninsulas, east of Puget Sound.[12]

According to that story, W. J. Kennedy and R. E. McClean caught the "uncanny monster" on June 5th, near the mouth of the Humi-Humi River, and displayed it alive in Seattle and Tacoma. As described in print, it measured 7'2" long, with a body "spotted and ribbed like that of a rattlesnake. Its movements are serpentine in character. It is about as thick as a man's thigh at the neck, gradually tapering to a point at the tail... It is finned somewhat like a halibut, having a dorsal fin the entire length of its vertebrae, while underneath is a similar fin, extending from the stomach to the tail." Stranger still, the beast possessed "the head of a dog and the fangs of a tiger."[13]

Bizarre, indeed, but not, it seems, all that unusual. Only three weeks earlier, Kennedy "had caught one of the same species, but it made such a fight when hauled into the boat that it had to be killed." In fact, a second "sea serpent," presumed to be the captive's mate, had tried in vain to rescue it on June 5, before Kennedy and McClean stabbed it with a steel gaff. Yet another specimen was "now on board the United States Fish Commission steamer *Albatross*, caught some time ago."[14] Clearly, the "monster" was an oarfish — and not a very large one, at that, since specimens measuring thirty-six feet have been documented, and some researchers speculate that oarfish may reach fifty feet in length.[15]

Ballard's "sea serpent" was an obvious hoax. *Courtesy of the Library of Congress.*

Washington's next "sea serpent" was an unmitigated hoax, crafted from a wooden pole or tree trunk and fitted with a fierce-looking head, mouth agape. Two photos of the "monster" with its makers, posed on Ballard's rocky beach, were published in 1906 and 1910, respectively. Both appear to have been taken at the same time, from different angles and ranges.[16]

"Colossal Claude"

The Columbia River's mouth is notorious for its treacherous currents and for the Columbia Bar, a giant offshore sandbar blamed for some 2,000 shipwrecks and seven hundred deaths. Mariners long ago dubbed the coastline between Oregon's Tillamook Bay and Vancouver Island "the Graveyard of the Pacific."[17] It comes as no surprise that such waters might harbor a monster, but the first record of cryptids in the neighborhood is relatively recent, dating from the 1930s.

Sometime in 1934, crewmen aboard the Columbia River lightship and its tender, the *Rose*, saw an unidentified animal swimming near the river's mouth. According to first mate L. A. Larson, "It was about forty feet long. It had a neck some eight feet long, a big round body, a mean looking tail and an evil, snaky look to its head." A newspaper report of the incident declared that "[m]embers of the crew, after studying the monster for some time with field glasses, wanted to lower a boat and go after it, but the officers discouraged the plan for fear it would swamp the boat."[18]

The creature — dubbed "Colossal Claude" at some uncertain point in its recorded history — apparently did not resurface until 1937. Captain Charles Graham, of the fishing trawler *Viv*, told reporters in Astoria that he had seen a "long, hairy, tan colored creature, with the head of an overgrown horse, about forty feet long, and with a four-foot waist measure."[19]

Several months later and 150 miles farther south, a Mr. and Mrs. White were surf-gazing at Devil's Churn when they beheld a fifty-five-foot creature with an upraised fifteen-foot neck resembling a giraffe's or camel's, except that it trailed a brown mane. An unidentified trucker stopped to gape at the beast, then the Whites jumped into their car and pursued it toward Heceta Head, where the animal veered out to sea and vanished from sight.[20]

On April 13, 1939, crewmen aboard the *Argo* were trawling for halibut when they met Colossal Claude near the Columbia's mouth. It passed within ten feet of the boat, raising its neck an equal distance above the ocean's surface. Captain Chris Anderson intervened when one crewman jabbed a boat hook toward the creature, later saying, "He could have sunk us with a nudge. His head was like a camel's. His fur was coarse and gray. He had glassy eyes and a bent snout that he used to push a

Oarfish, like this one that was captured by U.S. servicemen in Vietnam, may explain some sea serpent sightings.

twenty-pound halibut off our lines and into his mouth." Some sources claim that the *Argo's* crew saw Claude on other occasions, but they offer no details.[21]

After the *Argo* sighting was reported, college student "Rusty" Beetle of Port Angeles claimed an encounter with Claude preceding the initial incident from 1934. While vague on dates, Beetle said he was fishing off Dungeness Spit, at the northern end of the Olympic Peninsula, when a forty-foot serpentine creature surfaced in the Strait of Juan de Fuca, displaying a horse-like head and mane.[22]

We have no date or specific location for the sighting reported by salmon fisherman George Saggers, somewhere off Washington's Pacific coast. The creature he saw was "a mottled color of gray and light brown." Its neck rose four feet above the water's surface and was eighteen inches in diameter, decorated with a mane of sorts that "seemed like bundles of warts rather than hair. It looked something like a mattress would, if split down the middle allowing rolls of cotton batting to protrude." The beast stared at Saggers with protruding black eyes, three inches in diameter.[23]

Other undated sightings occurred along Oregon's coast at Bandon, Lincoln City, Nelscott, and Waldport. At Bandon, south of the Coquille River's mouth, the sea tossed up a still-unidentified twelve- and a half-foot carcass "with a bulbous nose and a cow-like body covered with brownish hair." Some three dozen witnesses, including members of the Women's Christian Temperance Union from Willamette Valley, watched a thirty-foot creature with "a slender neck, a snake-like head, and a fan-shaped tail" paddling along Nelscott's reefs on several occasions, while slightly farther north, Lincoln City produced at least two sightings.[24]

Sometime in 1942, witness Frank Lawson saw a smaller mystery creature at Long Beach, Washington. As described in a 1997 letter to oceanographer Paul LeBlond, the animal was sixteen feet long, with large fins and a coat of brown hair. Long Beach, coincidentally, is also home to "Jake the Alligator Man," a mummified "half-man, half-alligator" displayed at Marsh's Free Museum, a local tourist trap.[25]

Post-War Serpents

March 1950 saw another enigmatic carcass beached on Oregon's coast, this time at Delake. The incident began on March 3, when Henry Schwering and Bert Vincent were fishing at nearby Devils Lake, linked to the Pacific Ocean by the 120-foot D River (renowned as the shortest river on Earth). The lake is three miles long, one-third of a mile wide, and twenty-one feet deep at its lowest point. The anglers were relaxing, waiting for the next strike, when Schwering "suddenly noticed that the fish had stopped biting. Then I noticed fish scooting away and the water started boiling. Then I saw a huge, round head break water not far from the boat."[26]

Understandably perturbed, Schwering and Vincent rowed for shore and left the scene, but Vincent returned on March 4th to find a 22-foot hairy carcass beached at the D River's mouth. Other gawkers arrived, some two hundred in all, to examine the creature. One witness said, "It had the body of a cow, approximately nine tails, and is covered with hair all over the body and legs." Town marshal Andy Allum pegged its weight at 1,000 pounds (though some estimates tripled that figure), and his teenage daughter Marybell dubbed the creature "Old Hairy." Allum's sister-in-law described the carcass as having "gray and white feathers on its underside." Richard Liftin, a British correspondent for *United Press*, described a body "three or four feet thick and four feet long, [with] a long main tail extending eighteen feet, plus seven subsidiary tails eight feet in length, as well as a medium-sized one of twelve feet." When witness Peter Cheadle kicked the corpse, it "shivered and shimmied." A tow-truck driver, called to haul the beast away, arrived too late. It was reclaimed by the Pacific surf.[27]

What was Old Hairy? Professor Fred Kohlruss from the University of Portland declared, "It's an elasmobranch. It's a sea inhabitant whose bones remain in the cartilage stage." The subclass Elasmobranchii includes all sharks, skates, and rays, so the professor's verdict was suitably vague. Dr. E. W. Gudger, speaking for the American Museum of Natural History, was more specific. "It's a whale shark, undoubtedly," he said.

An apparent sea monster was stranded at Devils Lake in 1950. *Courtesy of U.S. Dept. of Fish & Wildlife.*

Some analysts believe "Old Hairy" was a whale shark, the world's largest fish. *Courtesy of the U.S. National Oceanic and Atmospheric Association.*

"A harmless critter with the body shaped like a tadpole." An unnamed biologist with the Oregon Fish Commission begged to differ, branding Old Hairy a mound of whale blubber.[28]

Late April 1958 brought the next "serpent" sighting, from Whidbey Island in Puget Sound, thirty miles north of Seattle. Rev. John Oosterhoof of Mount Vernon Presbyterian Church was among the witnesses who described a twelve-foot creature, one foot in diameter, undulating on the surface with motions that rendered further description fruitless.[29]

Three years later, in March 1961, Margaret Stout and her sister-in-law were strolling on Dungeness Spit with their sons, aged four and five, when they saw a strange object offshore. Mrs. Stout later wrote:

It was a dark, drizzly, and quiet day. We could see Vancouver Island vaguely through the mist. Ships in the channel were easily visible. We were at the beginning of the spit. We were watching a large freighter far out in the channel. It was moving up the Strait [of Juan de Fuca] towards Port Townsend. When it was about 45° northeast of us, out attention was drawn to a long thin object about 25° northeast and probably a quarter of a mile from us. At first, we thought it was a tree limb. It disappeared abruptly beneath the surface and in a few seconds appeared again, much closer. We could see that it was some kind of creature and distinctly saw that the large flattish head was turned away from us and towards the ship. I think all of us gasped and pointed. We could distinctly see three humps behind the long neck. The animal was proceeding westward at an angle toward us. It sank abruptly again and reappeared closer, almost due north of us. In the dim light, we could distinctly make out color and pattern, a long floppy mane, and the shape of the head. My small son grabbed me and started to cry with fear. At the same time, the animal seemed to become aware of us and sank again. It reappeared in a few seconds, still proceeding westwards, but a little way from us. I reassured the youngster, saying that it was obviously wary of us. It sank and reappeared once more while near enough to observe it closely.... As a trained biologist, including marine and fresh water biology, I could not accept that long floppy mane or fin. Yet we all say it. We deduced that the humps were at least five feet [long]. Again, I simply could not accept their arrangement.[30]

"Marvin the Monster"

In 1963, a pair of divers employed by Shell Oil Company were exploring Oregon's coastline for potential drilling sites when they videotaped an unknown creature at a depth of 180 feet. Its fifteen-foot serpentine body was ridged and laden with barnacles, swimming with the corkscrew motion of a drill bit. Those who viewed the tape, including an anonymous panel of "the nation's leading marine biologists" drawn from universities in Washington, California, and Texas, plus the Scripps Institute of Oceanography, offered conflicting identifications. Experts in Washington and California pegged the creature as a jellyfish, but could not decide if it was a ctenophore (one of the comb jellies) or a siphonophore (colonial jellies). Scripps thought it was a salp (a barrel-shaped, free-floating tunicate), while the University of Texas opined that it might be "a creature left over from prehistoric times." Nicknamed "Marvin the Monster," the beast remains unidentified today.[31]

On September 29, 1963, while experts were still examining Marvin's video debut, Ruth Cobert found a rotting carcass half-buried in the sand on Whidbey Island's Sunset Beach. The body measured twenty-five feet long, with a twenty-inch skull resembling that of a horse. Its spine was six inches in diameter at the neck, tapering to two inches at the tail. Beside the corpse lay a quantity of cartilaginous material. Dr. A. D. Welander, from the University of Washington's Fisheries Department, examined photos of the carcass and identified it as a basking shark on October 3rd.[32]

Clearly, "Marvin" was still at large.

In September 1967, *Portland Oregonian* reporter Peter Ciams described a sighting off the coast of Empire "several years ago." According to Ben Tanner, captain of the fishing vessel *Gold Coast*, a large unidentified creature approached the boat, "smacked its mouth, rolled its long lashed eyes at the crew, then pointed its tail in the air and dived straight down."[33]

It was no shark that Rea Avery Jr. glimpsed swimming offshore from Westport, Washington, in the summer of 1971. The gray creature had a neck six to eight feet long, which it raised above the waves to stare at Avery with a "curious" expression. Its eyes and mouth were clearly visible. Eight years later, back on Whidbey Island in October 1979, Kathryn Schaff and her husband watched a beast resembling "a huge diver wearing a helmet" as it swam along the coastline, blowing spouts of air at five-minute intervals.[34]

Colossal Claude's Return?

Another decade elapsed before the next alleged encounter with an aquatic unknown, this time upstream in the Columbia River. Local fisherman Donald Riswick of Astoria, Oregon, was trawling the river at an estimated depth of thirty feet, when something snagged his net and stalled his boat. Riswick throttled forward and escaped the snag, only to find a large hole in the net when he hauled it aboard. That incident, while unexplained, sparked rumors of "Colossal Claude's" return.[35]

A year later, in June 1990, Michael Cenedella and Joanne Rauch were strolling along a beach at Cape Meares, at the south end of Oregon's Tillamook Bay, when they found a strange carcass stranded before them. Cenedella paced off its length, some thirty-three feet, and snapped a series of photos that later appeared on various Internet websites. An unidentified spokesperson for Oregon State University's Hatfield Marine Science Center opined that the beast might be a decomposed gray whale (*Eschrichtius robustus*), which may exceed fifty feet in length but which does not possess the apparent dorsal fin shown in Cenedella's photos. Cenedella himself has seen four gray whales beached at various times, insisting that "[n]one looked remotely like this. The grays don't taper nearly so much at the tail and don't taper at all at the head. The heads are massive." Cenedella also questioned whether the cadaver's lone appendage was "a bent leg" or "a grotesque penis." No samples of the creature's flesh were saved for DNA analysis.[36]

A year later, on Johns Island in the Haro Strait, retired Seattle pharmacist Phyllis Harsh allegedly found a two-foot-long "baby dinosaur" stranded, and placed it back in the water. When describing that experience to author Edward Boufield three years later, Harsh also claimed an undated discovery of a "small dinosaur" skeleton near a bald eagle's nest on Johns Island. She did not preserve that specimen for study.[37]

Unusual Suspects

There is no doubt that large marine creatures appear sporadically off the coasts of Oregon and Washington, or that they sometimes die and wash ashore. The question now remains: What are they?

Mainstream science, while granting the near-certainty of many still undiscovered marine species, stops short of accepting "sea serpents," per se. And, indeed, the movements of some classic "serpents" — specifically their flexure into vertical coils or humps — are impossible for reptiles or fish, whose spines bend only in the horizontal plane.

An unidentified "globster" was beached at Tillamook Bay in 1990. *Courtesy of U.S. Dept. of Fish & Wildlife.*

What, then, remains?

Aside from deliberate hoaxes, marine biologists contend that most (if not all) sea monster sightings involve misidentification of known species or objects — whales; large sharks, rays or eels; giant squids; oarfish; porpoises swimming in tandem; flocks of birds skimming the ocean's surface; the lion's mane jellyfish (*Cyanea capillata*), whose tentacles may top one hundred feet in length; floating colonies of pelagic tunicates (family *Salpidae*), which may exceed thirty feet; or floating logs and seaweed. Beached "globsters," they contend, are generally rotting sharks or whale blubber.[38]

Oarfish certainly inhabit Pacific Northwest waters. The "monster" caught alive by W. J. Kennedy and R. E. McClean in 1896 was undoubtedly an oarfish. Another washed ashore near Seaside, Oregon, in July 2006, and yet another turned up in an Oregon cannery the following year. While normally dwelling at depths of 3,000 feet or more, where they feed on zooplankton and small fish, oarfish have been hooked by anglers fishing from shore in Great Britain and elsewhere.[39]

Large squids are also supposed to be deep-water feeders, but 610 giant squids and twenty rare colossal squids (*Mesonychoteuthis hamiltoni*) were beached or netted between 1545 and 2008. Author Stan Allyn, who founded Tradewinds Sportfishing at Oregon's Depoe Bay in 1938, once claimed a sighting of fourteen-foot tentacles as "thick as a man's thigh" rising from the surf near his seaside home, but he waited four years to report the event.[40]

Another oddity from Depoe Bay, reported in February 2009, involved two alleged sightings of sea otters (*Enhydra lutris*) gamboling offshore from the Oregon Parks and Recreation Department's Whale Watching Center. While that event might not seem unusual, author Loren Coleman notes that Oregon's sea otters seemingly vanished in 1906. Other supposed otter sightings were reported from Beverly Beach in May 2008, from Yaquina Head in January 2009, and from the Columbia River's mouth in March 2009. Jim Price, coordinator of the Hatfield Marine Science Center's Oregon Marine Mammal Stranding Network, told reporters, "There have been sightings through the years, so it's not unprecedented. But most of the so-called sea otter sightings have been river otters. It's a good likelihood this is a wandering animal from Washington or California."[41]

While even a theoretical return of sea otters to Oregon's coast excites marine biologists, the largest specimens on record barely reach five feet and tip the scales at ninety-nine pounds — hardly the model of a massive sea monster.[42]

Some crypto-theorists suggest that "sea serpents" may be survivors from the Mesozoic Era, often dubbed the Age of Reptiles for the dinosaurs that flourished on land, while winged pterosaurs filled the skies and Earth's seas teemed with aquatic ichthyosaurs, plesiosaurs and mosasaurs. A model of one such giant, *Kronosaurus queenslandicus*, is displayed at Aquarium Village in Newport, Oregon, with a plaque reading: "Nessie: The World Famous Yaquina Bay Sea Monster." While tradition claims the plaster beast was "found by a night watchman in 1992," its origins remain obscure. As suggested by its scientific name, the first Kronosaurus fossil was found in Australia, in 1924. Remains of a second species, K. boyacensis, surfaced in Colombia during 1992. None thus far have been unearthed in North America.[43]

A prehistoric reptile that did find its way to Oregon, albeit posthumously, was the *Dakosaurus andiniensis*, a marine species initially discovered in Argentina, in 1996. Eleven years later, in March 2007, new fossils surfaced in Oregon's Blue Mountains, but paleontologists agreed that the specimen — Oregon's oldest fossil to date, at an estimated 150-180 million years — probably died in Southeast Asia and was carried eastward over time by plate tectonics. Nonetheless, Stanford University researcher Adrienne Mayor noted the fossil's "remarkable" resemblance to nineteenth century Kiowa drawings of a legendary water serpent, suggesting that early tribesmen may have found similar fossils.[44] Or, perhaps, observed a living creature in the flesh?

While mainstream scientists steadfastly ignore "sea serpents," various authors have attempted to identify and classify them since 1892, when Anthonie (Antoon) Cornelis Oudemans published his classic work *The Great Sea Serpent*. Oudemans reviewed 162 reports published between 1522 and 1890, concluding that most could be explained by the existence of a single beast — a long-necked seal some fifty to one hundred feet long, which he christened Megophias megophias.[45]

British naval officer Rupert Gould wrote two books on unknown aquatic creatures, *The Case for the Sea Serpent* (1930) and *The Loch Ness Monster* (1934). He concluded that three unknown species explained most sightings: a long-necked seal, a giant turtle or turtle-like creature, and a relict Plesiosaurus larger than either. In closing, Gould wrote, "I do not suggest that the last-named is actually a Plesiosaurus, but that it is either one of its descendants or has evolved along similar lines."[46]

Nearly three decades later, zoologist Bernard Heuvelmans published his analysis of 587 sea monster sightings reported between 1639 and 1966. He dismissed fifty-six as hoaxes, fifty-two as "certain or probable mistakes," 121 as "vague and therefore doubtful," forty-one as "ambiguous periscopes," and nine as "incomprehensible," leaving 308 reports that he deemed credible. From those, he offered a tentative list of nine separate species, including a "long-neck" (eighty-two sightings), a "merhorse" (seventy-one), a "many-humped" creature (fifty-nine), a "super-otter" (twenty-eight), a "many-finned" beast (twenty-six), "super-eels" (twenty-three), "marine saurians" (nine), a "yellow-belly" (six), and a "father-of-all-the-turtles" (four). Having furnished that list, Heuvelmans then dismissed the giant turtle as "too doubtful and suspect." Five of his remaining eight proposed species were mammals, with one reptile and one fish, leaving the yellow-belly "on ice" as a possible unknown species of shark.[47]

Five years later, oceanographers Paul LeBlond and John Sibert published the first analysis of the Pacific Northwest sea monster sightings, collected between 1892 and 1969. They proposed three mammalian species, equivalent to the long-neck, merhorse, and many-humped creatures described by Heuvelmans.[48]

Researcher Gary Mangiacopra winnowed the Heuvlmans roster for a series of articles published between 1977 and 1981, identifying four supposed species of sea monsters. They included a "dorsal finner" roughly analogous to the Heuvelmans many-humped creature, a "maner" virtually identical to the merhorse, a "horn head" closely resembling the long-neck, and a "multi-coiled" species that Mangiacopra equated with the super-eel.[49]

Subsequent attempts to classify marine unknowns all owe a heavy debt to Heuvelmans. Author Bruce Champagne reviewed 1,247 published sightings in 2001, selecting 351 that he deemed credible. From those cases, he identified a multi-humped creature (fifty-one sightings), an eel-like species (forty-five), and a long-necked animal (thirty), while the beasts seen in 225 cases (sixty-four percent of the total) remained unclassifiable from the available descriptions.[50]

LONG-NECKED

MERHORSE

MANY HUMPED

Bernard Heuvelmans hypothesized nine species of unknown sea monsters. *Courtesy of Bernard Heuvelmans.*

Most recently, in 2003, authors Loren Coleman and Patrick Huyghe published a list of fourteen aquatic unknowns, four of which are apparently confined to freshwater habitats. Their list of marine cryptids includes a "classic sea serpent" (combining Heuvelmans's many-humped, super-eel and super-otter), a "waterhorse" (merging the long-neck and merhorse), a mystery cetacean, a giant shark, a mystery manta ray (confirmed and classified in 2008), a "great sea centipede" (analogous to the many-finned species), a mystery saurian, a cryptid chelonian

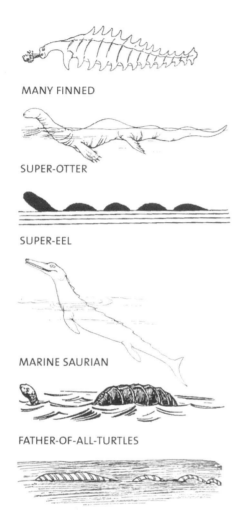

MANY FINNED

SUPER-OTTER

SUPER-EEL

MARINE SAURIAN

FATHER-OF-ALL-TURTLES

YELLOW-BELLY

Bernard Heuvelmans hypothesized nine species of unknown sea monsters. *Courtesy of Bernard Heuvelmans.*

(identical to the "father-of-all-the-turtles"), a mystery sirenian (with an apparent freshwater subspecies), and an unclassified giant octopus.[51]

"Caddy"

The sea monster most often seen in Pacific Northwest waters is an apparent mammal, dubbed Cadborosaurus (or "Caddy") by the *Victoria Daily Times* in 1933, for its frequent appearance in Vancouver Island's Cadboro Bay. Some published accounts call it Cadborosaurus willsi, in honor of Archie Wills, the newspaper's managing editor.[52]

In 1995, authors Paul LeBlond and Edward Bousfield analyzed sightings of Caddy reported from 1881 through 1994, plus eleven strandings and alleged captures of unknown creatures logged between 1930 and 1991. In six of the latter cases, experts identified the beached remains as those of five sharks and one supposed elephant seal.[53]

Based on eyewitness descriptions of Caddy, the animals are serpentine in form, ranging from fifteen to fifty feet in length. Their heads are commonly described as resembling those of a camel, giraffe, horse, or sheep. Depending on the individual's size, its flexible neck may be three to thirteen feet long. Behind that neck, humps or "loops" often appear, suggesting spinal flexibility in the vertical plane. Anterior flippers are sometimes reported.

The tail, often described as toothed or spiky, is horizontally split into flukes. The creatures swim at high speed on the surface, sometimes topping forty knots (forty-six miles per hour).[54]

No animal known to science matches Caddy's description, though it shares traits in common with the merhorse and long-necked "sea serpents" proposed by Bernard Heuvelmans. Its movements and eyewitness references to hair resembling a seal's or "coconut fiber," with visible ears and whiskers, plus occasional records of hissing or spouting, reinforce the impression that Caddy must be a mammal. Reports of Caddy chasing fish and seabirds indicate a predatory lifestyle. Two specimens, an apparent adult and juvenile, were seen together on three occasions between 1934 and 1939. Aside from Phyllis Harsh, witness William Hagelund also claims to have captured a baby Caddy, in Canadian waters, during August 1968. Like Ms. Harsh, he returned the sixteen-inch creature to the sea. Hagelund sketched the animal, but took no photographs.[55]

Another possible Caddy specimen was photographed at Naden Harbor, on British Columbia's Graham Island, in the summer of 1937. Employees of the Consolidated Whaling Corporation were gutting a sperm whale, hoping to find ambergris in its stomach, when a strange carcass spilled out. G. V. Boorman, the whaling station's first-aid officer, snapped two photos of the creature after it was laid out on a makeshift platform. A caption describes the beast as "The remains of a Sperm Whale's Lunch, a creature of reptilian appearance 10'6" in length with animal like vertebrae and a tail similar to that of a horse. The head bears resemblance to that of a large dog with features of a horse and the turn down [sic] nose of a camel." The photos were published in October 1937, whereupon Francis Kermode, director of Victoria's Provincial Museum, opined that "there was little doubt" the creature was a fetal baleen whale of indeterminate species (suborder Mysticeti), which had been born prematurely at sea.[56]

Authors Paul LeBlond and Edward Bousfield note that Kermode began his career at the Provincial Museum as a sixteen-year-old office boy, graduating to taxidermy and then to the director's post without any formal education in zoology. Three years before the Naden Harbor incident, when another carcass washed ashore on Henry Island, Kermode had pronounced it a specimen of Steller's sea cow (*Hydrodamalis gigas*), presumed extinct since 1768. In fact, professional biologists identified that carcass as a basking shark. In 1937, Dr. Ian McTaggart-Cowan, curator of vertebrate mammals at the Provincial Museum, disputed Kermode's identification of the Naden Harbor carcass, stating that the

Cadborosaurus is the Northwest's most famous sea monster. *Courtesy of William Rebsamen.*

creature resembled nothing known to science. No trace of the carcass remains today in the museum's collection.[57]

Another possible photo of Caddy exists, snapped October 4, 1936, after skeletal remains were beached near Camp Fircom, on Vancouver Island. The photo was printed as a postcard — and then forgotten for six decades until Dr. Karl Shuker discovered and published a copy of it in 1996. It remains unidentified today.[58]

Chapter Four

Lake Monsters

Worldwide, more than nine hundred lakes and rivers lay claim to resident freshwater monsters. Forty percent of those identified to date are found in North America.[1]

The Pacific Northwest is particularly wet. Washington, with 3,508 lakes and 6,269 rivers or streams, has 4,756 square miles covered by water. Oregon, despite its larger number of lakes and rivers — 5,273 and 12,100, respectively — places second with 2,384 square miles under water. Oregon also boasts 147 swamps identified by name, compared to sixty-five in Washington.[2]

Some confusion surrounds the identity of specific Northwest "monster" lakes. Author Loren Coleman named six for Oregon and five for Washington in 1983 and 2001, then dropped one from Oregon's list and added four to Washington's (including the Columbia River) for his collaborative work with Patrick Huyghe in 2003. In 1998, cryptozoologist John Kirk listed eight for Oregon and five for Washington (counting the Columbia River for both states). George Eberhart, writing in 2002, listed five Oregon lakes and eight in Washington.[3]

In Oregon, all sources agree that cryptids have been reported from Crater Lake, Crescent Lake, Forked Mountain Lake, and Wallowa Lake. In Washington, the only unanimous vote goes to Rock Lake. Authors Coleman, Huyghe, and Eberhart agree on reports from Oregon's Upper Klamath Lake, plus Chelan, Omak, Quinault, and Washington Lakes in Washington. Coleman listed Oregon's Hollow Block Lake in 1983 and 2001, but cut it from his list in 2003, while Kirk included it in 1998. Coleman omitted Washington's Moses, Spirit, and Steilacoom Lakes from his first two lists, then added them a year after they surfaced on Eberhart's roster. Kirk agreed on Moses and Spirit Lakes, but he stands alone in naming Oregon's Willamette River and Washington's Pend Oreille River.[4]

This chapter omits the Columbia River, since "Colossal Claude" has only been seen at its mouth and received full coverage in *Chapter Two*, as did Oregon's Devils Lake and D River — neither included on any prior published lists. Since most tales of Pacific Northwest lake monsters are rooted in Native American legends, their dates of origin untraceable, we shall review them alphabetically.

Crater Lake, Oregon

Crater Lake is a flooded volcanic crater, formed by the eruption and collapse of Mount Mazama in the Cascades, around 150 B.C.E. Originally christened Deep Blue Lake in 1853, it was renamed Lake Majesty during the Civil War, and finally received its present name in 1869. Crater Lake

Crater Lake's monster inspired a low-budget horror film in 1977.

is six miles long and five miles wide, with an average depth of 1,148 feet and a maximum recorded depth of 1,949 feet. It thus ranks as the deepest lake in the United States, and is often cited as the seventh-deepest lake on Earth. A volcanic cinder cone, dubbed Wizard Island, protrudes 755 feet above water at the lake's west end.[5]

Klamath tribesmen claimed that Crater Lake was home to a species of huge horned serpents called to kas, known for their aggressive pursuit of humans.6 According to folklorist Charles Skinner:

Crater Lake, Oregon, was a haunt of water-devils that dragged into it and drowned all who ventured near. Only within a few years could Indians be persuaded to go to it as guides. Its discoverers saw in it the work of the Great Spirit, but could not guess its meaning. All but one of these Klamaths stole away after they had looked into its circular basin and sheer walls. He fancied that if it was a home of gods they might have some message for men, so camping on the brink of the lofty cliffs he waited. In his sleep a vision came to him, and he heard voices, but could neither make out appearances nor distinguish a word. Every night this dream was repeated. He finally went down to the lake and bathed, and instantly found his strength increased and saw that the people of his dreams were the genii of the waters—whether good or bad he could not guess. One day he caught a fish for food. A thousand water-devils came to the surface, on the instant, and seized him. They carried him to a rock on the north side of the lake, that stands two thousand feet above the water, and from that they dashed him down, gathering the remains of his shattered body below and devouring them. Since that taste they have been eager for men's blood. The rock on the south side of the lake, called the Phantom Ship, is believed by the Indians to be a destructive monster, innocent as it looks in the daytime.[6]

Hollywood discovered Crater Lake in March 1977, releasing a low-budget horror film titled "The Crater Lake Monster." Writer-producer-director William Stromberg depicts a meteor strike at the lake, which hatches a long-dormant dinosaur egg. The reptile, once full-grown, proceeds to menace humans until it is destroyed by a brave local sheriff and visiting scientists. Reviewer George Reis panned the movie as "one of the worst giant monster flicks of all time."[7]

A quarter-century elapsed before the next news flash from Crater Lake occurred in May 2002. On that occasion, the *News-Press* of Fort Myers, Florida, reported the tale of former Oregon resident Mattie Hatcher, retired from nursing and living in Albany, Georgia. Recalling events from some unspecified year, Hatcher described a boating excursion with friends on Crater Lake, during which she glanced into the water and "felt her heart freeze." Hatcher and her friends beheld an "unbelievably big" creature, swimming deep below their small rowboat. "That thing must have been a block long," Hatcher said in 2002. "I have never been so scared in my life. What we saw that day was a monster. To me, it looked like a dragon."[8]

In October 2003, the Farshores website received an email report from an alleged witness, "Zathan," describing an encounter with a beast he dubbed "Cassie." Zathan — who described himself as "a real Loch Ness freak" — was hiking on Wizard Island with his mother when he glimpsed an unknown creature "swimming out in the deep blue water[,] going underwater and surfacing." The animal resembled "a very large lizard" and "swam back and forth like a snake," propelled by a tail the same length as its body. Those movements were accompanied by "a faint peeping sound."[9]

Zathan wrote back to Farshores in April 2005, expanding his original account. On that occasion, he described Cassie as possessing "a very, very, very long body around sixteen to twenty feet long." The creature was black or dark brown, "swam side to side like a lizard," had a large head with a "huge eye ball" and "a massive sea monster like jaw," and sported "a fin like protrusion" (which did not appear in a sketch attached to the email). The unknown author speculated that the beast was "a big eel," introduced to the lake by wildlife biologists.[10]

Crescent Lake, Oregon

Crescent Lake lies thirty miles north of Crater Lake. Named for its shape in July 1865, it is five miles long and four miles wide, with a surface area of 4,547 acres. Its average depth is 124 feet, with a maximum recorded depth of 265 feet.[11]

Author Betty Garner claims that monster sightings from Crescent Lake have been logged "since white people came to the area" (in 1846), but the only specific case located during research for this volume resulted from a journalistic error.[12]

Writing for the *Portland Oregonian* in 1967, Peter Ciams described an undated sighting at Crescent Lake by fishermen Henry Schwering and Bert Vincent, repeating verbatim Schwering's description of events at Devils Lake in 1950 (already quoted in *Chapter Two*).[13]

Forked Mountain, Oregon

Confusion surrounds this location and its legendary cryptids. It is best, perhaps, to start with Charles Skinner's summary of local native legends. He wrote:

The monster Amhuluk, whose home is a lake near Forked Mountain, Oregon, had but one passion — to catch and drown all things; and when you look into the lake you see that he has even drowned the sky in it, and has made the trees stand upside down in the water. Wherever he set his feet the ground would soften. As three children were digging roots at the edge of the water he fell on them and impaled two of them on his horns, the eldest only contriving to escape. When this boy reached home, his body was full of blotches, and the father suspected how it was, yet he went to the lake at once. The bodies of the children came out of the mud at his feet to meet him, but went down again and emerged later across the water. They led him on in this way until he came to the place where they were drowned. A fog now began to steam up from the water, but through it he could see the little ones lifted on the monster's horns, and hear them cry, "We have changed our bodies." Five times they came up and spoke to him, and five times he raised a dismal cry and begged them to return, but they could not. Next morning he saw them rise through the fog again, and, building a camp, he stayed there and mourned for several days. For five days they showed themselves, but after that they went down and he saw and heard no more of them. Amhuluk had taken the children and they would live with him forever after.[14]

Author Richard Eberhart places the unnamed lake — and Forked Mountain — somewhere west of Forest Grove, but exhaustive research for this volume revealed no such mountain anywhere in Oregon. In fact, the only Forked Mountains found in the United States are located in Arkansas and North Carolina. Oregon has a South Fork Mountain, but it stands in Clackamas County. Other accounts describe the unnamed lake abutting "Forkend Mountain," which exists nowhere in the United States.[15]

Encyclopedist Carol Rose confuses matters further, claiming that the Amhuluk inhabited several lakes, all vaguely dubbed the Wells of Amhuluk, whose enchanted waters possessed the power to transfigure ordinary animals. Thus, some grizzly bears that swam in those lakes mutated into monsters known as antukai or atunkai, resembling "huge grotesque otters."[16]

Lake Chelan, Washington

Lake Chelan — from the Salish Indian word for "deep water" — is located in north-central Washington's Chelan County. It measures fifty-five miles long and is one and a half miles wide at its broadest point. Its average depth is 474 feet, while its maximum recorded depth of 1,486 feet makes it Earth's twenty-fourth deepest lake.[17]

Native mythology claims that Lake Chelan and its surrounding mountains were created in prehistoric times, by epic battles between a voracious monster and the Great Spirit, who triumphed after multiple attempts to slay the vicious beast. Nonetheless, it later returned in serpent form to prey on tribesmen who dared cross the lake in canoes.[18]

The first recorded sighting of Lake Chelan's cryptid dates from November 1892, but since it describes an amphibious flying monster, it is described in *Chapter Five*. George Eberhart dates that incident from 1895, apparently because local hunter Clarence Andrews told the story to a *Seattle Times* reporter in December of that year.[19] No other sightings were discovered during research for this work.

Lake Quinault, Washington

Located in western Washington's Grays Harbor County, Lake Quinault is relatively small: 3.8 miles long, two miles across at its widest point, with a maximum recorded depth of 250 feet. Its scientific claim to fame is its location — in the midst of the northern hemisphere's only temperate rain forest.[20]

According to aboriginal folklore, a monster large enough to swallow whole canoes with all their occupants once lived in Lake Quinault. Its end came when it ate the brother of Kwatee, the Changer or Trickster god of tribes dwelling near Puget Sound. Kwatee retaliated by heating boulders and dumping them into the lake, thus boiling the monster alive. The treatment must have been successful, since no modern sightings from the lake exist.[21]

Lake Steilacoom, Washington

Lake Chelan is said to harbor a monster. *Courtesy of U.S. Dept. of Fish & Wildlife.*

Lake Steilacoom lies two and a half miles southwest of Tacoma. It is a man-made reservoir dating from 1853, when settler Andrew Byrd built a gristmill and dammed Chambers Creek to harness its power. The modest lake covers fifty-three acres, with a mean depth of eleven feet and a maximum depth of twenty feet.[22]

Those facts make it difficult to reconcile aboriginal folklore describing a female monster, called Whe-atchee, said to inhabit the lake. Traditionally, the beast lies nearly submerged, revealing only its head and right arm, flashing a version of the manual "OK" signal at human passers-by and calling out, "This is my Whe-atchee." While no modern sightings are reported, several authors assert that Nisqually tribesmen shun Lake Steilacoom to this day, refusing to fish or swim in its waters.[23]

In theory, some unexpected creature may have found its way into Lake Steilacoom from the Pacific Ocean, since Chambers Creek still drains into Puget Sound, but science recognizes no animal resembling the Whe-atchee, and most marine species cannot survive long in fresh water.[24]

Lake Union, Washington

Lake Union, found within the city limits of Seattle, appears on no previous lists of American "monster" lakes for the simple reason that it has spawned no recorded sightings. I include it here because a "documentary" film produced in 2005 used Lake Union as its setting to relate the story of Willatuk, a "famous" monster that somehow eluded the notice of historians, folklorists, and cryptozoologists until the movie's release.

Lake Union is a glacial lake, gouged out some 12,000 years ago by the same Vashon glacier that carved Seattle's Bitter, Green, and Haller Lakes. Duwamish tribesmen called it Small Lake, while Lake Union owes its present name to Thomas Mercer, for his 1854 prediction that canals would someday link Puget Sound to nearby Lake Washington in a "union of waters." Lake Union covers 570 acres, with a mean depth of thirty-three feet and a maximum depth of forty-nine feet.[25]

Actor-turned-writer/director Oliver Tuthill Jr. conceived Willatuk as a happy merger of his fascination with Native American folklore and Scotland's Loch Ness Monster. The *Seattle Times* found him filming his faux documentary at Lake Union in October 2005, employing a rarely seen benevolent cryptid, whose trappings included "two green latex heads, vaguely gator-like in shape and size, with golden eyes." Meanwhile, in a neat piece of guerrilla advertising, Tuthill created a website for *Willatuk*, including a timeline of fictional sightings in salt and fresh water, spanning 266 years between 1736 and 2002. Scheduled to include interviews with fictional cryptozoologists "Dr. Henry McCarton" and "Professor Luis (or Miguel) de la Reyo" of Brazil, *Willatuk* had not been released when this book went to press in 2010.[26]

Despite its shallow waters, Lake Steilacoom has a history of monster sightings. *Courtesy of U.S. Dept. of Fish & Wildlife.*

Lake Washington

Lake Washington presents us with multiple cryptids, one of which has been identified beyond question. The largest lake in King County, and the state's second-largest (after Lake Chelan), Lake Washington is twenty-two miles long and covers 21,600 acres, with a mean depth of 108 feet and a maximum recorded depth of 214 feet. Named by Thomas Mercer in 1854, in honor of President George Washington, today the lake lies surrounded by cities: Seattle to the west, Bellevue and Kirkland to the east, Kenmore to the north, and Renton to the south.[27]

As with so many other lakes in the Northwest, native tribesmen — the Duwamish, in this case — described Lake Washington as the lair of a lurking monster. Unlike the serpents reported from other bodies of water, however, Lake Washington allegedly harbored "huge, monstrous octopi [sic]" adapted to life in fresh water. Some accounts suggest that they are sighted to the present day, declared to be "quite timid actually, but very frightening to look upon when spotted by a diver unexpectedly."[28]

A very different creature, dubbed the "Madrona Monster," appeared in Lake Washington in 1947. A gardener known only as "Thomas" was working on Mary Barrie's property, in the Seattle suburb of Madrona Beach, when he saw a "hump" break the surface. Mrs. Barrie also saw the creature, describing "a dark, crinkly backed object moving south in the lake." She told the *Seattle Times*, "It was about one hundred feet long, but I could only see the middle, which was about twenty-five feet... I thought its tail and head were submerged." She added, "It was either a monster of a submarine" — a suggestion quickly refuted by Navy spokesmen.[29]

The next witness was Ivar Haglund, owner of a local aquarium and adjacent seafood restaurant on Pier 54. Haglund initially thought he was seeing a line of ducks, swimming in single file, but told *The Times*, "I took a picture anyway. Five minutes later the thing submerged and didn't come up again." The blurry photo, he averred, "clearly shows an uncommon creature."[30]

Other sightings followed, transforming the lake monster into a sea serpent. Ballard resident Ray Lichtenberger saw some unknown creature swimming out to sea, while A. T. Goodman, assistant lockmaster for the Hiram M. Chittenden Locks, opined that a wise creature might have escaped by shadowing a vessel in transit through Seattle's Lake Washington Ship Canal. An unnamed expert chipped in with the observation that "sea monsters can survive on salt water, fresh water or bourbon and water."[31]

Whatever the beast was, it seemed to have vanished. In March 1947, Ivar Haglund complained to *The Times*, "I've spent the past twenty-four hours scanning the waters of Puget Sound along with every fisherman I know. All we've seen is debris. I don't know which I saw the most of — flotsam or jetsam." Still, he added, "Who are we to say that from the boundless depths of the ocean all the mysteries have been uncovered and brought to the surface?" Author Betty Garner, writing in 1995, claimed that the Madrona Monster "is usually seen on hot sunny days in July," but she offered no sightings to prove it.[32]

The proximity of urban residents and industry fouled Lake Washington with pollution throughout the twentieth century — so much, in fact, that in October 1963 the *Seattle Post-Intelligencer* dubbed it "Lake Stinko." Public outcry prompted clean-ups, and by the turn of the next century Lake Washington boasted waters twice as clean as those surveyed in 1950.[33]

Six months after the lake received its malodorous nickname — on April 6, 1964 — retired Army Colonel Henry Joseph was boating with his wife and their six-year-old son on Lake Washington, at the north end of Mercer Island. Around 4:30 p.m. they were startled by the appearance of a thirty-foot object, some three hundred yards in front of their boat. Colonel Joseph first mistook it for a log and then saw it was alive. "In my thirty years of service," he declared, "I've seen sharks, whales, blackfish, porpoises, and manta rays, but nothing like this."

An octopus was pulled from the Metolius River in 1936. *Courtesy of U.S. National Oceanic and Atmospheric Association.*

The creature submerged as they passed it, but the Josephs' saw "an end of it" protruding from the water forty-five minutes later. "When we were within 100 yards or so," Colonel Joseph explained, "the creature just disappeared beneath the surface."[34]

There matters rested until November 5, 1987, when an eleven-foot, 900-pound white sturgeon (*Acipenser transmontanus*) was found floating dead, offshore from Kirkland. State wildlife officials believed that the fish had died from old age — which, in the sturgeon's case, may indicate an age exceeding 100 years. Skeptics proclaimed the mystery of the Madrona Monster solved, and while white sturgeons may reach twenty feet in length, with a record weight on 1,798 pounds on file, none yet seen rival the Madrona Monster's reported dimensions.[35]

In October 1999, local writer Dave McBee was prowling the lake's shoreline near Seattle's Washington Park Arboretum when he sighted — but failed to photograph or capture — a turtle the size of a "manhole cover." While the reptile eluded him, McBee claimed that his "monster" was a common snapping turtle (*Chelydra serpentina*), normally found in

America east of the Continental Divide, ranging from the Midwest states southward, through Mexico and Central America. Average specimens have shells ten to eighteen inches long, and boast a record weight of seventy-five pounds. McBee's specimen was thus a true giant — unless, perhaps, he glimpsed an alligator snapper (*Macrochelys temminckii*), another exotic transplant that may reach thirty-two inches in length and weigh up to four hundred pounds.[36]

In *Chapter Two*, we examined reports of phantom caimans in Lake Washington, seen in 1967 and the mid-1980s. Echoes of those sightings were heard in March 2005, when Medina police logged reports of a beast with "the head of an alligator" paddling around the docks in Fairweather Bay, not far from the home of Microsoft mogul Bill Gates. According to police spokesperson Shannon Gibson, two witnesses reported separate sightings. "Both were essentially the same," she told the *Post-Intelligencer*. "The people said they saw something that seemed to be a small alligator. The one report said 'head of an alligator.' Both were seen from the docks of their residences."[37]

Sergeant Kim Chandler, speaking for the Department of Fish and Wildlife, said, "Well, after that cougar was found in Discovery Park back in the 1980s, I've learned never to say never. But, in this case I'd have to say, even if it were a caiman, it would be highly unlikely to see it in that lake this time of year. Know how cold that lake is right now? Probably something like forty-seven degrees, which means an animal like that would last for, oh, maybe twenty minutes."[38]

Nine days later, with no crocodilian in sight, Officer Gibson told the *Mercer Island Reporter*, "At this point it's just a wait-and-see. They wouldn't be able to survive long in this water." Still, talk of a local "Loch Ness Monster" sold newspapers, and prompted state legislators to debate an Exotic Pets Bill. As finally enacted, the new law banned private possession of "potentially dangerous animals" after July 2007. According to that law, "A potentially dangerous animal includes but is not limited to large cats, wolves, bears, hyenas, non-human primates, elephants, alligators, crocodiles, water monitors, crocodile monitors; and various species of venomous snakes."[39]

In May 2005 a team of fisheries researchers from the University of Washington inadvertently netted another large sturgeon at Lake Washington, photographed the five and a half-foot fish, and then released it. The story broke in June, prompting reporter Lewis Kamb at the *Post-Intelligencer* to speculate that "maybe, just maybe, the recently netted specimen — or another of its ilk — could be the culprit behind a recent rash of reported Lake Washington reptile sightings."[40] Perhaps, but the case remains unproved.

Lake Washington's next cryptid, first "sighted" in October 2005, was wholly fictional. Director Oliver Tuttle's Willatuk, said to roam at will from Puget Sound to Lake Washington, via Lake Union, failed to reach theater screens, but Tuttle's advertising did land the beast its own Wikipedia entry.[41]

Moses Lake, Washington (1992)

Moses Lake consists of three arms drowning 6,800 acres. Its longest arm measures eighteen miles from north to south, and is one mile across at its widest point. The lake's mean depth is nineteen feet, with a maximum recorded depth of thirty-eight feet. Its present size dates from 1900, when a dam erected as part of the Columbia Basin Project expanded a smaller, salty predecessor called Salt Lake. The new, improved lake is named for Chief Sulktalthscosum of the local Sinkiuse-Columbia tribe, also known as Chief Moses. A town on the lake's shore, named Neppel in 1910, was also renamed to honor the chief in 1938.[42]

Aboriginal tales of Moses Lake describe multiple resident ghosts, including a female specter with "the head of a goblin," but the first recognizable cryptid sighting dates from April 15, 1992, when witness Cliff Johnson saw "a large reptile-like animal" swimming near Marsh Island, in the lake's southernmost arm. The creature raised its head in snakelike fashion, and Johnson claimed that head was the size of a human's. Author John Kirk notes that Moses Lake had no prior record of sightings, logging Johnson's beast as "the newest of the breed."[43]

Metolius River, Oregon (1936)

Metolius River is a tributary of Lake Billy Chinook, located in central Oregon's Cove Palisades State Park. The lake was created by construction of the Round Butte Dam, in 1964. The Metolius flows north from springs near Black Butte, and then turns sharply eastward to complete its twenty-nine-mile course, draining a 315-square-mile basin that contains forty-two lakes, 121 ponds, and 110 miles of perennial springs.[44]

More than a quarter-century before the Round Butte Dam's construction, in March 1936, the Metolius produced its own cryptid.

Fisherman Jack McDaniels hauled an octopus from the river on March 15 and placed it on display in Redmond's general store. The creature measured twenty-eight inches long and ignited a fierce controversy.[45]

Oregon naturalist William Finley, vice president of the National Wildlife Conference, instantly dismissed the capture as a hoax, insisting that a cephalopod "couldn't possibly have traveled up the Columbia over the Cascades and the Celilo Falls, and up the falls of the Deschutes and into the Metolius." Edward Averill, Oregon's ex-game commissioner, added his voice to the cries of "Hoax!" Stanley Jewett, head of the United States Bureau of Biological Survey (now the U.S. Fish & Wildlife Service), viewed the specimen March 16, telling the *Portland Oregonian*, "The Redmond octopus is real, but I am not convinced of its origin."[46]

More journalistic ridicule ensued. On March 17, George Aitken, speaking for the Deschutes County Sportsmen's Association, told the *Oregonian* that, while McDaniels indeed pulled his catch from the Metolius, "the octopus arrived here overland from California about 10 days ago, I have been reliably informed." Secretary W. S. Rice of the Oregon Wildlife Council went further the next day, declaring that the octopus had been preserved in brine and was "very dead" before McDaniels snagged it with his hook. All accounts suggest that McDaniels was an innocent victim of hoaxers that remain unidentified today.[47]

Omak Lake, Washington

Omak Lake is a saline endorheic lake — a closed drainage basin that retains water and permits no outflow to rivers, other lakes, or oceans. It is the largest saline lake in Washington, with a surface area of 3,244 acres and a verified depth of 325 feet.[48]

Residents of the surrounding Colville Indian Reservation, established in April 1872, maintain a long-standing tradition of monsters or spirits inhabiting the lake, but details are vague and no reports of modern sightings appear in cryptozoological literature.[49]

The sole attempt to document Omak Lake's cryptids is an 82-page book written by tribal lawyer Frank LaFountaine in 2005, titled *The Omak Lake Monster: A Modern Tale of a Lake Monster Encounter*. LaFountaine says that local residents believe the lake's creature "is real and menacing to anyone not giving it space," but his claim is undermined by reference to an expedition led by a nonexistent "respected scientist," one "Dr. Warren Earlhand" — and by his publisher's description of the book as fiction.[50]

An octopus was pulled from the Metolius River in 1936. *Courtesy of U.S. National Oceanic and Atmospheric Association.*

Pend Oreille River, Washington

The Pend Oreille River is a tributary of the Columbia, beginning at Idaho's Lake Pend Oreille and flowing westward for 130 miles, passing through Washington's Pend Oreille County and looping through British Columbia for fifteen miles, before it meets the Columbia five miles south of Montrose, B.C. In Canada, the river's name is generally spelled "Pend d'Oreille."[51]

John Kirk III, a founder of the British Columbia Scientific Cryptozoology Club and editor of its quarterly newsletter since 1996, is the only author on record who lists the Pend Oreille River as a cryptid habitat, and his published citation provides no details. Research for this volume uncovered a possible source for Kirk's listing, in folk tales of the aboriginal Pend d'Oreille tribe, also known as Kalispels, who preceded white settlers in Montana and Washington.[52]

According to those legends, a huge monster once inhabited the Pend d'Oreilles' homeland, until their chief deity — known as "One Who Sits on Top" — dispatched a fox and coyote to slay the menacing beast. The monster, disguised as a bighorn ram, pursued the new arrivals and dashed itself to death against a massive tree. The legend suggests no surviving river monsters, but Montana's Flathead Lake is famous for a cryptid seen sporadically from 1885 into the 1990s. No traceable reports expand its range to include the Pend Oreille River.[53]

Rock Lake, Washington

"Rock Lake" is a popular name for bodies of water in Washington State, which boasts ten lakes so named. They include one each in Chelan, Douglas, Skamania, and Whitman Counties, with two each in King, Lincoln, and Okanogan (which also boasts a third body of water dubbed Rock Lakes).[54] Our first report of monstrous activity, penned by folklorist Charles Skinner in 1896, reads simply:

> So with Rock Lake, in Washington. A hideous reptile sports about its waters and gulps down everything that it finds in or on them. Only in 1853 a band of Indians, who had fled hither for security against the soldiers, were overtaken by this creature, lashed to death, and eaten.[55]

But which Rock Lake? Here, the Internet comes to our rescue, placing the lake in question near a town named Rock Lake, in Whitman County. This particular Rock Lake is seven and a half miles long, one mile across at its widest point, and boasts a maximum recorded depth of 375 feet.[56]

The same website provides a summary of "serpent monster myths/stories/realities" related to Rock Lake, including a report published by the now-defunct *Palouse News* in the late nineteenth century. According to that story, one J. C. Cady was hunting along the lake's shore when he saw an apparent large animal swimming just below the surface. As it drew closer, Cady made a startling discovery. He explained:

> "At last it dawned on me. Only a few feet away and directly below me was a solid column of suckers. The column was as large around as a man's body and about ten feet long. Each sucker was standing straight up in the water. The top of the column was about a foot below the surface of the water. After watching this strange phenomenon for a while, I took a shot with my rifle at the fish.

Instantly it broke from its unity into a thousand fragments, each fragment being a sucker. Had the fish not been so near the shore that I could see them distinctly I should have been convinced that the body disturbing the water was the wonderful monster about which so much had been written. I believe that what I saw solved the mystery of the Rock Lake sea serpent [sic]."[57]

Suckers are fish from the family *Catostomidae*, including some eighty-six species worldwide, inhabiting freshwater lakes and rivers. Most species reach maturity below two feet in length, though some may reach 3.3 feet.[58]

Despite Cady's explanation, occasional cryptid sightings persist from Rock Lake. A local family, the Smiths, have collected several monster reports from the lake, which they relayed to John Kirk. The tales include the disappearance of three Native American women, snatched from their canoe on Rock Lake and never seen again, plus two sigtings of a creature resembling a floating log. An in-law of the Smiths, the late Fred Wagner — known as "a religious man [who] wouldn't lie" — was passing Rock Lake with an employee when both men saw an animal initially mistaken for three men in a canoe. Family spokesman Leroy "Pete" Smith, of St. John, believes the resident cryptids are sturgeons, though none have been hauled from Rock Lake within living memory.[59]

Spirit Lake, Washington

Spirit Lake lies north of Mount St. Helens, in Skamania County. Before the catastrophic volcanic eruption of 1980, Spirit Lake was surrounded by lush forests and claimed a maximum recorded depth of 189 feet. Outpourings of lava blocked the North Fork Toutle River at its outlet, raising the lake's surface elevation more than two hundred feet, while reducing its surface area by ten percent (to 3.9 square miles) and leaving Spirit Lake with a maximum depth of 117 feet, as recorded in October 1986.[60]

Fish did not reappear in Spirit Lake until 1993, and they were a far cry from the resident monster feared by aboriginal inhabitants, described as "a demon so huge that its hand could stretch across the whole lake." When Canadian artist Paul Kane passed through the district in 1847, he found no local tribesmen willing to hire on as guides, but they warned him of Spirit Lake's man-eating monster, as well as "a strange fish with the head of a bear." Kane met neither, and no sightings of any unusual beasts in the lake have been logged in modern times.[61]

Upper Klamath Lake, Oregon

Oregon's largest lake lies in Klamath County, east of the Cascades. It measures twenty miles long and eight miles across at its widest point. Upper Klamath Lake is fed by several streams, including the Williamson River, but the U.S. Bureau of Reclamation has regulated its depth since 1917, ranging from eight to sixty feet at various times.[62]

Nineteenth century author Charles Skinner reports that local tribesmen "avoided Klamath Lake because it was haunted by a monster that was half dragon, half hippopotamus," but no reports allude to any sightings by Anglo-American settlers since their arrival in 1846.[63]

Wallowa Lake, Oregon

OLregon's most famous "monster" lake lies one mile south of Joseph, at the far northeastern corner of the state. It is a ribbon lake, created when a glacier's sharp-edged boulders gouge a long depression in softer bedrock, dammed by moraines. Wallowa Lake is five miles long and one mile wide at its broadest point, with a maximum recorded depth of 283 feet.[64] Those depths allegedly conceal a cryptid known as "Big Wally."

And, as at Lake Washington, published reports suggest that it is not alone.

Before they were driven from their homeland by duplicitous politicians, in 1877, local Nez Perce tribesmen feared a great horned beast said to dwell in Wallowa Lake. Accidentally discovered by a native hunter, the monster devoured him when he followed it into the water. Others suffered a similar fate, until Indians shunned the lake entirely. A Shakespearean touch was added when the monster ate young lovers Wahluna and Tlescaoe, the son and daughter of two warring Blackfoot and Nez Perce chiefs, memorialized as an aboriginal Romeo and Juliet.[65]

Other native legends claim that Wallowa Lake is bottomless, perhaps connected to other American lakes by a maze of subterranean caverns. Proponents of that tale cite the undocumented case of a fisherman who drowned in Wallowa Lake and allegedly surfaced in Lake Erie, 1,800 miles to the east.[66]

The first white settler's sighting of a Lake Wallowa cryptid appeared in a local newspaper, *The Wallowa Chieftain*, on November 5, 1885. It read:

A prospector, who refuses to give his name to the public, was coming down from the south end of the lake on last Friday evening in a skiff shortly after dusk, when about midway on the lake he saw an animal about fifty yards to the right of the boat, rear its head and neck up out of the water ten or twelve feet, but on seeing him it immediately dived.

The prospector ceased rowing and gazed around in astonishment for the strange apparition which he had just seen, abruptly raised about the same distance to the left, this time giving a low bellow something like that of a cow. It also brought its body to the surface, which the prospector avers was one hundred feet in length.

The monster glided along in sight for several hundred yards. It was too dark to see the animal distinctly, but it seemed to have a large, flat head, something like that of a hippopotamus, and its neck, which was about ten feet in length, was as large around as a man's body.

This story may have been coined in the imagination of the narrator, but he was very earnest in his recital. However, it is a known fact that there is a tradition among the Indians that the lake has a big sea cow in it, which on one occasion, many years ago, came up one evening and swallowed a young warrior and his dusky bride as they were gliding over the surface of the lake in a canoe. And to this day an Indian of the tribes who formerly frequented its shores cannot be induced to go upon its waters.[67]

Spirit Lake, the alleged habitat of a man-eating monster. *Courtesy of U.S. Dept. of Fish & Wildlife.*

Sea cows (*Hydrodamalis gigas*) were large sirenian mammals once abundant in the North Pacific, where they reached lengths of twenty-six feet and averaged eight to ten tons in weight. Discovered in 1741 and reportedly exterminated by 1768, they were toothless relatives of the manatees and dugongs, sharing the herbivorous diet of those surviving species. None were man-eaters, and none are believed to have dwelled in freshwater lakes.[68]

Published descriptions of Big Wally contradict each other radically. Some refer to a "Chinese dragon" twelve feet long, sporting the "head of a hog," with or without a rhinoceros-like horn on its snout. Others compare the beast's head to that of a bison, with eyes set fourteen inches apart. Still others refer to a fish like a giant sturgeon or shark.[69]

Twentieth century witnesses compound the confusion. Their tales apparently begin with Irene Wiggins, who bought the Wallowa Lake Lodge in 1945 and ran it until 1988. She claimed several sightings of Big Wally spanning four decades, but details are sparse.[70]

Other reports include:

- **1950**: The Portland Oregonian reported that three witnesses had seen Big Wally feeding on Kokanee salmon (Oncorhynchus nerka). They described the creature as sixteen feet long, with a skull "as wide as a buffalo head."[71]
- **July 1952**: Mr. and Mrs. Daniels were boating on Lake Wallowa when they saw three sturgeon-like animals "basking and playing in the sun." Since the apparent fish were larger than any boat on the water that day, the couple fled to shore, fearing their own boat might be capsized.[72]

Wallowa Lake, home of "Big Wally" and other cryptids. *Courtesy of U.S. Dept. of Fish & Wildlife.*

- **July 1955**: Members of the Christman family and other unnamed witnesses watched two huge "fish" cavorting on the lake's surface, raising large waves as they chased one another in circles.[73]
- **1978**: A couple named Bryant logged their first sighting of Big Wally while driving along the lake's shore. In fact, they saw three objects "like the top half of a loop," each two feet wide, spanning some twenty-five feet. After submerging once, the undulating beast resurfaced, swimming back the way it had come. A year later, in July 1979, the Bryants saw a twenty-foot serpentine form swimming across Wallowa Lake.[74]
- **June 30, 1982**: Marjorie Crammer and Kirk Marks saw a different beast, swimming alone near the lake's northeastern shore. It was fifty feet long, displayed seven dark humps on the surface, and left a large wake as it passed.[75]
- **Early 1980s**: Witnesses Joe Babic and Bert Repplinger saw a serpentine creature swimming in Wallowa Lake, head and neck raised three feet above the surface. Three unnamed women confirmed the sighting, according to author John Kirk.[76]

There matters rest, but Big Wally is not forgotten. In March 2004, Portland State University adjunct biology professor Douglas Larson penned an editorial inviting the monster to stage a comeback and repel housing developers who threatened to encroach on Wallowa Lake's north shore.[77]

Willamette River, Oregon

This tributary of the Columbia River does not appear on any published list of "monster" habitats, but it may hold surprises in store for visiting fishermen. On July 4, 2005, Ted Sowers of Salem, Oregon, was angling for bass in the Willamette River, when he hooked a catfish nearly three feet long. Once landed, the fish measured thirty-five and a half inches and tipped the scales at fifteen pounds, ten ounces.[78]

Sowers later told Salem's *Statesman Journal*, "I was just shocked it was a catfish. Then we couldn't figure out what kind it was. It was almost ugly, you know. We landed it, and we looked at it for quite awhile, and there were no spots on it anywhere, no coloring other than what you see (in the picture), and the eyes were WHITE. The eyes just seemed like they didn't have any color." [Emphasis in the original.] The fish remained unidentified when the story was reported on July 21.[79]

Catfish (order *Siluriformes*) are found on every continent except Antarctica, with thirty-seven families and 872 species presently recognized. Sponsors of the All Catfish Inventory Survey suggest that another 1,750 species await discovery worldwide. Known species range in size from .39 inches to 8.2 feet. The largest specimens on record in America are a blue catfish (*Ictalurus furcatus*) weighing 124 pounds and a flathead catfish (*Pylodictis olivaris*) weighing 123 pounds and nine ounces. The flathead is sometimes called the yellow catfish, but its normal range does not extend west of the Mississippi River. The same is true for another species, the yellow bullhead (*Ameiurus natalis*). No known species features all-white eyes.[80]

The Willamette River flows for 187 miles between the Oregon Coast Range and the Cascades, with a maximum depth of 130 feet reported from Portland. Anglers who try their luck along its shores may not hook yellow, white-eyed catfish, but they have a chance of landing white sturgeon. Legal size limits imposed by the ODFW range from thirty-eight to fifty-four inches, depending on the geographical location. Fisherman Chris Brooks and his son Jacob landed eleven sturgeon on September 11, 2005, fishing on the Willamette near Portland's St. Johns Bridge.[81]

Blue catfish are among the Pacific Northwest's largest known freshwater species. *Courtesy of U.S. Dept. of Fish & Wildlife.*

The Wishpoosh

Our last supposed lake monster is a creature of Nez Perce legend, described as a giant beaver with enormous claws, said to inhabit an unnamed "vast lake." It preyed on tribal fishermen until the Nez Perce called on their trickster god Coyote for assistance. Coyote not only managed to kill the monster, but also used parts of its carcass to create new tribes, including the Chinook, Klickitat, and Yakima.[82]

Our only clue to the location of the monster's former habitat is the modern-day Wish Poosh Campground, at Cle Elum Lake, located in Washington's Wenatchee National Forest. While hardly "vast," at 7.1 miles in length and one mile wide, with a capacity of 436,900 acre feet, Cle Elum Lake is larger today than in olden times, thanks to a 165-foot dam built in 1933.[83]

No modern sightings of the wishpoosh are recorded, but reports of giant beavers have been logged from other parts of North America. Aboriginal folklore includes tales of huge beavers ranging from eastern Canada and New England to British Columbia, and fossilized remains of an actual giant species (*Castoroides ohioensis*) were found near Nashport, Ohio, in 1837. That specimen measured 8.2 feet long, with an estimated live weight of 130 to 220 pounds. Several lakes in Utah still produce occasional sightings of giant beavers, the most recent logged from Lake Powell in August 2002.[84]

Chapter Five

Winged Wonders

Cryptids are not confined to land or water. Some of the most startling and elusive soar above our heads, amazing witnesses who glimpse them briefly, then are left to cope with ridicule when they report their sightings. Some winged creatures seen in Oregon and Washington resemble species long believed to be extinct, while others are the stuff of nightmares, unlike any denizen of Earth from past of present.

Thunderbirds

Throughout North America, aboriginal folklore and legends describe giant raptors resembling huge eagles or vultures, known by many names in native dialects, collectively dubbed "thunderbirds." Tireless researcher Mark Hall has compiled thunderbird legends and modern sightings from coast to coast, including certain stories relevant to the Northwest.

Prehistoric teratorns resemble the "thunderbirds" of Native American legend.

According to Hall, Washington's Olympic Peninsula "is certainly the hub of western Thunderbird lore." Chinook and Chehalis tribesmen dwelling around Grays Harbor called the birds hahness while the Kathlamet of the lower Columbia River called their thunderbirds "abductors of maidens," describing them as relentless hunters of humans. Along the western face of the Olympic Mountains, members of the Hoh, Klallam, Makah, Quilleute, and Quinault tribes all described their giant birds for anthropologists during the 1930s. Twana tribesmen, inhabiting the Hood Canal on Puget Sound, described huge bird's nests littered with whalebones. The Quinault passed down the story of a whale found on a mountainside, still breathing, with its dorsal fin ripped off by the raptor that dropped it.[1]

Nor were the fearsome birds regarded as extinct by local tribes. Researcher René Dahinden collected tales of living thunderbirds from Washington, during his search for Bigfoot in the 1960s, and relayed them to Mark Hall in 1980. Long before that, on February 7, 1954, witness Gladie Bills and her teenage daughter saw six birds "the size of airplanes" circling above Hillsboro, Oregon.[2]

If thunderbirds exist, what could they be? Officially, Earth's largest living bird is the Andean condor (*Vultur gryphus*), a native of South America that boasts a ten-foot wingspan, a record beak-to-tail length of four feet three inches, and a top weight of thirty-three pounds. Its northern cousin, the endangered California condor, is North America's largest land bird, roughly equal in size to the Andean species. Both are vultures, presumed to dine primarily on carrion, and neither grows large or strong enough to lift humans, much less whales.[3]

The only other known living species likely to be mistaken for thunderbirds are eagles, of which North America harbors two species: the golden eagle (*Aquila chrysaetos*) and the bald eagle (*Haliaeetus leucocephalus*). Golden eagles are slightly larger, with a record wingspan of eight feet, a top length of just over forty inches, and a record weight of fifteen and a half pounds. The largest bald eagle on record had a wingspan of 7.6 inches, was forty inches long from beak to tail, and weighed fifteen pounds.[4] Yet neither is likely to be mistaken for an airplane at any distance.

Larger raptors did exist in prehistoric times, but modern science dismisses any possibility of their survival to the nineteenth century, much less the present day. They were the teratorns (family *Teratornithidae*), with four species known from fossil remains spanning the Miocene and Pleistocene epochs, from twenty-three million to 12,000 years ago.[5] In order of descending size, those species included:

- *Argentavis magnificens*: A true monster boasting a 26-foot wingspan, a length of eleven and a half feet, and a standing height of six and a half feet, it tips the scale between 140 and 180 pounds. Paleontologists estimate that individuals lived fifty to one hundred years and flew primarily by soaring on updrafts, like modern vultures.[6]
- *Aiolornis incredibilis* (formerly *Teratornis incredibilis*): North America's largest flight-capable bird; fragmentary fossils found in California and Nevada suggest a seventeen-foot wingspan and a top weight around fifty pounds.[7]
- *Teratornis merriami*: Known from more than one hundred fossil specimens found throughout Arizona, California, Florida, and Nevada — though most were found in southern California's Rancho La Brea Tar Pits — the *T. merriami* boasted a twelve-foot wingspan, stood thirty inches tall at rest, and weighed about thirty-three pounds.[8]
- *Cathartornis gracilis*: Known only from a couple of fossilized leg bones found at Rancho La Brea; based on that minimal evidence, the species was slightly shorter and more slender than *Teratornis merriami*, but no estimates of wingspan are available.[9]

Modern reports compiled by Mark Hall and other researchers strongly suggest that birds resembling *Argentavis magnificens* were known to North America's aboriginal tribes — and still appear to witnesses in the twenty-first century, ranging from the Alaskan wilderness to Pennsylvania.[10]

Pterosaurs at Large

If avian survivors from the Pleistocene ice age seem improbable, what are we to make of reports that describe apparent living pterosaurs from the Triassic and Cretaceous periods, 220 million to 65.5 million years ago? The notion seems fantastic, but eyewitness sightings are on file from 1892 to 2007.

Pterosaurs ("winged lizards") were the first known vertebrates capable of powered flight. Although reptiles, they were not dinosaurs — a name properly reserved for terrestrial reptiles of the *superorder Dinosauria*, also excluding aquatic reptiles such as the *ichthyosaurs*, *plesiosaurs*, and *mosasaurs*. The order Pterosauria includes two suborders and sixteen recognized families. The largest known species, *Quetzalcoatlus*, boasted a wingspan of thirty-three to forty feet, tipping the scales at 200 to 550 pounds. All species are presumed extinct today.[11]

And yet...

On November 19, 1892, Montana's *Bitterroot Times* published the story of three travelers who met an amphibious flying monster at Lake Chelan, Washington. As described in that account, after a night of camping at a lakeside spot called Devil's Slide, one of the men arose to bathe in the shallows. Moments later, his companions were roused by his screams, arriving in time to see their friend submerging, pulled by one leg. They grabbed his arms and hauled the unfortunate victim ashore...

"... but what was their surprise to see the monster also emerge from the water firmly attached to the man's leg by its teeth. It was a horrid looking creature, with the legs and body of an alligator and the head and restless eye of a serpent. Between its fore and hind legs, on either side, were large, ribbed feathery looking wings. The tail was scaled but not barbed like that in the picture of the typical dragon. With the exception of the under part of the throat and the tips of the wings, feet and tail, the creature was a beautiful white and its skin as soft as velvet. Knives, sticks and stones, and everything else, which were brought to bear upon the monster, proved unavailing, and at last the ingenious travelers bethought themselves of a heroic measure. They built a good fire and pulled the neck and belly of the beast, bird, or fish across it, taking good care not to burn the leg of their comrade in the operation. After a while the scorching heat aroused the animal from its torpor. It began to move its body and to stretch out its leathery wings after the manner of a bat, and suddenly flew into the air, still holding the man by the leg. After rising to a height of about 200 feet it took a 'header' downward toward the lake, into which it plunged with a splash, burying itself and victim out of sight."[12]

The story smacks of fabrication, from the anonymity of its alleged participants to the confusion of "feathery" and "leathery" wings, through the description of a hungry predator lapsing into "torpor" with a meal still in its jaws. Nonetheless, it was repeated in abbreviated form by the *New Orleans Daily Picayune*, two weeks later.[13] The rest is silence... at least, for the next 115 years.

Wenatchee, Washington, lies thirty-six miles south of Lake Chelan. On December 27, 2007, an unnamed local resident crashed his car into a streetlight while driving through the community of 28,000 residents. When police arrived and asked what caused the accident, the twenty-nine-year-old driver replied with one word: "Pterodactyl." During treatment for his minor injuries at Central Washington Hospital, the motorist was subjected to a breathalyzer test, which revealed "a minimal amount of alcohol." He was released without any charge or citation for driving while intoxicated. The alleged flying reptile remains elusive.[14]

A Flying Man

If prehistoric reptiles winging overhead strain credulity, flying humanoids are even more bizarre, but that has not prevented their appearance throughout modern history in various parts of the world. One such event occurred at 3 p.m. on January 6, 1948, in Chehalis, Washington.

That afternoon, 61-year-old Bernice Zaikowski was relaxing in her home when she was roused by startled cries from several children playing in her yard. Stepping outside to investigate, she heard "a sizzling and whizzing" sound that drew her attention to a point twenty feet in the air above her nearby barn. There, Mrs. Zaikowski saw a man equipped with artificial silver wings, strapped to his shoulders, performing aerial maneuvers while manipulating a set of controls attached to his chest.[15]

The strange figure soon departed, flapping out of sight, and while military officers drove forty-three miles from McChord Air Force Base to examine the scene, they dismissed the sighting as "one of those [flying] saucer deals." Author Loren Coleman claims that the story ended there, but Mrs. Zaikowski insisted that she "talked to some people in Chehalis that tell me they saw the man, too, and that he flew south from Chehalis and apparently came from the north or east."[16]

Three months later, on April 7, witnesses Viola Johnson and James Pittman saw "three men in dark drab flying suits flying through the air" above their workplace in Longview, Washington. As Johnson described it, the figures were "about 250 feet high, circling the city, going about as fast as a freight train. I couldn't see any motors or propellers on them, but I could hear motors like airplane motors, but not as loud. They had some kind of apparatus on their sides which looked like guns." According to UFO researcher Albert Rosales, "other residents reported hearing plane motors and seeing three planes circle at a high altitude."[17]

Rosales also logs the year's final sighting of winged humanoids, carelessly citing two different locations separated by three counties. He initially places the event near Grassy Butte, Oregon (Deschutes County), then at Grassy Mountain (in Malheur County). The latter must be correct, since witness Fred Scott was engaged in a marathon hike from Antelope (in Wasco County) to Rome (Malheur County) when the incident occurred, and a side trip southward to Deschutes County is both exhausting and illogical. According to Rosales, Scott was passing Grassy Mountain when he glanced at the sky and beheld two "flying persons" winging eastward in tandem, at an altitude of 150 to 250 feet. Neither airborne figure flapped its wings, which were "narrow and rounded at the tip." Scott deemed their legs "unusually short, almost as if cut off at the knees." He watched them slowly pass from sight, while he walked on for another half-mile or more.[18]

Italian Renaissance man Leonardo da Vinci sketched many inventions throughout his illustrious life, including a series of mechanical devices intended to grant human beings the power of flight. Drawn in various forms, including one apparatus patterned on bats' wings, these "ornithopters" were never constructed or tested, as far as we know.[19] If some successor to da Vinci managed to perfect such a system in the 1940s, it remains a closely-guarded secret.

Batsquatch

An even more bizarre departure from perceived reality is "Batsquatch," an alleged real-life version of the winged monkeys seen in "The Wizard of Oz," purportedly inhabiting the neighborhood of Washington's Mount Rainier. As readers might suspect, the creature's label is descriptive, portraying a Sasquatch-like monster with wings resembling a bat's.

Batsquatch's first appearance has proved difficult to trace. One Internet website dates sightings from "1980 to present," but offers no substantiating details. Columnist C. R. Roberts penned the first published tale of a sighting for the *Tacoma News Tribune* on April 24, 1994.[20]

That column related a story told by eighteen-year-old Brian Canfield, describing events that allegedly occurred on the night of April 16. At 9:30 that evening, while he was driving back from Buckley to Camp One, an "isolated settlement...located in the Mount Rainier foothills above Lake Kapowsin," Canfield's car unaccountably died. Seconds later, he saw a winged, nine-foot-tall creature with "blue-tinted fur, yellowish eyes, tufted ears and sharp straight teeth" land on the pavement before him.

Canfield told Roberts, "It was standing there staring at me, like it was resting, like it didn't know what to think. I was scared. It raised the hair on me. I didn't feel threatened. I just felt out of place."[21]

Providing further details, Canfield said, "Its eyes were yellow and shaped like a piece of pie with pupils like a half-moon. The mouth was pretty big. White teeth. No fangs. The face was like a wolf [sic]." After several minutes, the beast unfurled its wings and flew off toward Mount Rainier.[22]

C. R. Roberts assures us that Canfield was "an average, normal kid" who abstained completely from alcohol and drugs. Still, something is wrong with his story. Exhaustive research for this chapter indicates that no "Camp One" exists in Pierce County, Washington. There is such a settlement in Pacific County, but two other counties — Thurston and Lewis — separate Pierce from Pacific. All the other landmarks mentioned in the Roberts article, meanwhile, are found within Pierce County.[23]

Another 1994 report of Batsquatch, mentioned on various Internet websites, smacks of a hoax. The witness, one Butch Whittaker, is described as a mountaineer, a liquor store owner, and an "expert in paranormal activity and unexplained phenomena."[24] The nature of his expertise is also unexplained, and Whittaker remained untraceable at press time for this book.

As described on the Web, Whittaker was preparing to ascend Mount St. Helens, fifty miles south of Mount Rainier, on some unspecified date in 1994, when he saw Batsquatch in broad daylight. Whittaker allegedly snapped several photos of the creature, which remain unpublished. (The Internet photos of a purple creature alleged to be Batsquatch are obvious, comical fakes.) In the wake of his encounter, Whittaker supposedly remarked, "I'm not surprised. These things happen to me all the time." Whittaker's comment, allegedly quoted from an unnamed "prominent Washington periodical," has likewise proved unverifiable.[25]

The same website that offers Whittaker's observation and several hoaxed photos of Batsquatch also includes an anonymous sighting report from February 1998. That tale, beginning with the observation that "It was a dark and stormy night," relates the author's alleged sighting of a Batsquatch on the slopes of an unnamed Washington peak. Amid much melodrama, including claims that "my silence has caused the death of so many animals and put a town at risk," the author — "A Believer" — describes a purple beast resembling something from "a bad Jimmy Osmond dream." Ludicrous in the extreme, the story ends with an observation that "my worst fears are that I will be traced by my e-mail address and someone would know my location. Thus making me a laughing stock of my community and ending my rather prestigious position within the city. If you would like to hear more of the story, you may e-mail me. However, should you make any attempt to trace my e-mail address, I will deny everything."[26]

Another Internet report, dated May 7, 2009, transplants Batsquatch to the vicinity of Eugene, Oregon, where a "very trustworthy" teenage witness named "R. Lee" allegedly saw a seven-foot creature with "red reflecting eyes and very large wings" lurking around his home at 1:15 a.m. A proposed plan to catch the monster with shark hooks and a lamb carcass presumably proved fruitless.[27]

Wings over Mount Pilchuk

Our next flying monster almost seems to be a hybrid cross between Batsquatch and Chelan County's elusive pterosaur — in short, a winged creature of more-or-less humanoid form, but with reptilian features. Its one and only appearance, near Mount Pilchuck, reportedly occurred in 1981, but remained unpublished for another quarter-century.

Mount Rainier, the supposed domain of Batsquatch. *Courtesy of U.S. Dept. of Fish & Wildlife.*

According to British author Neil Arnold and an Internet poster known only as "Alien Embryo," the incident in question occurred near Mount Pilchuck, a 2,860-foot peak in the Cascade Range, surrounded by Mount Pilchuck State Park and the larger Mount Baker-Snoqualmie National Forest. No date beyond the year is known, but since the six elderly witnesses were en route to a picnic, we may safely assume that the season was spring or summer.[28]

The story's source remains obscure. Arnold cites none, while "Alien Embryo" vaguely attributes the tale to "a friend." Both versions describe a meeting between the witnesses — two carloads of anonymous sexagenarians — and local police, at an unnamed restaurant in Granite Falls. The picnickers had stopped to photograph Mount Pilchuck when they noticed an airborne object resembling a man with a hang-glider. As it drew nearer, they made out the creature's inhuman appearance. It was, they said, "at least seven to eight feet tall, [with] leathery skin, large wings, big feet and hand-like claws, somewhat humanoid, and lizard looking."[29]

Understandably frightened, the seniors piled into their two cars and raced toward Granite Falls, pursued by the monster. It swooped from the sky to attack them, scarring the paint on both cars with its talons. One driver allegedly suffered a heart attack or stroke, swerving off the highway and into a ditch, while his friends in the other car fled

Reports of winged monsters persist from Mount Pilchuk. *Courtesy of U.S. Dept. of Fish & Wildlife.*

to get help. Both versions of the tale describe police returning to the scene and firing at the beast without effect, then summoning military personnel who arrived "within an hour," taking charge of the witnesses and their damaged vehicles. Further research is hopeless, we are told, since "the police department burned down two years later, losing all records."[30]

That tale reads like an episode of "The X-Files," with its trappings of conspiracy. Inquiries to the local newspaper and public library produced no further information by the time this volume went to press.

Stranger Still

The year 1996 brought two more reports of weird things with wings, closing our inventory on a typically strange note. Motorist Lynn Johnson was driving through Lane County, Oregon, south of Cottage Grove, when a bizarre creature ran onto the pavement. Johnson estimated its speed at sixty to seventy miles per hour, but her description of the beast is even more remarkable. She said it was "the size of a deer, four feet tall, legs like a deer, clove hoofed [sic], and on two legs." Seeing her car, the creature spread "gray leathery wings" and "shot almost straight up" into the air, flying northward. Internet archivist Albert Rosales later claimed "the wings, with feathers, seemed too small to support the body," with an approximate length of eighteen inches.[31]

Rosales also logged the next report, omitting a specific date, but noting that the incident occurred at 11:30 p.m. An unnamed female witness allegedly saw "a gigantic winged creature" flying over Spokane, Washington, alternately rising and descending "at a leisure[ly] pace." That said, Rosales concludes that the witness "watched it, stunned as it flew quickly away towards Canada."[32] Fast or slow, the thing remains unidentified.

Chapter Six

Bigfoot in Oregon

While every American state except Hawaii has Bigfoot sightings on file, most authorities regard the Pacific Northwest as the epicenter of encounters with large unknown bipeds in North America.

Sadly, there is no central database for sightings of cryptids or footprints and none of the sources agree on the final tally. For example:

- The Seattle-based Sasquatch Information Society (SIS) listed twenty-six Oregon Bigfoot reports in October 2009, while removal of one duplicate entry reduced the total to twenty-five.[1]
- Authors Colin and Janet Bord list sixty-seven sightings from Oregon between 1885 and 1980.[2]
- John Green, writing in 1978, claimed 176 Oregon sightings of Bigfoot and/or footprints.[3]
- Christopher Murphy, in 2006, also claimed 176 Oregon sightings.[4]
- The Bigfoot Field Researchers Organization (BFRO) claimed 213 Oregon cases in October 2009, but six of those "cases" were newspaper articles duplicating field reports.[5]
- The Oregon Bigfoot website listed 676 Oregon reports in October 2009, of which 101 came from the BFRO.[6]
- Before its disappearance in March 2009, the International Bigfoot Society (IBS) website claimed 1,277 Oregon cases, but deletion of 281 duplicate entries reduced that total to 996. Other IBS entries include vague retellings of aboriginal legends and irrelevant reports of other cryptids, "giant chicken tracks," and so forth.[7]

Research for this book revealed a total of 1,402 alleged Bigfoot encounters from Oregon, spanning four centuries. Of those, 694 involve eyewitness sightings; 247 report discovery of footprints; and 461 describe sounds, smells, or other evidence attributed to Bigfoot without physical sightings.

In the Beginning

Long before the first European explorer set foot on the continent, aboriginal tribes recognized the existence of hairy forest-dwelling giants, known by many names in various dialects. Names applied in the Pacific Northwest included Choanito ("night people"), Hecaitomixw ("dangerous beings"), Qui yihahs ("five brothers"), Sasahevas ("wild men of the woods"), Sc'wen'ey'ti ("tall burnt hair"), See'atco ("one who runs and hides"), Skanicum ("stick Indians"), Skookum ("evil god of the woods"), Steta'l ("spirit spear"), Ste ye mah ("spirit hidden in the woods"), Tah tah kle' ah ("owl monster woman"), Tsadjatko ("giants"), Xi'lgo ("wild woman"), Yayaya-ash ("the frightener"), and Yi' dyi'tay ("wild men").[8]

It remained for twentieth century journalists to coin the names most often applied to large unknown bipeds. Canadian reporter J. W. Burns combined various aboriginal names to create "Sasquatch" in April 1929. The term "Bigfoot" first saw print in 1958, after huge tracks appeared around a road construction site in northern California.[9] By then, sightings of the creature known as Bigfoot/Sasquatch spanned more than 150 years.

Oregon's earliest claim of a Bigfoot encounter — perhaps North America's first — dates from 1752, but was not reported until 1846. Dr. John McCoughlin, chief factor of the Hudson's Bay Company's Columbia Fur District at Fort Vancouver, moved to Oregon City

Artist's conception of the elusive beast known as Bigfoot or Sasquatch. *Courtesy of William Rebsamen.*

in 1846. There, he interviewed a 106-year-old native who reminisced about events from his childhood. Around age twelve, the tribesman had observed a Sasquatch snatching salmon at the Willamette River Falls.[10]

Meanwhile, in 1811, the first discovery of an apparent Bigfoot track was logged from the Rocky Mountains in "Oregon Country," which is today part of Idaho. Witness David Thompson, an agent of the fur-trading Northwest Company, recorded the event on January 7, in a journal entry that read:

"I saw the track of a large Animal...has four large toes [about] three or four [inches] long and a small nail at the end of each. The Ball of his foot sank [about] three [inches] deeper than his Toes...the hinder part of his foot did not mark well. The whole is about fourteen [inches] long by eight [inches] wide and very much resembles a large Bear's Track. It was in the Rivulet in about six [inches of] snow."[11]

Later, in Thompson's "Narrative of His Explorations in Western America," he added: "We were in no humour to follow him; the Men and Indians would have it to be a young mammouth and I held it to be the track of a large old grizzly; yet the shortness of the nails, the ball of the foot, and its great size was not that of a Bear, otherwise that of a very large old Bear, his claws worn away, the Indians would not allow."[12]

Whatever Thompson's guides meant by a "mammouth," it seems unlikely that they were referring to the prehistoric elephant first recognized by science in 1728.

The Reverend Elkanah Walker was a missionary to the Spokane tribe from 1838 until his death in 1877. Initially based in Washington, he later settled at Forest Grove, Oregon. In 1840, Walker transcribed Spokane legends referring to hairy giants dwelling in remote portions of the Oregon Territory.[13]

Our next tale is vague, referring merely to "the 1800s," but investigation helps narrow its scope. The initial report describes residents of Thompson Flat being terrorized by a "wild man." According to the Coos Bay Historical Society, "In the old days, after all the miners had been run off by the Wildman, one brave miner decided to stay.... Some time later they found him at his sluice box with his head bashed in by a bloody rock, which was still lying nearby. At the time, the old miner was the only living soul in the area." The first gold strike at Thompson Flat occurred in 1852, and Curry County was created on December 18, 1855.[14]

Our next account — North America's first report of a Bigfoot kidnapping — was published on the front page of Salem's *Oregon Statesman* in 1857.[15] It described events occurring on the South Umpqua River, near Roseburg. A man and boy were camped, when a "loud plaintive cry" woke the youth at midnight.

> He observed an object approaching him that appeared like a man about twelve or fifteen feet high...with glaring eyes, which had the appearance of equal balls of fire. The monster drew near to the boy...and seizing him by the arm, dragged him forcibly away towards the mountains...with a velocity that seemed to our hero like flying.

> They had traveled in this manner perhaps an hour, when the monster sunk upon the earth apparently exhausted. Our hero then became aware that this creature was indeed a wild man, whose body was completely covered with shaggy brown hair, about four inches in length; some of his teeth protruded from his mouth like tuskes [sic], his hands were armed with formidable claws instead of fingers, but his feet, singular to relate, appeared natural, being clothed with moccasins similar to those worn by Indians.

> Our hero had scarcely made these observations when the "wild man" suddenly started onward as before, never for a moment relaxing his grip on the boy's arm.... They had not proceeded far before they entered an almost impenetrable thicket of logs and undergrowth, when the "wild man" stopped, reclined upon a log, and gave one shriek, terrific and prolonged...[,] immediately after which the earth opened at their feet, as if a trap door, ingeniously contrived, had

just been raised. Entering at once this subterranean abode by a ladder rudely constructed of hazel brush, they proceeded downward, perhaps 150 or 200 feet, when they reached the bottom of a vast cave, which was brilliantly illumined with a peculiar phosphorescent light, and water trickled from the sides of the cave in minute jets....

As our hero thus closely observed the interior of this awful cave, the "wild man" left him.... Presently the huge monster returned by a side door, leading gently by the hand a young and delicate female of almost miraculous grace and beauty, who had doubtless been immured in this dreadful dungeon for years... The young lady fell upon her knees, and in some unknown language... seemed to plead for the privilege of remaining forever in the cave.... This singular conduct caused our hero to imagine that the "wild man," conscience stricken, had resolved to set at liberty his lovely victim, by placing her in charge of our hero, whom he had evidently captured for that purpose. As this thought passed through [his] mind his ears were greeted with the strains of the most unearthly music....

The "wild man" wept piteously...and sobbing like a child, his eyes moist with grief, he raised her very carefully from her recumbent posture, and led her gently away as they had come.

A moment afterwards, the damsel returned alone, and advanced toward our hero with lady-like modesty and grace, placed in his hands a beautifully embossed card, upon which appeared the following words, traced in the most exquisite hand evidently the lady's own, "Boy, depart hence, forthwith, or remain and be devoured."[16]

The Chetco River, scene of an alleged double-homicide by Bigfoot in 1890. *Courtesy of U.S. Dept. of Fish & Wildlife.*

The boy then escapes, is found by miners, and reunites with his parents, who welcome him home with no thought of pursuing the Wildman.

In 1934, Tillamook tribeswoman Clara Pearson related stories from her childhood to author Elizabeth Jacobs, who published them in 1959. One story described the appearance of a hairy "wild man" and "wild woman" on the Nehalem River, during 1870.[17]

Fifteen years later, in December 1885, two unnamed but "well-known reliable citizens" of Lebanon spied a "wild man" in the woods, devouring the raw flesh of a deer. According to the witnesses, "The man was entirely destitute of clothing and his body was covered with long hair like an animal's." Nonetheless, they claimed that he "very strongly resembled" one John Mackentire, a Lebanon hunter who had vanished in the wilderness four years earlier. At their approach, the man-thing fled "with the swiftness of the wind." Other unnamed witnesses came forward with similar reports, but plans for a search of the region proved fruitless.[18]

Our next incident allegedly occurred in 1890, but was not reported until author Ivan Sanderson published an account in 1961, without citing sources. According to Sanderson, settlers residing at the mouth of the Chetco River had been "bothered for some time by really gigantic footprints" resembling a human's. Later, the action moved fifty miles inland, to a mining camp where nocturnal vandalism resulted in posting of guards. The watch was doubled after one sentry was "chased into camp by something very large, the looks of which he did not wait to investigate."[19]

Soon afterward, disaster struck. As Sanderson told the tale:

> One couple going to relieve a watch found their two companions dead and really grossly mutilated. They had in fact been literally smashed and apparently by being picked up and slammed repeatedly into the ground so that they looked as if they had fallen off a high cliff onto rocks. The account specifies that there was nothing anywhere near off which they could have fallen. The wretched men had emptied their rifles and there was both spoor and a large blood-trail leading off into the bush.[20]

On March 31, 1897, the *Burns Times-Herald* reported that "[a] trapper by the name of Powell who has been hunting and trapping on the Malheur River south of the Agency Valley this winter reports seeing a very strange animal roaming around in those parts. *The Advocate* says it is a biped of giant stature, being at least seven feet high, having long and massive arms that reach to its knees, while the whole body is covered with curly, glossy hair."[21]

The last report of the nineteenth century involves two prospectors named Bensen and Robbins. While scouting the headwaters of the Sixes River in 1899, they met a yellow-haired "devil" which stood six feet six inches tall. The beast hurled some of their camping gear over a cliff, then fled under fire from the prospectors' rifles.[22]

1900-1949

The first half of the twentieth century produced a meager fifteen Bigfoot sightings from Oregon, plus one record of footprints, one presumed Bigfoot encounter without a visual sighting, and two vague reports of multiple encounters without any useful details.

Early 1900s

First comes the tale of an elderly Oregon resident, recorded by researcher Peter Byrne. The informant claimed that in 1900, a huge foul-smelling biped "charged" his father and several friends, in the woods east of Eugene. Despite its speed and ferocity, the witnesses escaped unharmed.[23]

The winter of 1900-01 brought reports of a "kangaroo man" from Coos County, but the "very good looking" creature bore so little resemblance to the Bigfoot.[24] The Kangaroo Man is covered separately, in *Chapter Eight*.

In April 1904, the *Lane County Leader* reported that "a wild man or a queer and terrible monster" had troubled residents over the past decade. Three sightings had occurred since March 10, two logged by miner William Ward and his neighbors at Thompson Flat. Ward fired at the prowler, who responded by lobbing a four-pound stone at Ward's head, but both missed their targets.[25]

1920s

Two decades elapsed before the next recorded sighting from The Dalles. In 1925, a local farmhand twice saw a "gorilla" on his employer's property, resigning in fear after the second incident.[26]

A year later, "many sightings" were allegedly reported from Yankton, but they rated no newspaper coverage until August 1963, when passing mention of the incidents appeared in *The Oregon Journal*. The sole specific case involves a nameless motorist's report that a Sasquatch ran beside his pickup truck, peering through the driver's window.[27]

1930s

- An **undated** sighting involved hunter Bob Bailey glimpsing a Bigfoot along Mosby Creek, but no further details are available.
- **August 1933** produced three sightings of a "shaggy-appearing human" with "an animal-like face" from Clatsop County. Before 1933 came to an end, a hiker found humanoid footprints accompanied by a "rank, porky smell" along the Calapooia River.
- In the **winter of 1937-38**, witness Carol Cole logged a sighting involving two large bipeds holding hands and walking through snow near Mazama Lodge, at the foot of Mount Hood.[28]

1940s

The next decade produced seven Sasquatch sightings. One, simply dated from "the 1940s," comes to us from Wyeth, where a hairy biped allegedly raided a farmer's duck pond, killing several birds.[29]

1942

In late summer, Don Hunter and his wife saw Bigfoot standing in a meadow near Todd Lake. They stopped to observe it more closely, whereupon the creature retreated into the nearby forest.[30]

1943

Confusion surrounds our next case, from the month of October. Witnesses Bill Cole and O. R. Edwards placed the encounter south of Mount Ashland, but author John Green suggests that it occurred in neighboring California. Cole and Edwards were hunting some distance apart, when Edwards heard strange sounds, then "saw a large manlike creature covered with brown hair, about seven feet tall. It was carrying in its arms what looked like a man — I could only see legs and shoes — straight down the hill on the run." Despite surmising that the beast had snatched Cole, Edwards returned to his car, where Cole joined him a half-hour later. Green reports that neither spoke of the incident until they were separately interviewed, years later. On that occasion, Cole admitted colliding with a Sasquatch, but denied being carried.[31]

1944

An unnamed witness claimed a Bigfoot encounter on Lincoln County's Lobster Creek. Large footprints accompanied the sighting, but they were not photographed or preserved.[32]

1945

A witness, "Kathleen," and her husband were driving south of Roseburg when they saw "a huge man" sprawled in the highway. Clad in coveralls, the figure lay "draped from the yellow divider line well onto the shoulder, covering at least ten feet" of pavement. Kathleen noted that "it didn't move, but I could see its huge eyes, and its head was on an elbow, like it was resting." Driving cautiously around the figure, they proceeded on their way and kept the incident secret for years afterward. When interviewed in the 1980s, Kathleen "couldn't even recall if it was hairy or not, but the memory of the huge eyes and feet stuck" with her.[33]

Bigfoot was seen on the Calapooia River in 1933. *Courtesy of U.S. Dept. of Fish & Wildlife.*

1949

Two reports this year complete our survey of the decade. August brought a sighting from Fairville, where a couple idling on a moonlight drive beheld a "very large black creature" on the roadside. Racing home, the young man told his father of the sighting, and was then regaled with claims that a local farmer had recently fired on a similar beast. That incident may be the one reported during 1949 from a farm near Oregon City, where a farmer shot a hairy prowler in the act of eating "raw albino turkey." Although wounded and bleeding, the creature hurdled a fence and escaped.[34]

The 1950s

Oregon produced eighteen eyewitness sightings in this decade, plus two discoveries of tracks and four reports of other evidence.

In the summer of 1950, four members of the Hoage family, camped near Bend, were startled by "a low deep sound" and saw a "very dark shadow-like creature" run past their campsite. They later estimated that the beast was eight feet tall.[35]

Three years later, a fisherman saw a "huge hairy Bigfoot" watching him on Alder Creek. Colin and Janet Bord place the scene near Portland, but while Oregon boasts sixty Alder Creeks in fifteen counties, none are found in Multnomah.[36]

1954

Three reports were logged this year, though one is automatically suspect as it was relayed by notorious hoaxer Ray Wallace.

- Wallace's **undated** account came from "Chief Stokes," an untraceable Native American who supposedly saw three creatures — an "old Bigfoot and his female and baby" — standing near Blue Creek.
- Another **undated**, second-hand report describes a sighting of "a giant gorilla" that "did not look friendly," at Isthmus Slough.
- In **mid-October**, a report came from Allan Bossuyt, whose pickup stalled between Government Camp and Warm Springs. While examining his engine, Bossuyt heard "a very loud ungodly screaming roar, starting at a low pitch, and ending high...accompanied by large branches breaking or being knocked down." Bossuyt fled the scene at a limping ten miles per hour, without sighting the beast responsible for the noise.[37]

1956

In **July**, a child whose family resided near Lemolo Lake was hiking through the woods one afternoon when he saw a "pretty large" biped with "dark fur all over" crouched and drinking at the lake's shore. An uncle subsequently related a second-hand, undated tale of two horsemen who had met a Sasquatch family in the same vicinity. When seen, the male was "keeping watch," while its presumed mate sat nearby, breast-feeding an infant.[38]

In an **undated** report, a member of a Boy Scout troop hiking in the Columbia Gorge observed a creature that was silent, walking "sort of hunched over," and "smelled very bad, like rotten hay."[39]

1957

In autumn, the year's sole report came from hunters Gary Joanis and Jim Newall. Joanis shot a deer near Wanoga Butte and then watched a nine-foot Sasquatch emerge from the forest, pick up the carcass, and leave with the deer tucked under one arm. Furious, Joanis fired at the creature, but while it emitted "a strange whistling scream," the Sasquatch continued its leisurely retreat, soon vanishing from sight.[40]

1958

This year also only had one Bigfoot sighting. Two sisters outside Eugene observed a hairy biped running through the woods, but the girls kept silent about it until the late 1990s.[41]

1959

The decade's last year was also its busiest, with six alleged encounters reported. The only two with dates supplied occurred in October and December.

October's sighting, at an abandoned mill near Ten Mile, involved two youths who, after meeting Bigfoot, ran home for weapons and returned. The Sasquatch reappeared and "began chasing them, with its arms outstretched." The older boy fired "several good shots" with a .30-06, yet while the monster still pursued them, "it never caught up with them, although it easily could have." The incident led Colin and Janet Bord to speculate that "Bigfoot can't be killed," but poor marksmanship seems more likely.[42]

On December 1, 1959, a bow hunter observed three cryptids from a distance of eighty yards, on the fringe of Saddle Mountain State Park. He described them as "three black objects, heavily built," all roughly five and a half feet tall, "just standing around." When the hunter rapped on a tree stump, the "objects" fled.[43]

Four other reports from that year describe incidents in Clackamas, Josephine, Linn, and Marion Counties, including this attempted abduction:

Sasquatch sightings multiplied in the 1950s. *Courtesy of William Rebsamen.*

"Mrs. Carol," an employee of *Oregon City's Enterprise Courier* newspaper, logged the first one. En route to interview a paper carrier in Estacada, she stopped to relieve herself in roadside shrubbery. While thus engaged, she heard "a very high-pitched tone," lost consciousness, and woke to find herself tucked underneath a hairy biped's arm, being carried through the forest like a rag doll.[44]

The beast — "a young female" with small breasts and a full-body coat of light-brown hair — eventually dropped her, leaving the witness bruised but otherwise unharmed. Before the creature departed, Mrs. Carol — a self-described sensitive "able to commune with animals by picking up their vibrations" — allegedly engaged in conversation with her abductor, learning that the beast liked peaches. Later, Mrs. Carol returned to the site and left a basketful of peaches, which soon disappeared.[44]

By comparison, the other reports are relatively mundane: one witness glimpsed a malodorous biped near Murphy, while a startled trucker saw "a tall, white creature that resembled a gorilla" jogging at thirty-five miles per hour near Millersburg.[45]

Other 1950s Incidents

Four more sightings are simply dated from the "late 1950s," with one account vaguely relating multiple sightings of a creature dubbed the "Wildman of Winberry Creek," after its favorite haunt in Lane County. Also, children in Cottage Grove glimpsed a "gorilla like creature" near their home; and two other youngsters in Lake Grove saw an ape-like face ringed with white hair peering through their attic window, nine feet off the ground.[46]

The decade's most intriguing report is also the most frustrating. According to the SIS, a resident of Sisters "took a few [black and white] pictures of an old Sasquatch following him," but the alleged photographer remains anonymous and his photos — if they ever existed — have yet to surface.[47]

The 1960s

Alleged Bigfoot encounters nearly tripled in this decade, with fifty-five cases involving eyewitness sightings. Nine of them claim large footprints alone while fourteen offer other forms of evidence. Aside from those specific cases, two monster "flaps" in Lane and Linn Counties leave us with claims of multiple sightings, sans any details.

1960

While the Wildman of Winberry Creek continued its nocturnal antics, a new rash of sightings emerged from neighboring Linn County, where a trucker had reported a white Bigfoot jogging beside his vehicle in 1959. The albino creature resurfaced on July 31, 1960, frightening a group of teenagers at Conser Lake. Albany radio station KGAL broke the story on August 2, followed by a series of articles in the now-defunct newspaper *Greater Oregon*. Though *Fate* magazine picked up the story in January 1961, and Ivan Sanderson included it in a book published later that same year.[48]

In sum, while Colin and Janet Bord report "many sightings" around Conser Lake during 1960, details are sparse. Adults and teens alike went gunning for the beast, with one tracker reporting that two of his hounds were "literally torn to ribbons" by the monster. An imported telepath claimed contact with the creature and announced its name was "Flix," while doubters speculated that the monster was a fugitive baboon, on the run from a circus in Corvallis. Webbed handprints on a bedroom windowsill sparked speculation of aquatic origins. By October, the action had shifted to Sublimity — and then the monster vanished, apparently for good.[49]

While hapless hunters swarmed around Conser Lake, witness Sidney Morse reported a Bigfoot sighting from Prospect. Like the creature seen at Millersburg in 1959, this one ran alongside Morse's truck on an unpaved logging road.[50]

Two more sightings from 1960 are otherwise undated. Witness "Shirley" and her mother saw a Sasquatch cross the road near John Day, while Gary Carr reports that he and a friend were camped near Lost Lake, when large shaggy hands grabbed each boy by his hair. The prowler instantly released them, and a search of the camp revealed nothing.[51]

1961

- In an **undated** summer sighting, Betty Owen was poaching deer with friends near Dexter when a black bipedal creature interrupted their safari.
- Also **undated** was licensed hunter Larry Martin's Benton County face-off with a beast resembling "an ape or a gorilla or something like that," but Oregon's deer season spans a month between the last week of August and the end of September.[52]

1962

There were two Sasquatch sightings, but neither with specific dates.

Winberry Creek, alleged hunting ground of an elusive "wildman." *Courtesy of U.S. Dept. of Fish & Wildlife.*

- Ellen English was dozing at a campsite near Estacada when she was lifted by "something large, hairy, and very smelly, like someone who never took a bath." She credits her yapping poodle with saving her life, and reported only a glimpse of her would-be abductor, "a dark, dirty brown thing, rushing into the brush."
- Two hunters were also sleeping, in a station wagon near Mount Jefferson, when something with "a big black body straddled the side of the car and started rocking it."[53]

1963

- Between **August and September**, members of the same family camping on Quartz Creek reported Bigfoot sightings on three separate weekends.
- In two **undated** accounts, motorist Lourine Davis also saw an albino Bigfoot in the Quartz Creek area and witness Kelly Coryell saw a white Sasquatch emerge from a hollow tree outside Holland, describing it as six feet tall, with a pointed head.
- In **early October**, a former sheriff's deputy saw a Sasquatch cross the highway near Lebanon.[54]

1964

- In **June**, four hikers saw a large bipedal creature walking on a lakeshore, near Estacada.
- An **undated** sighting involved young "Kevin G.," who was hunting with a friend near Damascus when he spied a "broad shouldered hairy thing" with "a white front" reminiscent of a penguin.
- This **undated** case involved Keith Soesbe, who was roused from sleep to find a hairy monster peering through the window of his station wagon, which was parked near Elsie.[55]

1965

- There was an **undated** report of an alleged killing of a Sasquatch. This third-hand tale came from a railroad engineer whose train supposedly struck and killed a Sasquatch near Chemult in January. The train's crew said nothing at the time, since they feared accusations of drinking on-duty.
- In **July**, fifteen-year-old Fred Fuscus was riding with his parents on Highway 101, near Manzanita, when they saw an eight-foot Sasquatch.
- Also **undated** was Art Johnson and a friend hunting southeast of Astoria when a roaring monster chased them out of the woods. Returning the next day with police and game wardens, Johnson found a fir tree broken fourteen feet above the ground.[56]

1966

- In **mid-July**, ODFW employee Ronnie Smith saw a black Sasquatch cavorting in Island Lake.
- In **December**, several unnamed youths were cutting Christmas trees near Lakeview when a Sasquatch frightened them away.[57]

1967

- In **May**, teenage hunters, led by Dave Churchill, allegedly shot a seven-foot Sasquatch near The Dalles, but it smashed through a fence and escaped.
- In **October**, while cutting trees near Estacada, Glenn Thomas observed a Bigfoot family — male, female, and "a youngster" — eating rodents excavated from subterranean burrows.
- In **autumn**, Joe Jackson saw a Sasquatch standing beside Dead Horse Creek.[58]

1968

Bigfoot encounters multiplied rapidly this year, with twenty-five reports. Skeptics suggest that the flood of reports was caused by broadcasts of a film clip depicting a Sasquatch, made in northern California, on October 20, 1967. I leave the reader to decide which incidents seem plausible.

Winter-Spring Sightings

- In **March**, Richard Holzmeyer saw an eight-foot biped covered in short black hair, walking through the woods near Forest Grove.
- In **undated spring** reports, Glenn Thomas scored his second sighting of a Bigfoot picnic near the Clackamas River, watching a solitary female dine on leaves, while witness "Hansen," described a creature four and a half feet tall crossing Olson Road, near Colton.
- **June** brought a sighting of a Bigfoot "with no neck" standing in the woods outside Estacada.[59]

Summertime Sightings

- **July 4**: Witness Mac Conner saw a snarling, hissing biped "holding what appeared to be roadside garbage" near Dufur.
- **July 5**: A motorist saw a Sasquatch cross Highway 395 near Seneca.
- In **early August**, Anthony Anable described a twelve-foot-tall "silver and charcoal" creature that left fifteen-inch tracks separated by a 6.5-foot stride by Rogue River.
- Three **undated** cases include: Campers waking to find a Bigfoot spying on them, near The Dalles; witness "Richard," an employee of the U.S. Bureau of Land Management, seeing a black Sasquatch squatting roadside near Paulina; and a teenager meeting "a large animal, black in color and very wide," in the woods near Estacada.[60]

Fall Sightings

- In **October**, a fisherman in Hood River County; he claimed that the Sasquatch chased him through the forest to his pickup truck, but stopped to wait when the man fell, never really trying to catch him.

- **November-December**: Glenn Thomas finished the year with two more remarkable sightings: in November, he followed a line of sixteen-inch tracks to find a pair of female cryptids dozing and then waking to eat water plants from the Clackamas River. A month later, he met a nine-foot male in the same vicinity.[61]

Undated Cases

- A teenager saw a "bear" walking upright near Estacada's Ripplebrook Campground, whistling "like something where its nose was plugged."
- Carl Mathnay saw two large bipeds bathing in Marks Creek, in the Ochoco Mountains.
- Witnesses "Craig and Carrie" lost the mood for romance when a Sasquatch interrupted them near Cascade Locks.
- A porch-prowling creature in Hugo was nearly run-down by a truck as it fled, while a certain Mrs. Vallie almost struck another creature with her car outside Damascus.
- Finally, Idaho Bigfoot witness Naomi Cox reported "an experience" of her daughter's, at David Hill near Forest Grove, but provided no further details.[62]

1969

Sasquatch reports for this year include one witness's claim of "several" encounters.

Winter Reports

- In **March**, Washington County farmer "Richard H." logged a sighting west of Portland. While the creature stood at least one hundred yards away, subsequent measurement of surrounding trees pegged its height at "no less then seven and a half feet and no more than eight and a half feet."
- Around the same time, a logger saw Bigfoot wading in a small lake, somewhere along the Clackamas River.[63]

Summer Reports

- **June 26**: Doris Newton saw two black bipeds standing in a field near Dallas.
- In **August**, an unseen prowler rocked Jack Woodruff's mobile home, on the Coquille River's East Fork. The following night, a neighbor of Woodruff's saw a six-foot creature running through the woods.
- Also in **August**, witness Joe Bayless claimed multiple sightings of a six-foot Sasquatch along the Sixes River, near Port Orford.
- **August 24**: A shrieking "huge dark form" frightened campers at Babyfoot Lake.[64]

Undated Reports

- Ted Kiggins and another youth were fishing at La Dee Flat when they were frightened away by "a large Bigfoot that stunk like hell".
- Four teenagers driving near The Dalles observed a Sasquatch seated on a rocky roadside bluff.[65]

Other '60s Sightings

Three undated cases from the decade are of second-hand accounts:

- Scott Prior relayed his uncle's observation of a Sasquatch playing and sliding in the snow somewhere along the Rogue River.
- A member of the Western Bigfoot Society recounted the tale of a young mother from Elwood; she was so frightened when a Sasquatch approached her car near Bittner Creek that she subsequently moved away.
- Finally, "Greg" aired a friend's observation of a four-member Sasquatch family seen digging clams at the mouth of the Siuslaw River.[66]

The 1970s

This decade witnessed another explosion of alleged Bigfoot encounters, including 160 eyewitness sightings, twenty-nine discoveries of footprints, and sixty-seven cases citing other evidence of Sasquatch activity.

1970

Summertime Sightings

- In **June**, farmer John Fuhrman logged a report from Molalla after his guard dogs cowered from a visiting Sasquatch.
- **July** brought a "gorilla" sighting from the Umpqua River.
- **August 15**: A seven-year-old saw a shaggy creature with eyes "like twin red embers" strolling near Sheridan.
- **August 29**: Wilsonville resident was stalking trespassers when a foul-smelling Sasquatch grabbed her and tossed her over a fence.[67]

Late Summer-Fall Sightings

- In **undated** reports, a young couple driving a tractor near Delph saw Bigfoot watching from the treeline while a family camping in Silver Falls State Park met a towering biped along Howard's Creek.

- In **September**, Edward Flowers saw two creatures — one eight feet tall, the other roughly two feet shorter — running across a hillside near Coos Bay.[68]

Bigfoot appeared at Timothy Lake in 1970. *Courtesy of U.S. Dept. of Fish & Wildlife.*

Undated Reports

- In **October**, a teenage hunter saw a man-sized figure running with "amazing grace" through the Mount Hood National Forest.

- **Undated** sightings include "Chloe's" observation of a Sasquatch stealing food from her father's logging camp near Detroit Lake; "Ellen's" sighting of two twelve-foot creatures beside Eagle Creek; "Richard's" glimpse of a "possible black Bigfoot" near Hickman Butte; and a fire spotter's report of Sasquatch strolling past an observation tower near Timothy Lake.[69]

1971

- **June 4**: Three tenants of Pinewood Mobile Manor, a trailer park in The Dalles, saw a gray bipedal creature — seven and a half to eight feet tall — walk past their property.

- **June 5**: Richard Brown and his wife watched a ten-foot creature pass the trailer park. After observing it through a telescopic sight, Brown declared, "It seemed more human than animal."

- Also in **June**, two motorists would see a six-foot biped run across a road outside Boring.

- In **undated** cases, family members residing near Warm Springs watched a playful Sasquatch cavort on their porch, as if for their daughter's amusement, and Lola Smith swore off night work after a prowling "orangutan" spooked her in Buxton.[70]

1972

Winter Sightings

- In an **undated** February report, Jim Kunkle and a friend were hunting near Triangle Lake when they fired on a Sasquatch and watched it flee, "flailing its arms."

- **February 27**: Three loggers near Eugene saw Bigfoot from a distance of one hundred yards. Around the same time, Thomas Smith and a companion saw two hairy bipeds — one about six feet tall, the other two feet shorter — while fishing from a raft near Mount Jefferson.[71]

Summer-Fall Sightings

- **Early July**: Several boys claimed a moonlight sighting of a white Sasquatch while "partying" in the woods outside Banks.

- **July 20**: Our next witness was sober — a surveyor saw Bigfoot at the same McKenzie River site that produced the February 27 sighting.[72]

- In an **undated** report, a youth saw part of Bigfoot — one hairy leg from heel to mid-thigh — climbing an embankment in the Willamette National Forest. Years later, he recalled the creature's stench as "a concoction of burning human flesh, skunk spray, slurry hole, and rotten food all mixed with a strong scent of sulfur."

- **September 30**: Dewey Strong saw a Sasquatch standing beside a road in Lee Valley with its arms raised overhead.[72]

1973

Bigfoot Struck by Vehicle?

In **mid-January**, a trucker made the startling account of striking a Sasquatch while hauling logs near Grants Pass. The driver traveled another five miles before stopping to check his vehicle for damage, whereupon he found the front end smashed, but free of blood and hair. No effort was made to locate the "victim," and his story received little credence.[73]

Spring Sightings

- **April 5**: Don Stratton was driving east of Estacada when a five-foot-tall biped covered with silver-tipped hair hurled a tree stump in front of his car and then ducked out of sight in the woods.

- In **undated** May reports, a young man and his fiancée met a ten-foot creature in a wooded park in Sitkum and Sue Sebring was driving a school bus filled with children on Skyline Road in Portland's Northwest District when a Sasquatch crossed the road in front of them. Sebring claims the sightings became so frequent that her neighbors fondly dubbed the creature "George."[74]

Summer Sightings

- In **June**, Bigfoot visited a camper's fireside along the Collawash River. The man fired a gunshot, whereupon the creature fled screaming.

- **August** brought Jim Farley's sighting of an eight-foot biped near Wildwood and, from Douglas County, a five-year-old's report of his meeting with a "hairy man."

- An **undated** incident involved a hunter's sighting of Sasquatch along the Cascades Lakes Highway near Bend.[75]

Fall-Winter Sightings

- **October 1**: Hunter Rick Bladgen saw a six-foot-tall "barrel like" Sasquatch at Doctor Rock, near Big Flat.

- A second, **undated** report came from Baker City Gulch, where a hunter observed a silent Sasquatch "running as fluid and fast as any thing I have ever seen."

- A **winter** sighting was reported by witnesses "Pam and Terry," who saw a creature eight or nine feet tall at Hoodoo Camp near Marion Forks.[76]

Undated Reports

- A creature peered from the woods along Highway 126 near Eugene.

- A nocturnal prowler shook a parked car near Mount Hood, waking its lone occupant.[77]

1974

The year produced twenty reports, plus one vague claim of "several" sightings by a single family.

Winter Sightings

- In **January**, Deputy Sheriff Harry Gilpin saw a seven-foot biped cross a road near Rowena.

- **March 8**: Nine-year-old Nick Wells met a Sasquatch while walking to school in Florence. A follow-up investigation of that incident revealed two separate trails of footprints — fourteen and sixteen inches long.[78]

Spring Sightings

- In **May**, loggers Jack Cochrane, Fermin Osborne, and J. C. Rourke saw a six and a half-foot hairy man-beast on Fir Mountain on two consecutive days.

• June brought reports from Clackamas County, where two brothers saw a cinnamon-colored Sasquatch stroll past Sandy's Skyline Mobile Villa trailer park, and Warm Springs Indian Reservation, where a witness watched a shaggy biped excavate an anthill.[79]

Summer Sightings

In **July**, Michael Swink saw an eight and a half-foot "ape" with "really gigantic legs and a neck like a wrestler" wading in the South Umpqua River near Riddle. As he watched, the creature "jumped back and forth often and very easily," digging under stones for "something bug like," which it devoured. Despite its size, Swink surmised that it "was probably an adolescent."[80]

The month of **August** produced a vague account of "several" sightings by members of the Fitzgerald family somewhere in the Cascades and Tim Hayward surprised a Sasquatch as it slept beneath his family's hay wagon near the Estacada Airport. Another hairy biped, glimpsed by a child outside Canyon City, left large tracks verified by adults. Mac Connor was summer's last witness, reporting an encounter with a Sasquatch six to eight feet tall near Mount Hood.[81]

Fall Sightings

• **October 15**: Two men stranded by a stalled car near Powers met a blue-eyed Sasquatch with "long smoke colored hair."

• Also in **October**, Alex Filer's sighted a female biped hoisting boulders near Scio.

• In **November**, four loggers saw a Sasquatch with reddish-brown hair between Brookings and Gold Beach, and Rod Virell saw a six-foot creature with "skinny hips" standing on a log pile near Clackamas County's Nasty Rock.[82]

Undated Sightings

• "A huge black-haired ape-like creature" was seen by Jean Fitzgerald somewhere in the Cascades.

• A creature left "a giant heel print" after stepping over a six-foot fence near Yoder.

• A hulking silhouette was seen by Bert and Ernie Brown near Klootchie Creek.

• A shrieking seven-footer frightened "Laura" at Rocky Ford.

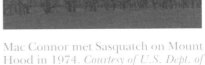

Mac Connor met Sasquatch on Mount Hood in 1974. *Courtesy of U.S. Dept. of Fish & Wildlife.*

• A beast left tracks on a Salmon Creek sandbar, and another red-haired creature seen near Canyon Creek.

• A hunter had a sighting at Bee Ranch.

• A beast "stood tall on two legs" outside Mist while a pair of malodorous bipeds were seen at Bagby Hot Springs.[83]

1975

Winter-Spring Sightings

• **January** brought a report from Portland security guards Gary Carr and "Joe H.," who glimpsed a pair of reflective eyes while patrolling Skyline Memorial Gardens cemetery. The orange orbs were seven or eight feet above-ground level, set eight to ten inches apart.

- In **June**, a camper watched Bigfoot for nearly an hour, somewhere in the Cascades.[84]

Summer Sightings

- In **July**, a "very tall" creature frightened swimmers in Wolf Creek and a "family" of three bipeds were seen drinking from a stream near Camas Valley.
- **August 15**: Two loggers saw an "enormous" Sasquatch near Dawson.
- **August 21**: "Laurie P." and seven other campers dodged stones hurled by three ape-like creatures along the Chetco River.
- An **undated** sighting had Robert Bellamy Jr. and five companions glimpsing Bigfoot while driving through Tygh Valley.[85]

Fall Sightings

- **October 1**: A hunter watched a hairy biped near Pilot Rock.
- **October 25**: Another hunter met a seven and a half-foot creature at Whiskey Peak. Around the same time, "Patti D." and four relatives saw a monster at Klamath County's "Starwin Camp," which proved untraceable.
- **November 1**: Leroy Lucas saw a seven-foot, dirty-gray Sasquatch near Mount Hood.
- **December 6**: Motorist Terry Reams and three passengers saw Bigfoot jogging along Interstate 84, near Hood River.[86]

Updated Sightings

- Carl and Debra Mathnay watched a creature nine or ten feet tall cross a highway near Zigzag.
- Heide Ballard saw a beige-colored "baby Bigfoot" in a tree outside Astoria.
- A Forest Service officer met Sasquatch at Lake in the Woods Recreation Site, while Betty Garmin saw one in her yard at Lakecreek.
- Correspondent "Gary" offers the secondhand tale of his grandfather watching a Sasquatch play in a stream at some undisclosed location.
- Jessie Humphreys and two companions were driving near Silver Lake when a hairy biped leapt from a roadside ditch.
- The strangest tale comes from a five-year-old who fell and gashed his head while playing at Lane County's Salt Creek Falls, later claiming that a "bear" carried him back to his family's campsite.[87]

1976

Winter-Spring Sightings

- Sometime early in the year, a mother with two children saw a "large dark creature" at The Dalles.
- **June 8**: George Morrison, chief naturalist at Crater Lake National Park, saw Bigfoot cross a local highway.
- **Undated** June sightings include Larry Baley and his wife meeting a seven and a half-foot biped on Highway 30, near the Trojan Nuclear Power Plant; two girls glimpsing

a red-eyed albino creature outside Philomath; and witness "T. G." and three friends watched Sasquatch drinking from a stream on Umatilla County's Emigrant Hill.[88]

Summertime Sightings

- **June 30**: One witness met Bigfoot during a Boy Scout gathering in Umatilla County.
- **Early July**: A bicyclist saw a seven-foot biped on Highway 101 between Nesika Beach and Wedderburn.
- In **August**, there were reports of an "erect black bear" stealing salt licks around Table Rock and a long-haired creature prowling the outskirts of Canyon City.
- **Early September**: A witness saw a Sasquatch step over a four-foot electrified fence near Cave Junction.[89]

Fall Sightings

- **October 3**: Rodney Boder saw a seven-foot creature standing on a hilltop near Glide.
- Also in **October**, a couple claimed two separate encounters with Bigfoot in northwestern Wasco County.[90]

Other Sightings

The year's undated cases include seven eyewitness accounts: a hiker saw Bigfoot somewhere in the Central Cascades while a young couple watched a Sasquatch cross Tanner Creek "in northern Oregon" — where three such creeks exist in different counties; a group of "reputable people" glimpsed a hairy biped while inspecting pipelines near Florence; a youth riding with relatives near Myrtle Point beheld another on a logging road; and witness Leroy Earley saw two creatures playing on a railroad track near Aumsville.[91]

Two other tales tax credibility. Twelve-year-old Liz Van Valkenberg saw a screaming creature attired in a short-sleeved shirt near O'Brien, while Rich Grumley relayed a secondhand claim that a ten-foot Sasquatch dismembered an unnamed hiker in the Mount Jefferson Wilderness. Grumley heard the story second-hand from witnesses, whom he described as a group of anonymous "girls from Vegas." Allegedly, the girls were detained by forest rangers who warned them, "Never come back!"[92]

1977

Leave Bigfoot Alone!

State senator Theodore Kulongoski sponsored a bill imposing two days of highway clean-up work on anyone caught "harassing, annoying, or intimidating" Bigfoot. The bill failed to pass, but Kulongoski survived hoots of ridicule to serve as Oregon's attorney general and win election as governor in 2002.[93]

Winter-Spring Sightings

- In **February**, "Bob and Scott" saw a creature resembling "Cousin Itt" from "The Addams Family" in Saddle Mountain State Park and a man walking his dog in Fort Stevens State Park saw a hairy biped cavorting on the beach.

Witnesses sometimes report unknown bipeds traveling in pairs or larger groups. *Courtesy of William Rebsamen.*

- **Early March**: A woman glimpsed an eight-foot creature standing near her barn somewhere in west-central Oregon.
- **March 10**: Joe and Sue Chane watched a nine-footer near the Sandy River outside Troutdale.
- **March 19**: A family of six saw Bigfoot cross Highway 126, east of McKenzie Bridge.
- **In April**, there was a sighting of an eight-foot albino creature crossing Canaan Road near Deer Island.[94]

Summer Sightings

- In an **undated** incident, Marion County deputies tracked a creature reported by campers who fired on the beast outside of Gates.
- **Early September**: A sighting of an eight-foot biped near Halfway was logged. The witness described a creature of "reddish color with spots of silver or white hair pretty much all over."[95]

Fall Sightings

- **September 27**: John Martin sighted a seven-foot biped crossing Highway 66 near Ashland.
- Early **October**: A violent episode from Bend was reported, four or five days after the incident on September 27. On that occasion, Gary Benson and Ronald Kershey fired shots at a seven-foot, silver-haired beast that "attacked" them without inflicting any injuries.[96]

Undated Sightings

- A farmer claimed that a white Sasquatch raided his chicken coop, near Otis, and knocked him down when he went to investigate.
- Witness "Robin W." saw five bipedal creatures — "three adults and two adolescents" — ambling past a truck weigh-station outside Memaloose.[97]

1978

Winter-Spring Sightings

- **Early January**: A Newberg resident claimed two encounters on consecutive nights. This resident describing a six-foot creature weighing some four hundred pounds.
- **February** brought a brief sighting from Carver, logged by witness "Glen."
- **Early May**: The Carver area produced another sighting. "Kevin" and a friend glimpsed a Sasquatch from their car, using a nearby tree to peg its height at seven feet.
- **May 15**: A witness living near Rainier told police of his encounter with a green-eyed prowler who peered through his second-floor window.[98]

June Sightings

- A couple hiking through the Central Cascades saw one Sasquatch — or "possibly two" — moving rapidly into the forest.
- Richard Wilson was walking his dog, near Chapman, when a shaggy biped emerged from the marshland and frightened him.

- Near Applegate, two equestriennes bolted from the sight of a long-haired creature eating blackberries. Another berry-picking beast frightened a child near Reedsport.
- Hikers saw a Sasquatch sitting on a stump near Biscuit Hill.[99]

That Hairy Thing

- An **undated** report from July had Marci Roberts spying "a big old hairy thing" on Highway 26 in Wasco County.
- In **August**, "a huge hairy man" with a "disgusting smell" spooked three campers outside Shady Cove. During the same month, witnesses saw a "very large" bipedal creature near Powers and two motorists logged a sighting between Barton and Carver.[100]

Fall Sightings

- **September 25**: Barbara Megli reported seeing a Bigfoot in southern Coos County.
- In **October**, Larry Waldo watched a creature engaged in "God-awful screaming" near Penland Lake; a hunter saw a black ten-foot biped near Mount McLoughlin; and a pair of gunmen near Yankton allegedly shot Bigfoot four times between the eyes and then neglected to guard its corpse, which vanished overnight.[101]

End-of-Year Sightings

- **December 18**: A woman walking her dog near Cleawox Lake met a wailing Sasquatch.
- **Undated** incidents for December include the sighting of a brown Bigfoot by "Mrs. Miles," west of Springfield, and a black creature seen near Mount Hood by Rick Schaffer and his friend "Dan." Dick Wildfang saw a male and female Sasquatch outside Dallas, while Alex Filer watched a screaming biped leave fourteen-inch tracks south of Sodaville.[102]

Undated Sightings

- A motorcyclist sighted a "brown creature" near Larch Mountain.
- A Sasquatch screamed at young swimmers on Gold Beach.
- A sighting of a beast "too big to be a person" in the woods near Cottage Grove; and a report of bipedal "bears" crossing a meadow in Willamette National Forest.[103]1979

1979

Winter-Spring Sightings

- **January 2**: Witness Goldberg gave a report from Gales Creek, west of Banks, of a shaggy beast that left clear footprints.
- In **April**, Monte Kauffman saw a "great big man-like ape" on Neahkahnie Mountain, estimating its weight at five hundred to six hundred pounds.[104]

Summer Sightings

- In **July**, one witness saw "a huge hairy man" near Shady Cove.
- **Early September**: Mark Osborne and four other hunters met Sasquatch and found its handprints on their truck near Burnt Woods.[105]

Fall Sightings

- In **October**, Betty Parks spied a Sasquatch near Wilsonville and recorded the second-hand tale of a woman whose son was touched by Bigfoot. During the same month, John Parsons saw a hulking creature in his Clatsop County apple orchard.

- **November 1**: Parsons also met an eight-footer at his hunting camp, near Wheeler.

- **December 1**: Jim Hewkin found three stocky creatures, all roughly five and a half feet tall, munching berries in Saddle Mountain State Park.

- An **undated** autumn case relates a camper's claim that he woke one night, near Diamond Lake, to find Sasquatch stroking his beard.[106]

Undated Sightings

- Witness "George" sighted a Sasquatch near Clatsop County's Big Creek fish hatchery.

- "Laree's" met a smelly biped atop Hungry Mountain.

- Mike and Betty Dobbins saw a six-foot creature cross an unidentified coastal highway while intoxicated teens claimed an encounter with the "Ooooeee Monster" in Damascus.[107]

Throughout the Decade

Twelve more reports are simply dated from the 1970s, without specific years.

- Mrs. Cleveland and her son met Bigfoot on Squaw Mountain.
- "James" relayed the second-hand tale of a girlfriend's sighting near The Dalles.
- Karl Blagge and unnamed "military people" glimpsed a Sasquatch from a helicopter between Estacada and Mount Jefferson. Blagge also snapped a still-unpublished photograph of Bigfoot near Ukiah.
- Herman Gertz and cousin "Darrel" met an eight-foot biped near Memaloose Creek.
- A "Ms. Grant" of Sweet Home reported a Sasquatch inside her neighbor's garage.
- Two couples camping near McKenzie Bridge glimpsed "something big" in the woods.
- A teacher hiking near Linton Lake saw a hairy beast "far too large to be a man."
- A Troutdale resident saw Bigfoot on a foggy night, later expanding that encounter into three.
- A policeman in Bend saw a full-figured female Sasquatch, sparking undocumented tales of slaughtered hunters in the same vicinity.[108]

The 1980s

Bigfoot sightings declined in the 1980s total two hundred reports, including 106 eyewitness sightings, thirty discoveries of tracks, and sixty-four cases involving other evidence.

1980

Winter-Summer Reports

- In **February**, "John R." sighted a six-foot, long-haired biped that crossed his newspaper route near Arago.

- **July 6**: Rainier resident Bill Buol saw a dark-haired biped lurking around his barn.
- In **August**, two fishermen on Davis Creek dropped their poles after sighting of a seven-foot monster and, on the 28th, Scott Ericson met a Sasquatch while posting a letter near Grants Pass.
- An **undated** case involves a motorist's sighting of "a large, light reddish brown, hairy man" outside Bend.[109]

Fall Reports

- In **September**, two hikers saw a "big and hairy" creature walking upright outside Sutherlin.
- **October 3**: Children heard whistling and scraping outside their trailer near Keno and then saw a "long shaggy finger" probing a vent on the roof.
- Other **October** cases include a Bigfoot sighting by three teenagers idling in Dabney State Park; a report of two creatures seen walking together outside Yoncalla; and a trucker's meeting with a red-eyed ape-like beast near Hardman.[110]

Other Reports

The year's undated sightings include some of Oregon's most dramatic.

- Two witnesses allegedly saw five hairy bipeds together at Memaloose Crossing, on the Clackamas River.
- A hunter saw Bigfoot snatch a fawn near Estacada while another beast harassed hunters at Browns Camp in Tillamook State Forest.
- "Jack B." saw a Sasquatch with "a light-colored face" step over a fence near Elsie.
- Two brothers driving near Anthony Lake spent five minutes watching Bigfoot cross an open field.
- A hunter saw Sasquatch pass the Musick Guard Station, near Cottage Grove.[111]

1981

- In **June**, a Deschutes County angler told a tale of "something brown" and "very heavy" stalking fishermen near Roseburg.
- In **September**, a "warm colored" Sasquatch with "human-like eyes" was sighted in Veneta.
- **Undated Cases**: Daniel Ranes saw an eight-foot biped near the Sandy River; Duane Richards met a similar creature at Horseshoe Lake, but mistakenly placed that body of water in Clackamas County (six Oregon counties have lakes of that name, but Clackamas is not among them.); and witness "Chuck" reported a big "black sucker" had toppled his camper at Badger Lake.[112]

1982

Summer's Reports

- In **June**, members of an unnamed family saw a six-foot, "very human looking" biped in Blue Mountain County Park.
- Also in **June**, Steven Fuller and friend "Dave" met a group of eight hairy creatures on Green Mountain, firing shots in the air when one Sasquatch charged them.

- In **August**, Jeff Greer and three friends glimpsed a howling beast near Bald Butte; Travis Cover saw a seven-foot biped outside Brookings.
- On **Labor Day**, John Parsons glimpsed an even larger Sasquatch in an apple orchard near Saddle Mountain State Park.[113]

Fall Reports

- In **September**, Robert Varner glimpsed a tall silhouette in the woods near Heavenly Twin Lakes.
- **October 20**: A hunter watched two creatures — one eight-footer and another half its size — through his rifle's scope near Dallas.
- **November** brought a report of a beast that resembled "a biker," seen near the site of John Parsons's September encounter, and Gary Weilert reported seeing a creature nine or ten feet tall near Milton-Freewater.[114]

Undated Reports

- Pamela Moore sighted a smelly Sasquatch stalking wild horses near La Pine.
- Joe Cary claimed he struck an eight-foot biped with his truck outside Chemult.
- "J. W." described a road-killed Bigfoot being spirited away by Forest Service officers at Frog Camp.
- Three hunters known only as "Crouse, Crowe, and Lyons" allegedly shot a Sasquatch near Yankton and then lost it despite a clear trail of blood and fourteen-inch footprints.[115]

Campers saw an eight-foot Sasquatch on Hoodoo Mountain in 1983. *Courtesy of U.S. Dept. of Fish & Wildlife.*

1983

Summer-Fall Reports

- In **June**, a six-foot hairy biped drove a family from their camp on Mosby Creek.
- In **early August**, teenage cousins met a pair of hulking creatures near Elmira.
- In **November**, two hunters saw a growling Bigfoot with "a bushy beard and hair like a man's" near Highway 26 in Tillamook County.[116]

Undated Reports

- Orey Inness saw a "black ape" sunning itself near Silverton.
- Thor Aronsen watched a Sasquatch jog along Fish Creek.
- "Wilbur" and a friend met Bigfoot while panning for gold near Mitchell.
- Campers "Pam and Terry" watched an eight-foot biped on Hoodoo Mountain.
- A resident of Warm Springs Indian Reservation saw Bigfoot hammer her home's rain gutters.[117]

1984

- **July 8**: There was a report of a stinking, "slightly hunched" biped at Green Lake.

- **August 17**: An encounter was reported near Yachats.
- An **undated** August incident involving two girls at Dickie Prairie.
- In **autumn**, "David H." and his son flushed a Sasquatch from cover while hunting in the Tygh Valley; Pat Carter allegedly played catch with a juvenile Sasquatch near Valsetz while its mother watched from the sidelines, cradling an infant; Alex Filer glimpsed a running biped at Round Lake; and a logger caught one watching him near Mount Hood.[118]

1985

- In **October**, Bigfoot watched a forest ranger fix a flat tire near Fish Creek and yodeled for witness Angie Butler near Neskowin.
- In **November**, George Lee glimpsed a Sasquatch while hunting near Birkenfeld.
- In **December**, a trucker stopped his rig on Cabbage Hill to let a hairy biped cross the road.
- **Undated** reports include Frank Kaneaster's sighting of a "pure black seven-foot ape" outside Colton; "Marietta W.'s" report of "a thing with big hairy shoulders" near Hood River; the tale of a couple who surprised Bigfoot sleeping in a roadside ditch near Veneta; and another sighting logged by National Guardsmen on maneuvers at Wolf Creek.[119]

1986

- In **June**, two girls claimed to have telepathic communication with a female Sasquatch and its child somewhere in "coastal northwest Oregon."
- **Mid-Summer**: Hikers "Jeff and Hugh" watched Bigfoot chasing a deer at Cascade Locks. Around the same time a motorist saw one cross Highway 97 near La Pine.
- **Late August**: Five teens met a pair of creatures — one eight-footer, another three feet tall — on Mount Hood.
- **November 5**: A seven-foot biped startled a driver near La Pine.
- Also in **November**, a hunter met a beast that "smelt like crap" at some undisclosed location.
- **Undated** reports include Gary Dotson's sighting of a Sasquatch jogging near Heppner; Harold Morris's encounter with a hairy biped on Chapin Creek; another sighting on Mount Hood, by Pat Manyhorses; a sighting by two college students, near Corvallis; a sighting of a creature "too big to be a gorilla" at Multnomah Falls; and Don Ratliff's second-hand tale of a minister's confrontation with a ten-foot biped near Wamic.[120]

1987

- In **June**, a Sasquatch crossed Highway 97 near Tiny Creek.
- In **August**, park ranger Richard Seifried saw Bigfoot in Crater Lake National Park.
- In **September**, Chris Johnson sighted a Bigfoot couple and their infant near Stayton.
- **Undated** tales include two motorists who saw a knuckle-walking ape at Cornelius Pass and a Sasquatch that robbed a hunter of his kill on Thomas Creek. Marion Kelley saw Bigfoot cross a road near Sweet Home, and a teenage witness watched a biped splashing "like an elephant" in a creek near Glide. Anonymous female witnesses saw separate creatures at Grants Pass and Paulina Peak. Finally, injured hiker "Jason" claimed that Bigfoot dug a snow cave to shield him from exposure in Lane County.[121]

1988

- In **February**, Earla Penn saw a nine-foot creature near Kings Valley while another biped frightened seven witnesses outside Chemult.
- **August** brought a sunrise sighting of two young Sasquatches playing at Sled Springs.
- In **October**, George Stott met Bigfoot near Tenmile Lake, while witness "C. J." saw a Sasquatch walking with a "playful" bear at Borden Gulch.
- Late **December**: Frank Portoghese and friend "Ed" saw Bigfoot running through the woods near Salt Creek.
- **Undated** reports include Peter Rockbadger's sighting of Bigfoot at Fall Creek; a "tall black figure" on Hungry Hill; a menacing biped near Tumalo; and a "big furry thing's" harassment of campers in Hells Canyon.[122]

1989

- **Undated**: Witness "Tom" reported a "possible Bigfoot" in Ecola State Park.
- In **May**, near Wyeth, Carlo Sposito and two friends saw "a large primate" chasing a deer.
- **July 8**: While searching for a lost child near Estacada, helicopter crewmen glimpsed "a huge object" through infrared gear.
- Also in **July**, Shawn Heist saw three creatures at Lee Falls.
- Late **September**: There was a sighting of something "as tall as a moose" near Molalla.
- In **October**, Mike Smith saw an eight-foot biped at David Hill and, later that month, Bigfoot startled a driver at Santiam Pass and ogled hunter Bob Prichard at Lost Lake.
- **Undated** cases include "Dan P.'s" encounter with Bigfoot near Music Creek, while other witnesses saw large bipedal beasts roaming around Cascadia, La Pine, and Forest Grove.123Other '80s Sightings

There were thirteen cases undated beyond reference to the decade: Large bipeds were seen stepping over a farmer's fence outside Elsie; trudging along the Trask River; prowling around Crater Lake; running beside Wolf Creek; watching loggers on Fir Mountain; visiting another farm near Sandy; picking berries outside Lincoln City; stealing scraps from a hunter's kill in Tygh Valley; frightening hunters near McMinnville; accosting fishermen on the McKenzie River; shifting boulders in Shower Creek; and hurling logs at teenage hikers, somewhere in the Central Cascades.[124]

The 1990s

The last decade of the twentieth century produced 544 reports of alleged Bigfoot encounters. The file includes 225 eyewitness sightings, 113 reports of footprints, and 206 claims of other supposed evidence.

1990

- **July and August**: Hikers saw a "dirt brown" seven-footer at Tenmile Lake; two others met an eight-foot specimen on Mount Hood's northern slope; and Mike Rinnan watched a twelve-foot giant crossing Highway 37 near Black Bear Swamp, where Richard Robinson also glimpsed a similar monster.

- **Early October**: "Larry W." met a shaggy biped at the Penland Lake Recreation Site and a logger named Cochran encountered a seven-foot beast on Fir Mountain.[125]

1991

- In **June**, two witnesses at Diamond Lake saw a creature that was "very tall, similar to a bull elk in the head, but not like a bear." That same month, dogs pursued "a large brown object moving fast" in the Rogue-Umpqua Divide Wilderness.
- **July** brought sightings of a blond Bigfoot from Portland Heights, a black eight-footer seen by Sam and April Jolly at the Salmon River's mouth, and a six-foot creature photographed by Alex Filer near Mill City on the 24th.
- **Undated**: Summer closed with the sighting of an eight-foot biped in Emigrant Springs State Park.
- **October** produced sightings of a crouching beast near Rice Hill and witness "Ivan's" report of a creature "possibly wearing a deer hide" at Tombstone Prairie.
- **Undated** reports describe two unnamed "college boys" attacked by Bigfoot outside Forest Grove, a black biped spying on campers near Grants Pass, a seven-footer "swaying back and forth" at Deadman Pass, and a creature that cured "Gene E.'s" wife's back pains on the Wilson River, using only "emanations."[126]

1992

Spring Sightings

- **Early Spring**: Witness "Ty" saw a black Sasquatch carrying a trash bag outside Salem.
- **April Fool's Day (the 1ˢᵗ)**: Hunter "Carl" claimed Bigfoot killed his seven dogs near Ukiah.
- In **May**, two brothers met a Sasquatch in Umatilla County.
- **June 1**: "James T." and friends encountered a blue-eyed seven-footer near O'Brien.[127]

Summer Sightings

- **July 15**: Bill Wheeler reported seeing Bigfoot picking berries near Allingham Guard Station on.
- **Undated** summer cases include a report of two bipeds from rural Umatilla County, Steve Carlson's sighting of a child-sized creature at Lost Lake, witness "Tim's" encounter with a "psychic" ten-foot specimen in Rooster Rock State Park, a report of two creatures uprooting trees beside the Wilson River, and a claim of five bipeds burying a sixth outside Estacada.[128]

Fall Sightings

- **September 22**: Rusty Dean saw an eight-foot creature near Kokostick Butte.
- In **October**, a Sasquatch frightened a woman on the lower Nestucca River.
- In **November**, Larry Waldo sighted a beast at Penland Lake and there was a report of a Sasquatch eating roadkill outside Eugene.

- **December 6**: An eight-foot monster visited Linton.
- **Undated**: Tom Olson's sighting from Sandy describes a snarling creature three and a half feet tall. Two other cases involve a red-haired seven-foot beast at Marcola and a Sasquatch seen wading across Scapoose Creek.129

1993

Winter/Spring

- **January 12**: Dr. John Esposito reported a seven-foot creature "doing knee bends" near The Dalles.
- In **February**, Ann Peterson and her parents met Bigfoot in the Stinkingwater Mountains.
- During the month of **April**, a soldier reported seeing three hulking bipeds on Saddle Mountain and Chris Jones met with a Sasquatch near Colton. Three more sightings from the same vicinity were collectively dismissed by Ray Crowe as "probable hoaxes."
- In **May**, at Saddle Mountain, witness "Colleen" reported a run-in with a Sasquatch, who also spooked hikers atop Big Craggies on Memorial Day.[130]

Summer Sightings

- **Undated**: There were seven sightings on the Bee Ranch in Clackamas County, where multiple witnesses described both male and female "conehead" creatures.
- In **June**, Bigfoot scouted a cabin near Rhododendron, brought its mate to pick berries on Trask Mountain, and survived a collision with Jackson Moore's car outside Colton.
- In **July**, a hairy biped jogged past West Fork Butte Lookout; a ten-footer leapt over a truck on Highway 211, near Clear Creek; and a seven-footer with a "disfigured face" spooked campers at South Sister.
- **August** brought Gary Dotson's sighting of a shy Sasquatch at Wahtum Lake.
- Early **September**: Sightings from Fort Stevens and Wildcat Mountain were logged.[131]

Fall's Sightings

- **September 24**: Paddy Sullivan saw Bigfoot near Breitenbush Lake.
- **September 25**: Jim Hewkin filed a sighting from Colton (branded a hoax by Ray Crowe).
- **September 28**: Another Colton witness glimpsed a female biped.
- **October 1**: Bill Wheeler and two friends saw a seven-foot beast in Forest Park.
- **October 4**: Wes Sumerlin spied a nine-footer on Meacham Creek.
- **October 4-5**: Dan and Laurine Davis logged two sightings of a five-foot biped from Cow Meadow.
- In **December**, a railroad inspector saw Bigfoot at Cornelius Pass, before a pair of Christmas Day sightings from Bee Ranch and Alsea.
- **Undated** sightings include John Rabon's encounter near Timber Junction, a "Mr. Cleveland's" report of Bigfoot stripping bark from trees on Squaw Mountain, and a berry-picker's claim that a Sasquatch "charged" his party on Rock Creek.[132]

1994

Winter-Spring Reports

- **January 8**: Members of the Jones family met Bigfoot at Bee Ranch.
- **January 26**: Jack and Rusty saw birds swarm a red-haired seven-footer near The Dalles.
- In **April**, Nathan Iness encountered a cave-dwelling creature in the Abiqua Basin, a teenager sighted one outside Plainview, Bigfoot was seen hurdling a six-foot fence near Oregon City, and Dan and Laurine Davis had a sighting near Bagby Hot Springs.
- In **May**, a Sasquatch frightened sheep near Turner and jogged along a beach near Tillamook.[133]

Summertime Reports

- In **June**, an eight-foot beast ran through a camp on the Bee Ranch; four albino specimens whistled along the Tualatin River, a "large animal" frightened campers on the Metolius River, and another slaughtered an elk on the Warm Springs Reservation.
- In **July**, sightings include a gray beast near Bee Ranch; a seven-foot reddish-brown creature outside Cascadia; three bipeds on McComb Butte; another crossing Highway 211 near Colton; an eight-foot "shadowy figure" at Santiam Pass; and a Sasquatch jogging by moonlight outside Detroit.
- **August** sightings include one from Richard Jacobs, on Goat Mountain; Becky Cunningham's report of a "bearded" Sasquatch at Blind Slough; a sighting by Steve Williams near Valsetz; and Pat Garnier's account of a seven and a half-foot female with lactating breasts near Pelican Butte.[134]

Fall's Reports

- In **September**, there was a hunter's sighting outside Tollgate, a child's account of a "slender-built" Bigfoot from Pendleton, and motorist "M's" encounter near Colton.
- In **October**, witness "Dan" saw "a tall hairy thing" outside Mist.
- **December** brought another report of a Sasquatch chasing sheep near Turner and "Larry W.'s" claim of wounding Bigfoot near Mount Washington.[135]

Undated Reports

- Cousins Jeremy and Steve Anderson saw a six and a half-foot creature making "monkey sounds" on Vinegar Hill.
- Mark Stanislawski glimpsed a "short hairy troll" near Silverton.
- Members of the Brown family reported a sighting near Colton (labeled a hoax by Ray Crowe).
- "Roger S." saw Bigfoot running across the Bee Ranch, while another spooked "J. W.'s" horses at Husband Lake.
- Other reports describe a "hairy man-like creature" in Portland; an eight-foot female with an infant on the McKenzie River; a fast-walking monster near Warm Springs; a beast with a "squashy-face" at East Lake; a creature "twice the size of a man" near McKenzie Bridge; a biped on the railroad tracks near Aumsville; and an eight-footer scouting roadkill near Sisters.[136]

1995

Winter/Spring Sightings

- **January 22:** Two hunters reported seeing seven creatures seen at Dutch Flat.
- **March** brought a vague sighting from Portland and a report of a "possible injured juvenile" on Interstate 84 near Boardman.
- On **April 5**, three boys met Bigfoot near Saint Helens. Nine days later, on the 14th, a hiker saw a Sasquatch splashing in Laurance Lake.
- In **May**, Ed Riddle sighted an "oily-shiny" beast on the Molalla River, a creature was glimpsed on Marys Peak, a "large black biped" at Crow Flat, and a seven-footer was seen at Skookum Lake (Clackamas County).[137]

July's Sightings

- Sean Kehr met with an albino Sasquatch near Willamette, Sue Sebring reported seeing Bigfoot drinking from Rock Creek, and a camper sighted one near Molalla.
- A railroad conductor glimpsed "something tall and hairy" near Bonneville Dam.
- A "large white creature" was seen at West Linn.
- A prospector met a smelly beast near Sweet Home.
- An eight-footer with glowing eyes was seen near Detroit.[138]

Late Summer/Fall Sightings

- **August 2**: A sighting was reported near Ecola State Park.
- **August 14**: A deputy sheriff "met" with a Sasquatch near Tillamook.
- **August 28**: A beach-combing creature was seen in the same vicinity two weeks later.

Bagby Hot Springs, scene of a 1994 Bigfoot sighting. *Courtesy of U.S. Dept. of Fish & Wildlife.*

- **Early September**: Tony Cole fired on "a whole family of 'em" near Wallace, while a hiker met a five hundred-pound specimen in the Three Sisters Wilderness.
- Also in **September**, twelve witnesses saw Bigfoot at Illahee Flats, but none recalled the date.
- **October's** reports include a sighting on Cathedral Ridge on the 24th; Kevin Jones's meeting with a seven-foot female and her offspring at Peavine Lookout on the 28th; and an undated report of "a large animal" chasing an elk in Silver Falls State Park.[139]

Late Fall Sightings

- **November 3**: Kevin Jones claimed another sighting at Peavine Lookout
- **November 14**: A hunter sighted a Sasquatch near Ash.
- **November 15**: A fisherman met Bigfoot in Hells Canyon.
- **November 23**: Tony Ellis saw a seven-footer near Timber.
- **November 25**: "Chase" and "Mark" saw a six and a half-foot biped near Molalla; and a bow hunter logged the month's last sighting near Colton.[140]

Undated Sightings

- Betty Garmin claimed "many sightings" around Mount McLoughlin.
- There was also a claim that Bigfoot was seen "about five times" on Porter Road near Estacada.
- A motorist saw Sasquatch outside Sweet Homer, while our least impressive sighting comes from a woman "tripping" on LSD at Multnomah Falls.[141]

1996

Winter-Spring Reports

- **February 13**: Witness "Barry" had an encounter at Tollgate.
- **April 8**: A red-eyed creature startled a Holley resident.
- **May 16**: Laurine Davis saw "a gorilla" outside Estacada.
- Undated **May** sightings found Bigfoot crossing Interstate 5 near Wilsonville, frightening children at Cornucopia, and pounding $1,100 worth of dents into a truck at Timber.
- **June 20**: Nathan Peak saw a seven-foot Sasquatch in the same vicinity.[142]

Summertime Reports

- **July 13**: Hav Tranh and wife Gioking were hiking in Deschutes National Forest when Hav broke his leg. Two "horribly ugly" bipeds, eight or nine feet tall, allegedly appeared soon afterward and carried Han to safety while his wife followed.
- **Late July**: "L. E." saw a tan "psychic" Sasquatch near Sisters, while a red-haired specimen visited Sublimity.
- In **August**, a "hairy man" was reportedly seen in Takilma.
- **September 15**: A hunter glimpsed a massive creature at Little Boulder Lake while Jerry Mitchell saw a nine-footer near Ripplebrook at around the same time.
- In **undated** reports, two motorcyclists met Bigfoot near Bandon and a strolling couple saw a Sasquatch walking in the surf near Garibaldi.[143]

Fall's Reports

- **September 22**: A beast with a deformed left foot made tracks around Three Lynx.
- **October 5**: Timber resident "Zuzanna" saw a male and female Sasquatch "jabbering at each other" in her yard.
- **October 12**: A hunter met Bigfoot near Soapstone Creek while another beast stole witness "Howard's" lunch on Goat Mountain.
- **October 26**: A silver-gray nine-footer surfaced at McKenzie Pass.
- **Early November**: A seven-foot creature crossed Highway 97 near La Pine.
- **November 17**: Willie Harges logged a sighting at Tioga Creek.
- **November 26**: Howard Hall saw a pair of creatures outside Molalla, claiming that the female "smelled faintly of almonds" and "appeared to be sexually interested in him."
- **November 28**: Orey Inness also saw two bipeds near Molalla.
- **Undated** November sightings include George Lee's encounter near Elsie, a teacher's sighting from Wilderville, Delora Dever's encounter at Lolo Pass, Scott Sebring's tale

of Bigfoot fleeing a fire near Willow Creek, a military policeman's report from Grants Pass, and the appearance of an eight-foot beast near Silverton.[144]

Undated Sightings

• Reports include another incident with Orey Inness, this one at Abiqua Falls, and Karl Breheim's claim that a Sasquatch took a bite out of his toolbox at Grants Pass.[145]

1997

Winter/Spring Reports

• In **February**, witness "Bob" described a screaming beast in Saddle Mountain State Park.

• **March 10**: Joe Chane saw a nine-footer in Troutdale.

• In **April**, a white Sasquatch startled a driver near Deer Island.

• **May 15**: Mat Bagley watched Bigfoot cross the Molalla River, while others surfaced in Timber and at Redmond's airport.

• **May 26**: "Josh C." saw a nine- and a half-foot female in Saddle Mountain State Park.[146]

Summertime Reports

• In **June**, a motorist claimed a sighting from Coquille.

• **July 28**: Bigfoot was seen pulling ferns near Sitkum.

• **August 27**: John Tingue saw a red-eyed creature at Beaverton.

• **August 30**: A creature visited Brooks.

• **Early September**: Dan Thorp encountered an angry seven-footer near La Pine and a hiker claimed that he shot a Sasquatch on Anderson Creek in Tillamook County.

• The **summer** ends with a miner's undated report of Bigfoot "striding" past Disston.[147]

End-of-Year Reports

• In **November**, Jarrell Rysavy's wife and two companions met a Sasquatch in the Tillamook State Forest.

• In **December**, Rick Wood snapped a photo of Bigfoot in Clackamas County, while a hunter claimed a sighting near Vernonia.

• **Undated** reports include a camper's sighting from Brookings and an off-roader's panicky account from Grant County's Bear Creek.[148]

1998

Winter-Summer Reports

• **February 26**: "Walt" saw Bigfoot eating crayfish from Cook Creek.

• In **March**, campers saw a nine-foot creature outside Chiloquin.

• **July 19**: A seven-foot monster demolished Scott Voet's camp near Estacada.

• **August 2**: "Shawn J." and "Kurt V." watched Bigfoot cross the Wilson River.

• **Late August**: Mike Rinnan saw another beast in Black Bear Swamp, an eight-footer visited Tiller, and another appeared on Mother Lode Creek.

- **September 5**: Johnny Mochea and "Jay" saw a "cinnamon brown ape" outside Estacada on.[149]

End-of-Year Reports

- In **September**, Alex Ivanoff sighted a seven-foot beast that "looked similar to a human" at his home in Cottage Grove.

- **October 21**: Orey Inness and two friends saw a towering twelve-to-fifteen-foot monster near Abiqua Creek.

- **Halloween (October 31)**: A mushroom hunter reported that a Sasquatch leapt from a pit near Coquille.

- An **undated October** sighting placed Bigfoot near La Pine.

Waluga Park, another source of alleged Sasquatch sightings. *Courtesy of U.S. Dept. of Fish & Wildlife.*

- **November 13**: Tanya Rysavy and friends watched two "very massive" bipeds running through the Tillamook State Forest.

- **Undated** sightings include a government employee's report of Bigfoot emerging from a cave in Abiqua Falls, an account of a "weird person" near the Wilson River, and a vague claim of "numerous Sasquatches living all throughout" Waluga Park.[150]

1999

- **February 2**: "Ian" reported a creature resembling "a walking tree" near McMinnville.
- **April 25**: Darin Richardson saw Bigfoot cross a field in Milo McIver State Park.
- In **May**, an eight-footer visited Sutherlin.
- **July 15**: Tourists "Glen and Melinda" accidentally videotaped "distant bipedal movement" outside Lorane.
- **July 21**: A "big hairy Indian" approached fisherman "T. M." at Detroit Lake, stealing his gear while growling, "All the fish in this lake are mine!"
- **August 28**: Joe Rabb saw Sasquatch cross a road near Saddle Mountain State Park.
- **September 18**: Barbie Kaneaster met a limping albino creature near the Clackamas River.
- **October 3**: Robert Windsor witnessed a seven-foot beast near Crater Lake National Park while campers near Takilma logged another sighting later the same month.
- **November 2**: Witness "Darin" saw coyotes chasing Bigfoot near Salmonberry.[151]

Other '90s Sightings

- A marijuana grower claimed that many bipeds occupy the Red Buttes Wilderness, displaying "territorial and aggressive" behavior.
- Bigfoot was seen wading a creek near the Wickiup Reservoir.
- A creature was briefly glimpsed outside Simnasho, ducking behind trees.[152]

A New Century

As of December 2009, the new century had produced 274 alleged Oregon Bigfoot encounters, including 107 eyewitness sightings, sixty-two footprint discoveries, and 105 cases claiming other evidence.

2000

Winter-Summer Sightings

- **February 3**: A "ten-foot black ball of hair" was seen near Carlton.
- **May 18**: A motorcyclist reported seeing Bigfoot at Grants Pass.
- **June 5**: An elderly woman glimpsed a Sasquatch near Orting.
- **June 29**: A forestry manager saw one outside Port Angeles.
- **July 1**: The year's most famous case emerged when psychologist Dr. Matthew Johnson caught a hairy biped spying on his family at Oregon Caves National Monument.
- **July 2**: "Clarissa" and her brother allegedly saw a dead Sasquatch on I-84 near Hood River, but fled without collecting any evidence.
- **July 15**: A live biped that smelled "like something dead" appeared near McKenzie Bridge.
- An **undated August** sighting of a "dirty-looking" Bigfoot came from Bend.[153]

End-of-Year Sightings

- **September 16**: A motorist met a Sasquatch near Grand Ronde.
- **Late September**: Undated sightings came from Conde Creek, Chesnimnus Creek, and the Calapooia River (where a female and her child were seen).
- **October 25**: A hunter reported a sighting near the Oregon Caves National Monument.
- **October 26**: Arthur Laird gave an account of two bipeds dragging a deer along Camas Creek (Coos County) while a trucker claimed a sighting from Highway 219, near Hillsboro.[154]

2001

Winter Sightings

- **January 7**: An SIS report was made, but "has not been validated or is being studied."
- **February 21**: "Rick S." saw Bigfoot cross a road near the Ripplebrook Ranger Station.
- **March 17**: Two bipeds were reported strolling near Brookings.
- **March 23**: A solitary "large figure" was seen near Horsfall Lake.
- **Late March**: A woman claimed two brief sightings of a screaming beast at Bend and a camper reported two creatures crouched in the forest near White City.[155]

End-of-Year Sightings

- **Mid-May**: A "friendly" Bigfoot visited a home near Christmas Valley, prompting claims that the creatures "often stop and watch" local residents.

- **June 4**: A beachcomber saw two "huge ape-man figures" near Brookings. That same month, three campers met a beast with glowing eyes near Three Sisters.

- In **July**, a Sasquatch frightened campers at Indian Crossing.

- **August** produced two sightings: one at Joe Graham Horse Camp on the 23rd and one north of Grants Pass, date unknown.

- **September 11**: Terrorism eclipsed a sighting near Roseburg and another that same month at Barlow Pass.

- **Undated** cases include a sighting by the mayor and port commissioner of Florence, near Coos Bay, and a beast with arms "like CO_2 cylinders for soda dispensers" seen outside Gresham.[156]

2002

Winter-Spring Reports

- **January 9 or 16** (reports differ): Linda Boydsdon almost struck an eight-foot creature with her car near Multnomah Falls.

- **February 6**: The SIS claimed another unvalidated sighting.

- **March 3**: Unnamed hikers met Bigfoot near Sweet Home.

- **April 19**: Hikers met Bigfoot at Coos Bay.

Many witnesses report sightings of adult and juvenile creatures together.
Courtesy of William Rebsamen.

- **June 8**: "J. W." spotted a Sasquatch near Grants Pass.
- **June 11**: A Sasquatch paced a truck outside Detroit.[157]

Summer Reports

- **Late July**: A motorist reported a sighting from Highway 199 near Cave Junction.
- **August 10**: Steve Branson had a sighting from untraceable "Tshudy's Pass."
- **August 20**: A stroller reported something "like an ape" from Lookingglass Valley.
- **August 24**: A six-foot creature was seen at Philomath.
- **Late August**: A driver met a seven-footer outside Weston and Matthew Johnson gave a vague report of a summer sighting, location unknown.[158]

Fall Sightings

- **September 24**: A hiker's botched an attempt to photograph Bigfoot on Ruckel Creek.
- **October 24**: Guests at Suttle Lake Resort saw an eight-foot Sasquatch and two smaller specimens crossing the grounds.
- **Late October**: A psychiatric nurse driving near Glide stopped his car to help a hitchhiker who proved to be a seven-foot apeman.
- **December 17**: Bigfoot peered through the windows of a house near Umatilla County's Pilot Rock.
- **December 21**: Another motorist met a Sasquatch on Cabbage Hill.[159]

2003

Winter-Spring Reports

- **February 15**: A "huge animal" was seen knocking on an apartment door in Welches.
- **Late February**: A growling "figure" appeared outside Sutherlin.
- **May 9**: An eight-foot "hairy ape" that smelled like "hanace garbage" startled hikers near Astoria.
- **June** brought sightings by fisherman "Dan" from Hermiston and another angler near Detroit.[160]

Summer-Fall Sightings

- In **September**, a driver reported a sighting from Three Pyramids.
- In **October**, sightings were logged from Prineville on the 10th, Roaring River on the 19th, and Cherry Grove on the 22nd.
- **November 8**: Two sightings included a seven-foot creature near Estacada and a shaggy jogger at Willamette Pass.
- **December 7**: Three drivers saw Bigfoot cross Highway 97 near Oakridge.
- **December 8**: Another Sasquatch appeared at Grand Ronde.
- An **undated** report placed a Sasquatch on Forest Road 4550, near Estacada.[161]

2004

Winter-Spring Sightings

- **January 27**: Two hikers saw a creature eight to nine feet tall near Eagle Creek in Clackamas County.
- In **February**, others met an amber-eyed beast beside the Rogue River.
- **March 18**: A hairy, seven-foot "possible human" surfaced in Tillamook County.
- In **April**, there was a sighting at an Estacada rifle range on the 22nd; another on the 25th, cited by the SIS with no details; plus two undated reports from Cave Junction and Huntington.[162]

Summer-Fall Sightings

- **June 10**: Two girls logged a Bigfoot sighting from Chip Ross City Park in Corvallis.
- **July 3**: There was a family's sighting on Prospect Highway, near Butte Falls.
- **September** proved more active: campers near the John Day Fossil Beds National Monument claimed three sightings in as many days; a motorist met "something big, tall, and hairy" near Chemult; another driver glimpsed Bigfoot at Cascade Summit; and a hunter fled from a Sasquatch near Detroit.
- In **October**, Bigfoot returned to Cave Junction the 10th and startled a driver near Troy on the 26th.
- **November's** sighting spooked another hunter outside Detroit.[163]

2005

- **January 14**: A Stanfield farmer fired on "something hunched over attacking [his] cattle," which uttered a "creepy scream" when wounded.
- **Early May**: Teenage hunters met a gray Sasquatch near Sweet Home.
- **May 16**: A motorist glimpsed a blackish-brown biped near Prineville.
- In **June**, a woman saw Bigfoot outside her home near Grants Pass, while another met a "very muscular" biped on Highway 22, outside Sheridan. There was also a report of a Sasquatch at Devils Flat.
- In **August**, sightings were logged near Dora on the 5th and from an undisclosed location on the 8th.
- **September 15**: Bigfoot was reported prowling Yamhill's outskirts.
- In **October**, a Sasquatch spooked a family driving near Canyonville.[164]

2006

- **January 2**: A reddish-brown Sasquatch left three footprints near Glendale, later cast in plaster.
- **January 27**: A "very bulky" eight and a half-foot creature showed itself near Cannon Beach.
- **May 6**: The SIS claimed a sighting, but did not provide the location or any other details.

- **July 22**: A Coos Bay resident saw Bigfoot near his home
- **July 24**: Bigfoot visited Government Camp.[165]

2007

- **April 12**: A couple "goofing off" near Sitkum met a Sasquatch more than nine feet tall.
- **July 9**: Six campers glimpsed Bigfoot's silhouette and measured its fourteen-inch tracks near Detroit.
- **August 16**: A couple saw "a dark figure running around" Prineville Reservoir Resort.
- **August 21**: A Bigfoot researcher got lucky with a sighting in Santiam State Forest.
- **October 5**: The SIS claimed a sighting, which "has not been validated."[166]

2008

- **July 31**: A motorist had a sighting near the Sandy River.
- **August 22**: A photographer snapped "something walking upright" near Gales Creek.
- **August 25**: Two motorists saw "an ape" cross Highway 26 near Rhododendron.
- **October 5**: The SIS claimed a sighting, but offered no details.[167]

2009

- **March 2**: Three travelers saw a "very large animal" near Dora.
- **March 17**: A motorist in Tumalo swerved to miss a shaggy jogger.
- **May 22**: A hiker at Cape Meares glimpsed a "very tall, thin to medium build" creature.
- In **September**, another hiker met an eight-foot biped on South Sister.[168]

Chapter Seven

Bigfoot in Washington

As with Oregon, reported tallies for Bigfoot encounters in Washington vary widely. Some of those offered include:

- John Green's tabulation of 281 in 1978.[1]
- Christopher Murphy's citation of 286 in 2006.[2]
- The IBS claim of 768 cases, lost when the website vanished in March 2009. Before it disappeared, I retrieved 625 case files, including 152 duplicates, two reports of a "giant rabbit," and several files with multiple sightings.[3]
- As of December 2009, the Oregon Bigfoot website listed 138 cases from Washington; the BFRO claimed 479 (including many general newspaper stories); and the SIS offered 1,813 — most "unvalidated" and excluded here for lack of any details.[4]

My own tally for Washington, drawn from those and other sources, lists 1,210 alleged Sasquatch encounters. Those include 639 eyewitness sightings, 206 reports of footprints, and 365 cases claiming other evidence.

Days of Yore

Aboriginal tribes of Washington State shared various names for Bigfoot with their Oregon neighbors, while adding some of their own. Aside from the aforementioned Choanito, See'atco, Skookum, Ste ye mah, and Tah tah kle' ah, the beasts were also called Nung-nung and Tyapish.[5]

While Rev. Elkanah Walker logged the first published account of native "giant" legends in 1840, and explorer Paul Kane recorded the first tales of cannibalistic "skoocooms" around Mount St. Helens in March 1847, John Green's archival research unearthed the earliest known tale of an actual sighting in the Evergreen State. Fur trader Rocque Ducheney saw an "ape" on Mount St. Helens around 1850, and fled when the beast beckoned him.[6]

Six years later, a group of See'atcos supposedly kidnapped a Nisqually tribeswoman from Fort Vancouver. In the early 1860s, two Burgoine brothers allegedly vanished from a cabin at Grizzly Lake during successive winters, one after scrawling a journal entry referring to "strange hairy monsters." Sadly, our only source for that report is "Eric Norman," a pen name shared during 1969-72 by sensationalist pulp authors Warren Smith and Brad Steiger. Compounding the confusion, Ray Crowe placed Grizzly Lake in Lewis County, where no such lake exists — although Grizzly Lakes are found in Skamania and Snohomish Counties.[7]

The nineteenth century ends with another kidnapping tale, more bizarre than the rest. Sometime in the 1890s, legend has it that a

Explorer-artist Paul Kane (foreground) collected native tales of forest-dwelling monsters. *Courtesy of the Library of Congress.*

newlywed Indian bride was abducted by a Sasquatch from Keller in Ferry County. She survived and escaped, but bore a hybrid child called Patrick, described as a "5'4" tiny man [with] very long arms reaching to his knees. [He] had a sloping forehead, a large lower jaw with a wide mouth with straight upper and lower lips, and straight protruding teeth. He was hump-backed, his ears were peaked, he had long fingers and large hands, and generally when at school was described as very ugly, although very smart." Despite his appearance, Patrick reportedly married and fathered five children before his death at age thirty.[8]

1900-1948

There are twenty-three Bigfoot encounters on file for the first half of the twentieth century, fifteen of them eyewitness sightings. Reports from 1900 include a Vancouver dairyman's claim that "a large hairy thing" grabbed his leg while he slept, before dogs chased it off, and a teenager's sighting of four bipeds dining on grubs outside Huntsville.[9]

A dozen years elapsed before the next report, in autumn 1912, when Bigfoot prowled and howled

Ape Canyon, scene of a supposed miners' battle with Bigfoot and several modern sightings. *Courtesy of U.S. Dept. of Fish & Wildlife.*

around a farm near Oakville. Five years later, in autumn 1917, a logger working on the Cowlitz River saw "a large ape-like something" roaming the woods.[10]

1920s

In 1920, a farmer saw three of the "biggest, strangest bears ever" near Coppei Creek. Soon afterward, his wife saw "a caveman" whom she said "was dressed up in furs and really needed a bath." The couple blamed Sasquatch for stealing several of their cows.[11]

Washington's next Bigfoot tale dates from July 1924, when a group of prospectors allegedly fought a pitched battle with hairy "mountain devils" near Mount St. Helens, at a site now called Ape Canyon. Survivor Fred Beck waited forty-three years to dictate his full report of the incident, replete with claims of telepathy and spirit guides, inter-dimensional travel, and religious epiphanies that strain credulity to the breaking point. Forest rangers called the incident a prank, and track-hoaxer Rant Mullens later claimed that he and an uncle had stoned the miners' cabin as a joke.[12]

Another claim of Sasquatch aggression comes from Quinault, sometime in 1927. Ex-policeman Fred Bradshaw relayed the story of two men found with "their rifles twisted and distorted, and with all their bones crushed and broken, like they had been repeatedly smashed against the ground." Sadly, all records of the crime had been discarded, and the case sounds so much like Ivan Sanderson's 1890 report from Oregon that we may question whether it occurred at all.[13]

1930s-1940s

Our next case comes from 1932, when Hite Center resident Ashland Hite saw "a tall bear-like creature" walking upright past his home. Three years later, hunter Datus Perry was stalking game near Augspurger Mountain when he spied a black-and-brown Sasquatch sleeping in a thicket.[14]

In autumn 1941, a young woman riding with her fiancé near Mount Adams Lake saw "a tall black creature covered with hair and very muscular" crossing a roadside meadow. Another 1941 witness, Clarence Fox, described a "naked man" seen "leaping from rock to rock on a mountainside" above Lichtenwasser Lake. Global events in the summer of 1944 eclipsed "David A.'s" sighting of a "tall ape-like creature" at Fragaria.[15]

Four sightings complete our record for the 1940s: In 1947, Bigfoot peered through a woman's windows and rifled her trash cans at the northern tip of the Olympic Peninsula; in 1948, Clarence Foster saw a slender Sasquatch crouched beside Mad Lake, while hikers Bob Ferris, Melrose Stevens, and Earl Willits met a foul-smelling eight-footer at Glacier Meadows; and an undated report describes a woman's sighting of "a creature, not a bear," picking huckleberries outside Carson.[16]

The 1950s

This decade produced seventeen alleged Bigfoot encounters, including eleven eyewitness sightings. Sadly, the most sensational report must be discarded as a journalistic hoax.

1950

On May 21, diabetic Joe Carter vanished while skiing with friends on Mount St. Helens. A two-week search proved fruitless and was halted on June 5, with Carter presumed dead. His remains were never found, and thirteen years elapsed before the *Longview Times* blamed Bigfoot for snatching "Jim Carter," fabricating statements from alleged searchers speculating that "the apes got him." Renowned Bigfoot hunter René Dahinden unwisely repeated the tale, complete with Carter's garbled name, in 1973.[17]

Another case from around the same time seems more credible. Three children at Mill A, near Gifford Pinchot National Forest, described "a figure" watching from the treeline as they played.[18]

1952-1956

Next come four vaguely-dated sightings spanning roughly four years.

- **July 1952** or **1953**: Witness "D. W." was hiking on his grandfather's farm near Longview when he saw "two large upright animals" near the Columbia River.
- **Early 1950s**: A North Bonneville motorist described a Sasquatch jogging alongside his car.
- Two boys from Holden saw a Bigfoot crossing Miners Creek in late July or early August, sometime between **1953 and 1955**.

- **Summer of 1955 or '56**: A dozen hikers, led by Paul McGuire, met a biped covered with "longish dirty-white hair" on Mount St. Helens.[19]

1957

- **May**: The only dated case comes from Charlotte Simons, who met a seven-foot monster near Malott.
- **Undated** sightings came from Bob Morgan, who saw "a gorilla" in Mason County; Danny Voyhles, who complained of Bigfoot stalking him at Vancouver Lake; Arlene Arp, who saw a beige seven-footer with "long silky hair" watching traffic near Amboy; and a driver watched a Sasquatch cross a highway north of Carson.[20]

1958-1959

- In **1958**, school bus driver Hubert Smith saw a Sasquatch cross a road near Arlington — a few days before tracks were found and preserved at nearby Jim Creek.
- Sometime in **1959**, an off-duty sheriff's deputy saw Bigfoot while fishing near Wind River.[21]

The 1960s

This decade produced 102 alleged Bigfoot encounters, eighty-five of them eyewitness sightings.

1960

- **July 18**: Unidentified honeymooners saw a Sasquatch "eating frogs" on Highway 101 near Shelton.
- **Undated** reports for the year include a seven-foot creature that explored the porch of a home near Gig Harbor and an albino biped that startled motorists outside Richland.[22]

1961

- In **March**, Roger Veach saw "a large hairy man" cross a road south of Yacolt.
- In **September**, a hiker glimpsed Bigfoot near Ross Lake, but failed to specify which one (lakes of that name exist in both Snohomish and Whatcom Counties).
- An **undated** motorist's sighting from Swede Pass completes the year's list.[23]

1962

- Sometime in **June-July**, Tex and Sandy Johnson claimed a sighting by their five-year-old daughter near Kalama.
- In **October**, Dutch Holler and his uncle saw a seven-foot biped in Spokane.[24]

1963

- **Undated** springtime reports saw campers frightened by a hairy prowler on the Dosewallips River while "a respected businesswoman" caught Bigfoot peeping through her windows on Toppenish Ridge.
- In **June**, Stan Mattson watched a female Sasquatch and her offspring drinking from the Lewis River, outside Yale.
- In **July**, Martin Hennrich and his wife saw Bigfoot and measured its sixteen-inch tracks near the Lewis River's junction with the Columbia; Gladys Herrarra glimpsed a nine-foot Peeping Tom at her home near Satus Pass; and motorist Paul Manley saw a shaggy "tree stump" climb out of a roadside ditch between Goldendale and Toppenish.
- Summer ends with an **undated** driver's report of a nine-foot creature crossing a highway near Sequim, where eighteen and half-inch tracks were found the next day.[25]

1964

- In **July**, a ten-foot creature frightened local residents at Lake Stevens and a motorist saw Bigfoot cross Highway 112 in three strides between Neah Bay and Sekiu in Clallam County.
- **Undated** sightings came from Ape Canyon and Cradle Lake.[26]

1965

- **July 30**: Campers "Craig, Jeff, and Dan" caught Bigfoot watching them at Kachess Lake.
- In **August**, several children glimpsed an eight-foot hairy creature on a farm at Parker.
- In **October**, Russell Geis and Dennis Lensgrave fired on a white seven-footer at Nisqually Head.
- **Undated** sightings include Sheriff Hank Deshard's report of a Sasquatch crossing Highway 14 near Carson and farmer "James K.'s" encounter at Loomis (Okanogan County).[27]

1966

- An **undated spring** report came from soldier Ken Gosline, who met a Sasquatch on maneuvers in the Olympic National Forest.
- **Summertime** brought three undated reports: An eleven-man party fired shots at an eight-foot, whitish-gray beast outside Richland; three boys saw a "white demon" near Sawyer; and the same thing (or its twin) chased a youth outside Yakima.
- **September 19**: Ken Pettijohn saw a seven-foot, gray-white beast near Yakima.
- In **October**, Carl Timberbrook watched a similar creature strolling along the Yakima canal while Mike Corey of Yakima fired on a beast that killed his dog.[28]

1967

Bigfoot mania took off with October's release of the Patterson film, but ten of Washington's eighteen reports for the year occurred before that event.

- **March** brought a hunter's sighting from Badger Mountain (Benton County).
- In **August**, Robert Emery and another soldier met three hairy bipeds at Fort Lewis

while another serviceman stationed there, Ed Bush, caught Bigfoot prowling the base before summer's end.

- In **September**, there were six separate sightings along the Nooksak River, involving seven witnesses, and Carol Davis saw a Sasquatch wading ashore near Bellingham.[29]

Eight sightings followed the Patterson film:

- In **October**, there were two reports from Frank and Rita Lawrence of a hairy prowler lurking near their Marietta home.
- **Undated** autumn sightings include Billy Brown's attempt to shoot a Sasquatch on the Chehalis River, a hunter's report from Spirit Lake, and George Hofmann's meeting with the "Brinson Monster" on a Lewis County farm.
- In **December**, Frank Lawrence saw Bigfoot again, outside Marietta; helicopter pilot Norman Winningstad logged a sighting while circling over Mount Zion; and Loren Kelley saw Bigfoot watching children at play on a farm near Woodland.[30] 1968

- **Mid-June**: Frank Lawrence claimed his third Bigfoot encounter, with a female and her child, near Clipper.
- In **August**, camper "S. F." woke to glimpse an eight-foot prowler on Icicle Creek.
- In **November**, two students met a nine-foot creature near Tieton.
- **Undated** cases include Art Gilbert's claim that Bigfoot assaulted an unnamed friend near Orchards and a tale from hikers who watched two creatures fight to the death on Copper Mountain, with a twelve-foot monster slaying its seven-foot rival. Oddly, while Washington boasts four Copper Mountains, none is found in Okanogan County as claimed by IBS researcher Mike Stevenson.[31]

Badger Mountain, where soldiers met three bipedal creatures in 1967. *Courtesy of U.S. Dept. of Fish & Wildlife.*

1969

This was the year that Skamania County's commissioners passed an ordinance making it a felony to kill Bigfoot. That law was revised in 1984, reducing the slaying of Sasquatch "with malice aforethought" to the status of a gross misdemeanor. Still, the decade's last year produced a record twenty-three sightings.

Winter Sightings

- **March 5**: Don Cox saw a nine-foot creature cross a road in Beacon Rock State Park.
- **Undated**: Ellen Satterthwaite had a similar encounter near Skamania later in the month.[32]

Spring Sightings

- In **April**, a woman saw two bipeds rifling trash cans somewhere between Bossburg and Northport.
- In **May**, Fred Bradshaw watched a seven-foot creature leave seventeen-inch footprints near Satsop.

- **Undated** sightings include Betty Peterson's report of two bipeds crossing a road near Kettle Falls, Don Cox's description of "a giant hairy ape" at Beacon Rock, and a four-witness sighting of a white eight-footer outside Marietta.[33]

Summer Sightings

- **July 26 or 27** (reports differ): Deputy Sheriff Verlin Herrington saw a female Sasquatch seven to eight feet tall outside Copalis Beach.
- **August 4**: Teenage campers Marshall Cabe and Mark Meece claimed that three hairy creatures chased them around Cub Lake.
- An **undated** August report had four teens night-riding near Copalis Beach logging a sighting.
- **September 13**: A lone youth saw a 5'3" creature at Deception Pass.
- **September 20**: Dick Hancock and Gary Johnson saw a Sasquatch collide with a highway sign, leaving it bent, in Fife Heights.
- **Undated** September reports include a Bellingham resident who saw a "huge, sad-looking face covered with white hair" peering through her bedroom window at 4 a.m., while fisherman Robert Parker and friends claimed an encounter with Bigfoot near North Bend.[34]

Autumn Sightings

- In **October**, Ross Hendrich watched two large bipeds climb a hill near Yakima.
- **November 1**: Sergeant Lloyd Stringer saw a brown six-footer cross a road near Saint Clair Lake.
- **November 15**: "S. H." reported a highway sighting east of Packwood.
- **November 23**: Charles Kent saw a "bear" walking upright on the Calkins Ranch, near Woodland.
- **Undated** reports for November include Louise Baxter's highway sighting at North Bonneville and Bigfoot's encounter with four loggers at Neah Bay, plus two anonymous filings from Ingalls Creek and Klickitat Valley.[35]

Other '60s Sightings

Seven undated cases for the decade range from the mundane to bizarre.

- Witness "Lopez" saw an eight-foot biped near Orchard sometime in the early 1960s.
- An unnamed witness claimed "a dozen" sightings at a dump near Yakima during the winter of 1961-62.
- Jim Mission dated his Yakima River sighting of a "tall animal with head set on shoulders" from the mid-1960s.
- Researcher Harry Oakes cited an unnamed sheriff's deputy as his source for a tale of "a big creature" killing a woman somewhere in the Olympic Mountains in 1964 or '65, but produced no evidence.
- Bill Gefroh met a Sasquatch near Mount Rainier and measured its sixteen-inch tracks sometime in the late 1960s.
- Witness "G. J." placed his sighting at the Salvation Army's Camp Arnold sometime between 1967 and 1970.
- "Hippie-type" Mark Mashosky cannot decide if his meeting with a small Bigfoot in the Olympic National Forest occurred in the 1960s or 70s.[36]

The 1970s

This decade produced 183 specific reports of Bigfoot activity, including 111 eyewitness sightings, thirty-three footprint discoveries, and thirty-nine cases with more ambiguous evidence.

1970

Winter-Spring Sightings

- In **March**, Bill Harwood met a nine-foot primate at Priest Rapids Dam and three unnamed campers woke to screams from a foul-smelling giant at an undisclosed location.[37]

- In **May**, witnesses Becky Figg, Diane Higby, and Rosemary Tucker saw a silver-haired seven-footer near Copalis Crossing.

- **June 14**: An "enraged" nine-foot creature trapped two young couples in their car, on a lover's lane, outside Yakima.

- Two **undated** June reports had Bigfoot chasing a car occupied by three teenage girls near Carlisle and hurling stones at Allan Ebling and his friends outside Taholah.[37]

Summertime Sightings

- **July 9**: Wayne Thureringer and a friend spent fifteen minutes watching a Sasquatch in Mount Rainier National Park.

- **July 10**: Several men fired on Bigfoot at a Yakima swimming hole — and then fled when the shots left it unfazed.

- **July 31**: An unnamed man surprised a sleeping monster in a cave at Beacon Rock State Park.

- **August 2**: Ronald Zimmerman saw a white Sasquatch with "a very large stomach" at Boston Basin.

- **August 15**: Motorcyclist Rich Myers glimpsed a twelve-foot biped in the Blue Mountains near Walla Walla.

- **August 19**: A Sasquatch watched Louise Baxter change a flat tire outside North Bonneville.[38]

Artist's conception of Sasquatch dining on berries. *Courtesy of William Rebsamen.*

Autumn Sightings

- In **October**, a teenage resident of Spanaway was frightened by a shaggy voyeur peering through windows of his home.

- In an **undated** report, fishermen Jim Peters and "Glen" logged a sighting from Spirit Lake, where "a big, hairy, dark brown thing" left fourteen-inch "human-looking tracks."[39]

1971

- **March 2**: A Sasquatch startled Charles Smith and Margie Baker by knocking on their car's roof in Tenin while a soldier saw Bigfoot prowling the grounds of Fort Lewis later in the month.
- In **June**, there was another window-peeping incident from Spanaway.
- In **August**, a Sasquatch scaled a hill north of Mount St. Helens.
- **October 2**: Elmer Wollenberg watched two bipeds strolling past Yale Lake.
- **December 15**: A family of four saw Bigfoot in their yard near Bremerton.
- **Undated** reports include Deputy Verlin Herrington's second sighting, near Aberdeen; George Hildebrand's report of a Sasquatch crossing Sherman Pass; and Mike Machheid's unsubstantiated claim that Bigfoot snatched a girl near Vader and then released her with minor scratches.[40]

1972

Winter-Spring Sightings

- In **February**, Don Waugh saw a black biped hurdle a ditch near Aloha; a Kapowsin farmer watched Bigfoot through a telescopic sight; and a Bremerton resident saw a reddish-brown seven-footer outside her home.
- **May 22**: Four witnesses saw "a large hairy creature" on Silver Star Mountain.
- **May 26**: James Figg glimpsed a black specimen near Copalis Crossing.
- An **undated** report also found Mike Hazenburg and a friend dodging stones hurled by Bigfoot at Stossel Creek.[41]

Summer-Late Fall Sightings

- In **June**, Allen Ebling and other witnesses saw an eight-foot biped roaming the Quinault Reservation.
- **August** brought sightings from Van Zandt, where a hulking silhouette frightened campers, and Satsop, where "something" with seventeen-inch feet stalked ballplayers "Kirk and Kelly D."
- On **Christmas Eve**, Julie Reed and a companion saw Bigfoot cross a road outside Aloha.[42]

Undated Sightings

Regrettably, these six cases include two filed by veteran hoaxer Ray Wallace. Other reports include:

- Dale Ulrich's report of "three bears" walking upright outside Cougar.
- Witness "Coleman's" claim that Bigfoot stole a logger's lunch near Mount St. Helens.
- Seven witnesses met a Sasquatch on a moonlight stroll near Clearwater, while another creature stoned Kevin Turner and four other campers at Haleys Dam.
- An unnamed witness met Bigfoot at Sherman Pass, while a malodorous creature visited a camp on the north fork of Logy Creek.[43]

1973

- In **February**, biker "Dan" saw a seven-foot biped outside Wenatchee.
- In **May**, two fishermen saw "a large dark hairy figure" crouched on the beach at Point Jefferson.

- An **undated** spring sighting had motorists meeting "a large chimp" jogging along Highway 169 between Auburn and Black Diamond.
- In **July**, two witnesses reported a six-foot creature outside Bonneville.
- In **September**, a seven-foot beast was described as running with upraised arms near Woodinville.
- **Undated** reports include Louis Awhile's highway sighting near Beacon Park and an unnamed Indian's claim that an angry Sasquatch peered through his window outside Omak, growling, "Somebody shot me and I don't like it!"[44]

1974

- In **January**, a husband-wife prospecting team glimpsed a creature that "smelled very funny," between Cook and Grass Lake.
- **June 9**: Driver Tony McLennan stopped to help an "injured dog" near Maple Valley, fleeing when it rose to eight feet tall on two legs.
- In **October**, there was another sighting from Woodinville.
- In **November**, a fisherman met a Sasquatch at Sunset Falls.
- In **December**, Richard Taylor swerved to miss a hairy jaywalker near Port Angeles, crashing his car and injuring passenger Larry Followell.
- In **undated** reports, motorist "Rhonda" struck the beast that crossed her path outside Poulsbo, but it suffered no apparent harm, and researcher Robert Morgan logged reports of primates burying their dead in lava tubes around Mount St. Helens, but offered no evidence.[45]

1975

- **May 25**: Anonymous report of "what may be a Sasquatch" on Whitehorse Mountain was received.
- In **July**, a mobile home near Eatonville was shaken by a grunting beast that left 21-inch footprints while a soldier at Fort Lewis logged a sighting of an eight-foot, red-eyed monster.
- **October 1**: Teenage campers Tom Gerstmar, Jerry Lazzar, and Earl Thomas faced a nine-foot creature at Section 3 Lake on Pinegrass Ridge.
- **October 22**: Lummi Indian Reserve police led by Sergeant Ken Cooper observed Sasquatch for "many minutes," before it was joined by a second creature.
- **Late October**: A Lummi police captain fired at a six-foot biped and another Sasquatch jogged alongside Sgt. Cooper's patrol car.
- **Undated** cases include a motorcyclist's sighting near Enumclaw, a report from horseman "Tim S." that Bigfoot spooked his mount on Hangman Creek, and a farmer's claim that Sasquatch killed one of his goats at North Bonneville.[46]

1976

- **Early July**: Mike Johnson photographed seven hump-backed creatures walking in single file at Royal Basin, but gave his film to an unnamed friend who lost it.
- In **September**, a Sasquatch stared down a trucker parked outside Eatonville.
- In **November**, a hunter saw a "large dark form standing upright" in the Goat Rocks Wilderness.

- **Undated** cases include a trucker's near-miss with Bigfoot outside Port Angeles, and a shaggy burglar's theft of food from a home in Okanogan.[47]

1977

- **March 16**: A soldier was treated for shock after he met Bigfoot while hiking near Eatonville.
- **July 13**: Three campers saw a musky-smelling "large, dark animal" at Little Falls.
- **July 19**: A Sasquatch crashed a party at the exclusive Cowlitz Timber Trails Association.
- **August 14**: A Skykomish driver met an eight-footer, but the report doesn't say where.
- **August 27**: Vernita Frazier met a screaming ten-footer at Clear Lake.
- **Undated August** sightings include a couple's report of "three brownish figures" on Nooksack River and a lone biped lurking around Lake Hannan.
- In **September**, a hairy night-prowler spooked camper Mildred Quinn on White Chuck Mountain.
- **Undated** reports include a child's sighting near Elma and Roger Veach's encounter with "a possible Bigfoot" on the Muddy River.[48]

Cryptozoologist Autumn Williams traces her interest in Bigfoot to early childhood. *Courtesy of Autumn Williams.*

Encountering the Sasquatch

Spring of 1977 also launched a two-year series of remarkable encounters logged by Sali Sheppard-Wolford and her daughter, famed Sasquatch researcher Autumn Williams. When Autumn was only two years old, Sali and her husband moved the family to Orting, in the foothills of Mount Rainier, and logged a Bigfoot sighting on their day of arrival. The rest of their story is best savored by reading Sali's book *Valley of the Skookum*. Suffice it to say that the tale is strange and thought-provoking, replete with Sasquatch encounters, "spirit journeys," and swooping aerial light shows. Autumn, meanwhile, launched her career as a Bigfoot researcher in grade school, collecting reports from her classmates.[49]

1978

- **April 3**: Report of four creatures "playing 'chase'" in Mount Rainier's foothills.
- **April 30**: Bigfoot surprised a fisherman at Logy Creek.
- **Undated April Sighting**: "Dr. D. E. M." saw two creatures walking near Beacon Rock.
- In **June**, a trucker met a Sasquatch on Highway 101 near Neilton.
- In **October**, Albert Permella told police that "a gigantic, hideous looking creature" assaulted him outside Yakima, leaving him bruised and his clothes torn.
- **November 6**: Jack Webb and four companions met an eight-foot biped in Skamania County.
- **Veteran's Day**: Two hunters saw a seven-footer near Grays River.
- **Undated** claims include a sighting from Highway 14 near Cape Horn (Clark County), another soldier's sighting at Fort Lewis, and a report of Bigfoot watching picnickers on Mount Rainier.[50]

1979

- In **April**, a Sasquatch returned to Fort Lewis.
- **May 8**: J. J. Senko saw an eight-foot "hairy thing" cross Highway 9 near Aberdeen.
- **August 1**: A six-foot creature stoned Richard Jacobs near Ape Canyon.
- **August 15**: A fisherman met Bigfoot at one of Jefferson County's several Jupiter Lakes.
- **October** sightings came from the Pacific Highway outside Bellingham and Germany Creek, where Bill Roseback watched an eight-footer leave 22-inch tracks.
- **November 22**: A nine-foot beast stopped traffic outside La Grande.
- **December 7**: A biped startled motorists near Vaughn.
- **Undated**: Teen witnesses "Mark and Rob" filed a report from Yacolt, where Sasquatch hammered on their car with massive fists.[51]

Other '70s Reports

- In the "early '70s," Richard Willman saw Bigfoot near Black Diamond.
- Ten intoxicated youths claimed a sighting from a Leavenworth pig farm.
- Cameron Blagg saw a biped at Hagen Creek.
- A Sasquatch made an appearance at Skagit Speedway.
- Young bicyclists glimpsed a bipedal creature at a gravel pit near Puyallup in 1973 or '74.
- A logger saw Bigfoot outside Longview, sometime between 1974 and 1977.
- Four climbers saw a Sasquatch on Mount St. Helens.
- A claim that campers stoned by multiple creatures at July Creek (Grays Harbor County) responded with gunfire.
- A complaint of Bigfoot snatching a steer outside Forks; and a Halloween clown's police report of a highway sighting between Amboy and Yacolt.[52]

The 1980s

Alleged Bigfoot encounters decreased to 165 in this decade, including eighty-six direct sightings, twenty-seven track reports, and fifty-two cases claiming other evidence.

1980

Winter-Spring Sightings

- **January 11**: A motorist reported a sighting from Highway 9, between Arlington and Marysville.
- In **April**, a DNR crew planting trees near Home Valley watched two strolling bipeds through their binoculars.
- On **Mother's Day**, motorists near Skagit County's Big Lake saw a creature "not a bear, nor a human" crossing Highway 9.[53]

Bigfoot or Volcanic Ash?

- A literal explosion of reports accompanied the eruption of Mount St. Helens on May 18, which killed fifty-seven people while destroying 250 homes, forty-seven bridges, 185 miles of highways, and fifteen miles of railways. It also spilled lava over 230 square miles. Fred Bradshaw's father claimed National Guard trucks removed "a group of bodies" from Green Mountain while researcher Joe Beelart says the U.S. Army Corps of Engineers found two more on Cowlitz River, airlifting them to parts unknown.[54]

The eruption of Mount St. Helens spawned tales of Bigfoot corpses recovered by authorities. *Courtesy of U.S. Dept. of Fish & Wildlife.*

Such tales are tantalizing, but none can be substantiated. Meanwhile, hairy survivors also were seen.

- Two hikers fleeing the eruption saw Bigfoot on Mount St. Helens while witness "Paul H." watched "a muddy orange colored monkey that looked like an orangutan" drinking from a stream near Augspurger Mountain. On June 28, backpackers glimpsed "a large, dark, human-like form" on Mount Pugh while a "giant gray figure with glowing eyes" frightened a driver outside Granite Falls on July 27.[55]

End-of-Year Sightings

- **September's** reports include motorist "Michael's" sighting from Interstate 5, south of Bellingham, and a hiker's report of "a large hairy manlike creature" outside Eatonville.
- **November 22**: Steve Moro saw Bigfoot standing beside an unnamed creek in Snohomish County.
- **Undated** reports include "Greg's" sighting of an eight-foot biped jogging near Stampede Pass, Mary Smith's claim that Bigfoot killed a deer at Summit Lake (Washington has nine Summit Lakes in eight different counties), "Mr. Jackson's" glimpse of a Sasquatch at Yacolt, and an anonymous sighting from Castle Rock's graveyard.[56]

1981

- **May 23-25**: Several children met Sasquatch near Alder Lake over Memorial Day weekend.
- **July 2**: A seven-foot voyeur peered through the windows of a home outside Colville.
- **September 13**: A young couple driving near Gig Harbor saw something "larger than any man and too tall for a bear."
- **Undated** reports include Fred Long seeing Bigfoot moving silently through woods north of Brinnon and a hunter's report of a Sasquatch on Mount Rainier.[57]

1982

- **June 4**: Bigfoot surprised teenage campers near Elma.
- **June 10**: Forest Service employee Paul Freeman saw a beast "big enough to tear the head right off your shoulders" outside Walla Walla, preserving one of its fourteen-inch

footprints in plaster. (Border Patrol spokesman Joel Hardin blamed a hoaxer for the prints, without specifically accusing Freeman.)

- **July 3**: A motorist watched Bigfoot cross Highway 101 near Port Angeles.
- In **October**, a hunter saw three bipedal creatures on Nestor Peak Trail, while Keith Graham and his sister spied a seven-footer on Eckler Mountain.
- **November 26**: Off-road drivers saw a biped with a "nondescript" face outside North Bend.
- **Undated** sightings include Vane Brouley's claim that he photographed a Sasquatch on Woodward Creek, Al Warner's encounter with "something of pretty good size" on Mount Adams, and "Nancy's" sighting of a "big brown hairy creature" on Whidbey Island.[58]

1983

- In an **undated spring** sighting, Thorne Barnes saw Bigfoot at a church camp on the Wind River.
- **April 13**: A driver and his passenger glimpsed a ten-foot, green-eyed creature with "no neck" on the Yakima Indian Reservation.
- **May 11**: A beast lumbered past Sunrise Elementary School in Puyallup.
- In **August**, another Puyallup encounter occurred at the site of the present-day Crystal Ridge housing development.
- Orval Zcholmer's undated report described a black biped seen near Ape Canyon.[59]

1984

- In an **undated February** report, soldier "Ben" and four fellow Army Rangers met an eight-foot howling biped at Fort Lewis.
- **Februaray 15**: A Sasquatch frightened an elderly couple on Cloquallum Road in Shelton.
- In **May**, a six-foot creature allegedly ogled a fisherman at Pattison Lake.
- **July 8**: Teenage hunter "David B." saw Bigfoot on Kelly Hill (Stevens County).
- **July 18**: Teachers and students on a field trip from summer school met "a black hairy bipedal creature" at Clallam Bay.
- **Undated July** reports found a Sasquatch stepping over a highway guard rail near Longview and prowling on Aberdeen's B Street.
- **August** brought sightings from Fairchild Air Force Base and from the outskirts of Wilkeson.
- **Late Summer**: Randy Trusty saw an "angry" biped with a "furled brow" on State Road 4 west of Longview.
- **October 20**: A hiker glimpsed a Sasquatch "mother and child" outside Shuksan.
- **Late October**: Hunters logged another sighting near Cumberland.
- **Late Autumn**: Witness "C. H." reported "a brachiating ape" on the Kalama River.
- In **December**, there was another shaggy window-peeper report in Shelton.[60]

1985

- In **June**, Fred Bradshaw reported seeing a ten-foot Sasquatch "swaying" beside the North River. Stepsister Carol Howell described the beast as "big...awesome...exciting."
- In **August**, Fred and Carol logged a second sighting from the same vicinity, describing an eight-foot creature, and Bradshaw allegedly dodged stones hurled by another ten-footer before the month ended, pausing long enough to measure its eighteen-inch tracks.

- **Late Summer**: A Boy Scout camped near Spokane saw a "large brown animal on two legs," but could not remember the date; Battle Ground resident "Darlene C." blamed Bigfoot for killing a deer and spooking her neighbor's horses; and "Paul" and two friends claimed that a monster with "a horrid smell like rotten meat or really bad BO" chased them near Wilkeson.[61]

1986

- **July**: Two hikers saw "something tall and heavily built" on the Yakima River.
- **Christmas Day**: A teenage resident of Kent spied a Sasquatch prowling around a relative's home.[62]

1987

- In **March**, a creature "like an ape, but also sloth-like" frightened two girls in Monroe on the 12th while a nine-foot albino biped with "angel hair" surfaced near Twisp later the same month.
- **July 5**: A ten-foot creature crossed State Route 706 near Ashford.
- **Autumn**: Dale Stenson and friends saw a nine-foot beast on Clallam County's Burnt Mountain while Barb Gardiner and friend "Gertrude" nearly struck "a huge ape" with their car at Snoqualmie Pass.[63]

1988

- In **April**, soldiers camped on the Nisqually River saw and smelled an eight-foot biped "with a slight hunch in its back."
- **Late Spring**: Kris Huckins saw a white Sasquatch near Longview while two hikers met a beast with "a huge upper body" outside Bangor.
- **July** brought sightings of a "tall tan dirty looking animal" from Crow Canyon on the 10th, and of "a hairy man-like creature" near Machias.
- **Late Summer**: A limping, blue-eyed albino Sasquatch appeared near Aberdeen while a biped with a "nasty stink" explored Camp Bonneville Military Reservation.
- **October 5**: Paul Freeman and son Duane photographed Bigfoot at Mill Creek Watershed.
- **November** brought another sighting from Fred Bradshaw, of a six-foot creature seen near Satsop.
- **Undated** reports include witness "Sally's" sighting of a "well built" creature that "stunk like rotting meat" from one hundred feet away on Wind River; "Jeff H.'s" encounter with a seven-foot monster outside Battle Ground; and a hiker's report of a "large white haired creature" watching wild horses outside Silver Lake.[64]

1989

- In **June and July**, members of the Goldammer family claimed "several" sightings at their Yacolt home, providing sparse details of two.
- In **August**, a traveler from Texas saw two creatures with glowing yellow eyes near Squaw Peak.
- In **September**, Jerrard Warner met a nine-foot biped at Status Pass.
- **October 30**: Lance Axtell and friend "Richard" saw a smoky-gray eight-footer at Stossel Creek.

- **Late Autumn**: At Ostrander, an unnamed child allegedly played with "little hairy monsters" while his parents watched, amused, and elk hunters fled from a ten-foot monster on Mount Rainier, somehow forgetting the date.[65]

Other '80s Cases

- Leonardo Thomas reported a female Sasquatch smiling at motorists outside Goldendale in "August 1981-83."
- Anonymous sighting of a "large figure" was seen near Battle Ground on January 15, "1983 or '84."
- A hunter reported an eight and a half-foot creature squatting on a road near Palmer in "October 1984-85."
- "Craig B." encountered a herd of twenty bipeds near Prindle sometime in 1988 or 1989.
- A Sasquatch rocked a canoe occupied by "two little Indian boys" on the Columbia River during the "late 1980s."[66]

The 1990s

Alleged Bigfoot encounters nearly doubled, with 298 reports that include 149 eyewitness sightings, sixty-eight track discoveries, and eighty-one cases citing speculative evidence.

1990

- In **February**, a hunter claimed that Bigfoot shadowed him and a friend near Fall City.
- In **May**, members of an Army airborne unit met the "Cat Lake Monster" at Fort Lewis and a girl saw a Sasquatch cross Trout Lake Creek Road, near White Salmon.
- **June 18**: The season's last sighting was of a "huge, upright animal" on Cyclone Creek.
- In **August**, witness "Doug" saw Bigfoot outside Trout Lake.
- **December 3**: A trucker filed the year's last dated report from North Bend.
- **Undated** reports include Dar Addington's sighting from the Mill Creek Watershed; Victor Bastulli's claim that he was stoned by a "gorilla-looking man" at Bonney Lake; "Connie's" encounter with a seven-foot prowler near La Center; and a report from four brothers who met a "big haired ape-like man creature" somewhere "in the mountains."[67]

1991

- In **April**, two hunters observed a seven-foot creature on Silver Creek near Lyle.
- In **May**, motorist "Brad" swerved to miss a five-foot "mugwump" outside Ione.
- **June 8**: Darin Richardson met an eight-foot beast with an "indescribable" odor near Mineral Lake while a fisherman glimpsed a seven-foot Sasquatch near Hood Canal Bridge and measured its sixteen-inch tracks later the same month.
- In **July**, Jim Avila and another climber "felt intelligence" from the biped they saw on Mount Adams.

- **Undated** reports for the year include a highway sighting near Randle and an unsubstantiated claim that Forest Service employees found a dead Sasquatch at Blewett Pass.[68]

1992

- In **March**, a child saw "something covered with hair" near Seattle.
- In **April**, two horsemen logged a report from Green River Gorge.
- Paul Freeman claimed two more sightings "in the Blue Mountains of Washington State" on **April 20** at an undisclosed location and **August 20** at Deduct Springs (actually located in Oregon), but his blurry camcorder tapes remain questionable.
- **May 26**: Residents of Carson claimed that Bigfoot ate their geese while Greg Hassler logged a nonviolent spring sighting from one of Skamania County's two Bear Lakes.
- In **August**, a Sasquatch approached two teens at Lake Cushman.
- In **October**, a Sasquatch surfaced twice: first frightening sisters Carrie and Loren Kelley near North Bonneville and then helping Phil Vauer butcher a bear he shot in North Cascades National Park. (Ray Crowe labels that report a hoax, though Vauer swore he was serious.)
- In an **undated** autumn sighting, Garett Suppah reported a tribe of six bipeds from Rattlesnake Creek.
- **December 26**: A motorist saw Bigfoot leap across a logging road near Naselle while several hunters filed an undated report after watching a Sasquatch through binoculars on the Humptulips River.[69]

1993

- In **February**, young brothers saw "what seemed to be like a gorilla" in Amboy.
- In **April**, Kalvin Dahl met Sasquatch while hunting bear near Centralia.
- **May 8**: Five hikers saw a six-foot-tall biped in the Indian Heaven Wilderness.
- In two **undated** spring sightings, poachers allegedly shot Bigfoot on Clark County's Larch Mountain and then lost it despite a clear blood trail, and a Clallam River fisherman saw a gray, bearded creature.
- In **July**, a "strangely colored" beast frightened a youth on the lower Columbia River.
- **July 23**: A Forest Service firefighter saw Bigfoot while battling a blaze near Skykomish.
- In **August**, Matthew Helberg and three friends reported a nine-footer outside Toutle.[70]
- **September 10**: Sightseers glimpsed a Sasquatch near Packwood.
- **October 15**: A homeless drifter saw an "absolutely huge" beast north of Shelton. Later that month, soldiers training at Fort Lewis met a seven- and a half-foot trespasser while another beast frightened drivers near Carson.
- **Mid-November**: Kalvin Dahl logged his second sighting from Bunker Creek.
- **Undated** reports include a sighting of a "giant man" near Prindle, a teenager's report from the Wind River, and a supposed photo of Bigfoot from Scotty Creek, dismissed by Forest Service analysts as a deer.[70]

1994

Springtime Reports

- **Second week of March**: two nocturnal fishermen caught Bigfoot wading in North River.
- In **April**, "John" and his son saw "something" devouring an animal's carcass at Gold Bar.

- **May 30**: Hikers met a "big, dark, square creature" near Skamania County's Swift Creek.
- **Undated**: "Andrew P." reported two hairy creatures wrestling near Wynoochee Lake and Dale Stenson met an eleven-foot beast acting "very aloof" at Ozette Lake.[71]

Summertime Reports

- In **June**, a Sasquatch startled a female motorist on Highway 14, west of Skamania.
- On **Independence Day**, witness "Trish" saw an eight-foot specimen walking beside the North River.
- **Late July**: Two youths saw a "strange colored" Sasquatch duck into a cave on the lower Columbia River.
- In **August**, separate berry-picking parties glimpsed two six-foot creatures together at Elephant Rock, near Quinault Lake, and met a lone "furry man" at North Bend.
- An **undated** sighting found a dirty-white beast prowling apple orchards outside Mineral.[72]

Autumn's Reports

- **September**: Jim Fielder saw a six-foot "reddish-brown bear-human like animal" in Mount Rainier National Park on the 24th, a couple driving through Trapper Creek Wilderness met a similar looking creature on the 26th, while undated reports describe a "massive" black beast near Cougar and a hairy biped watched by fishing guides at King County's Rattlesnake Lake.
- **October**: "Anna" sighted a six and a half-foot albino Sasquatch from Carson.
- **November 5**: Rip Lyttle saw a biped with a "long skinny body" and smelled its "urine odor" outside Prindle.
- **Undated** reports include a hunter's sighting at Forlorn Lakes, Bigfoot's encounter with Terry Reams near Lexington, and a "huge hairy thing" traipsing around Verlot.[73]

1995

Winter-Spring Sightings

- **January 15**: A teacher saw Bigfoot cross State Highway 105 near Aberdeen.
- **March 19**: A deputy sheriff watched two bipedal creatures cross farmland at Onalaska.
- **April 17**: A motorist met a Sasquatch outside Monroe.
- **May 26**: Five campers near Twentyeight Mile Creek saw a black beast "like the one in the movie taken in California, but not as filled out."
- **June 10**: Witness "A. Leverett" and a friend glimpsed Bigfoot briefly at Corral Pass.[74]

Summertime Sightings

- In **July**, "Shannon B." sighted a "fast upright animal" near Elma.
- **July 11**: A forest ranger photographed Bigfoot — or, critics say, a scale model — near Mount Rainier.
- **July 12**: Two brown seven-footers passed by Tahola, dodging gunshots from a frightened witness.
- **July 22**: John Gerhardt met a Sasquatch while panning for gold at Pinto Creek.
- **August 5**: Paul Freeman, Bill Laughery, and Wes Summerlin saw "a standing figure" at Biscuit Ridge while examining older footprints.[75]

Autumn Sightings

- **November 5**: Rip Lyttle followed rapping sounds near Prindle and saw a biped moving through the woods.

- **December 3**: A Sasquatch allegedly chased two witnesses at Elephant Butte.

- **Undated**: A Suquamish tribal forestry officer David Mills reported a sighting somewhere in the Olympic Mountains; a claim that Bigfoot killed a goat near Hamilton Creek; an anonymous hunter claimed he trapped a Sasquatch in a pit near Lava Butte; another sighting at Prindle; and vague "multiple daylight sightings in Suquamish."[76]

1996

Winter-Spring Sightings

- **February 8**: Three youths saw an eight-foot, green-eyed biped roaming around Hazel Dell.

- **March 16**: Kurt Armbruster saw a nine-foot creature with "a very long penis and testicles, like a small horse," using a stick to excavate snowbanks on Vulcan Mountain.

- **April 4**: Witness "Mary" met a Sasquatch near Naselle.

- **May 15**: Jim Steal crashed his motorcycle when a seven-footer startled him near Elma.

- **May 23**: A fisherman glimpsed a "fur covered, bipedal, short headed, ape faced" beast at Chopaka Lake.

- **May 26**: Owen Pate logged a sighting from the same lake.[77]

Summertime Sightings

- **Late June**: Two boys watched Bigfoot wading in a pond at Morton's Gus Backstrom City Park.

- **August**: Kelly Blomberg saw a "dark thing" north of Aberdeen, Laurie Duyck saw "a large figure" beside the Naches River, and skydiver "T. S." glimpsed a hairy creature from an airplane passing over Kapowsin.

- **September**: Ruth Steele reported seeing a seven-foot "humanoid" covered in "gray, white, and sometimes black fur" near Dryad; Mark Windus claimed Bigfoot answered his "rabbit call" in Rose Valley; and an unnamed couple reported watching four creatures — "two big and two smaller ones" — through binoculars at Mill Creek Watershed.[78]

Autumn Sightings

- **November**: Ruth Steele, accompanied by her daughter, claimed a second Sasquatch sighting outside Doty. "I. H." and his son saw a "large, upright animal" while hunting along the North River.

- **Undated**: A man seeking mushrooms met Bigfoot near the Satsop River, "Diane Y." sighted a "dark upright man-like figure" at McKenna, and a motorist met a Sasquatch outside of Oakville.[79]

1997

Summer-Fall Sightings

- An **undated** mid-year report has Paula Drake sighting a white biped crossing Highway 101 near Moclips.

- **July 19**: A hiker reported a Sasquatch lurking at Green Mountain Lookout.

- **July 25**: A forestry worker saw Bigfoot on Indian land, south of Kingston while summer's last report described a prospector's meeting with a "tall hominid male" at Ingalls Creek.

- **October 10**: Hoaxer Ray Wallace filed a report from witness "Buss" of an eight-foot creature "speaking" and hauling salmon from the Green River near Mount St. Helens.

- **October 11**: Anna Wood reported a Sasquatch sitting on a driftwood log and admiring the sea near Kalaloch.

- **Mid-October**: In an undated sighting, a hunter saw Bigfoot "strolling along" East Humptulips Road.

- **October 25**: Two other sportsmen claimed a sighting from the nonexistent "American River National Forest."[80]

End-of-Year Sightings

- In **November**, two hunters saw "something" near Cougar, reporting that it made "voice noises like talking."

- **Late Autumn**: Two more anonymous sportsmen's reports describe "a big gorilla" near Dixie and a Sasquatch that stole a bear hunter's kill somewhere in the Blue Mountains.

- In **December**, Darin Richardson complained of a "tan creature" rocking his motor home outside Fort Canby.

- **Undated** reports include Scott McDonald's vague claim of a sighting in the Olympic Mountains, "Sherri K.'s" encounter with a six-foot biped at Lemei Rock, and a logger's meeting with a "golden colored" beast near Goldendale.[81]

1998

Winter-Summer Sightings

- In **January**, two "trailer people" saw a white Sasquatch on Highway 101 above Moclips.

- In **April**, Matt West met a tan biped near Arctic Lookout.

- **June 1**: Mark Windus logged his second Rose Valley sighting.

- **July** brought Bryce Patnode's sighting from Wynoochee Lake and another of a black quadruped with "a human face but dog like teeth," seen at some undisclosed location.

- **August 5**: Brent Flye and friend "Mike" saw a seven and a half-foot Sasquatch on the Lewis River Trail while later that month, equestrienne "J. P." glimpsed "a large man-like figure" at Sultan Basin.[82]

Fall Sightings

- **September**: Rod and Georgi Cusik logged a Bigfoot sighting from Curly Creek on the 15th while an undated report, by ten-year-old "Brenden," placed a Sasquatch near Orting.

- **October 1**: A seven-foot beast shadowed fishermen at Willapa Bay.

- **October 12**: A couple saw Bigfoot in the Snoqualmie National Forest.

- **October 27**: A sighting from northern Seattle was reported while, in an undated report, Dale and Terry Stenson saw a screaming eight-footer on the Johns River.

- **November** brought yet another soldier's sighting from Fort Lewis.

- In **December**, Bigfoot frightened campers on Mount Rainier.[83]

1999

Winter Sightings

- **February 3**: "D. Adams" described a bipedal beast that left fifteen-inch tracks near the Wynoochee River.

- **March 15-18**: Jinks Bogar claimed four separate sightings along the Satsop River over a four-day period.

- **March 16**: "H. Rodregies" (or "Rodguis") allegedly saw a nine-foot creature kill a black bear on Jefferson County's Clearwater River.

- **March 19**: The BFRO reports another sighting in the same vicinity by an unnamed "Mexican brush picker."[84]

Spring-Summer Sightings

- **April** produced another sighting from Highway 101, this time near Forks.

- **May 20**: "Dan C." saw a nine-foot creature outside Hoquiam and measured its eighteen-inch tracks.

- In **June**, telephone lineman Michael Ford glimpsed Bigfoot between Carnation and Fall City.

- **July 16**: "Leonard S." saw "a large shadow" near Ione and then found humanoid footprints ranging from nine to seventeen inches long.

- **August 16**: A seven-foot "brown furry flash" frightened four Lake Cushman campers.[85]

Fall Sightings

- **Late September**: loggers saw another Sasquatch outside Goldendale.

- **October 9**: A hunter reported a sighting in the same vicinity of Glendale.

- **October**: On the 20th, near Randle, Bigfoot hunters led by "K. Y." claimed that an adult biped "lured us away from its young" (which were not seen). Three men "mudding" in an off-road vehicle near Onalaska met a large black creature in an undated report.

- Michael Hazenberg's **undated** report from Republic claimed a brief sighting and alleged that a Sasquatch stole part of a freshly-killed deer, leaving a six-point antler "in trade."[86]

Other '90s Sightings

- Sometime in 1990-91, "Warren" relayed a second-hand sighting by his daughter's boyfriend near Beacon Rock.

- Unnamed campers on Skamania County's Strawberry Mountain claimed that a "large hominid" disrupted their outing.

- Meanwhile, outside Elbe, on a January morning in the "early nineties," two "very believable" witnesses claimed they lobbed stones at Bigfoot and then watched it retreat through the woods.[87]

New Millennium Monsters

As this book went to press, the twenty-first century had produced 341 alleged Bigfoot encounters in Washington State, including 134 eyewitness sightings, fifty-five reports of footprints, and 152 cases presenting other evidence.

Some witnesses describe Sasquatch stepping over fences. *Courtesy of William Rebsamen.*

2000

Winter-Spring Sightings

- **January 24, 25, or 27** (reports differ): An anonymous report was received of a Sasquatch peering through the windows of a cabin near Starbuck.

- In **March**, a father and son met a "huge" biped with a "really low" fore-head outside Seattle.

- **April 15**: Three Morton residents saw Bigfoot step over a fence.

- Other **April** reports describe a Sasquatch washing a wound at a creek outside Everett, while something "tall, black, and running on two legs" appeared near Evans Creek. Unfortunately, Washington has three such creeks, and the SIS failed to specify a county.[88]

Late Spring-Summer Sightings

- **May 18**: Two sightings were reported, at Grants Pass and near Beacon Rock State Park.

- **June 1**: Forester David Mills met a Sasquatch on a tree plantation outside Indianola.

- **June 3**: There was a second sighting in the same vicinity while a motorist saw Bigfoot near Orting two days later.

- **June 29**: A forestry manager for the Suquamish tribe reported a biped prowling the Hoh Indian Reservation.

- An **undated** June report describes an eight and a half-foot "cave man" roaming near Elbe. The anonymous witness claims that he recovered hair samples, analyzed by Dr. Grover Krantz, who "confirmed it was gigantipithicus [sic]" — an obvious impossibility, since the prehistoric ape Gigantopithecus is known only from fossilized teeth and jaw fragments.[89]

Late Summer-Fall Sightings

- **July 24**: A motorist reported an eight-foot creature crossing a road near Tacoma.

- In **August**, three witnesses saw a "freaking huge" biped at Rattlesnake Lake.

- **September's** reports included sightings of seven-foot creatures at Skamania County's Jim Creek, and on the outskirts of Kingston.

- **September 22**: Members of a BFRO expedition made a plaster cast of a large impression found in soil at Skookum Meadow, describing it as the imprint of a reclining Sasquatch. (Critics claim it is the outline of an elk; the debate continues.)
- **September 25**: Chris Wright saw Bigfoot circling his home near Iron Mountain.[90]

End-of-Year Sightings

- **October 7**: "G. H." saw a "tall, hairy animal" cross the Orting-Kapowsin Highway near Graham.
- **October 8**: Fisherman "Mike H." and a friend saw Bigfoot near Easton.
- **October 11**: Dual sightings came from Morton, where multiple witnesses saw "a gorilla" on Highway 508, and Obstruction Peak in Clallam County, where a French hiker watched two hairy bipeds through binoculars.
- **October 20**: Fred Bradshaw and two friends glimpsed a Sasquatch near Newskah Creek and measured its seventeen-inch tracks.
- An **undated** sighting was reported by "Craig and friend" from Mount St. Helens.[91]

2001

Winter-Spring Sightings

- **March 10**: A camper saw two pointy-headed creatures prowling the woods outside Carbonado.
- **March 11**: A girl saw Bigfoot walking along Blacksnake Ridge.
- **March 24**: A white biped "played peek-a-boo" with Fred Bradshaw and Rick Long near Roy, leaving seventeen-inch tracks.
- **April 25**: "Diane Y." of McKenna logged her second sighting.
- **May 1**: Bicyclists faced a "black hairy creature" on the Carbon River, near Fairfax.
- **May 13**: "R. C." and his wife and son saw a Sasquatch cross Interstate 5, near Chehalis.
- In **June**, a Mason County resident glimpsed Bigfoot at some undisclosed location on the 3rd while a motorist claimed contact outside Glenwood (Yakima County) eight days later.[92]

Summer-Fall Sightings

- In **July**, a group of fishermen saw a Sasquatch wading in the Kalama River.
- **September 1**: Bigfoot frightened "Mr. G." and his family at Chinook Pass.
- **September 9**: "Joseph" and his wife watched "a tall, fast-moving animal" traverse a snowfield below Table Mountain in Whatcom County. Also in September, a hulking beast chased two teenage hunters through the woods near Quilcene.
- In **October**, Paul Freeman logged yet another sighting, with companions Bill Laughery and Wes Sumerlin, near Walla Walla; Brian Smith met a Sasquatch at Kooskooskie; and hikers saw another hairy biped on Blacksnake Ridge.
- **October 29**: Hunters saw a large, roaring beast near Yakima County's Rimrock Lake.
- **Undated** sightings came from Deckerville Swamp and two-time witness Scott McDonald, somewhere in the Olympic Mountains.[93]

2002

Spring Sightings

- In **April**, sightings were reported by two brothers camped near Walla Walla; campers at Pend Oreille County's Sullivan Lake; and Witness "Anthony" near Bellingham on the 28th.
- **May 9**: A hunter saw a "large black animal" walking along the Toutle River.
- **May 18**: motorists pursued a shaggy beast on Highway 504 near Mount St. Helens.
- Also in **May**, the SIS logged a sighting from "Port Colborne," but no such place exists in Washington — or anywhere in the United States. Another report is vaguely located in "eastern Washington," where unnamed campers saw two creatures walking together.[94]

Summertime Sightings

- In **June**, reports were made from a young couple in Bellingham and a Sappho resident who saw a "hairy, human-like creature" loitering near his home.
- **August 3-4**: Sightings were reported by fishermen at Lone Butte (Skamania County), kayakers on Pend Oreille County's Sullivan Lake, and tourists in North Cascade National Park.
- **Undated** August reports include a nine-foot creature seen near Marten Lake (misplaced in Okanogan County by the SIS) and a Sasquatch drinking from a stream near Cactus.[95]

Fall Sightings

- **September 5**: A "huge hairy giant tall man looking thing" frightened hunters near Seabeck.
- **September 14**: "R. G." and two other fishermen saw Bigfoot on the shore of Riffe Lake.
- **Undated** September sightings include Steve Peterson and his girlfriend seeing one biped and hearing another hooting near Mount St. Helens. A hunter met a seven-foot beast near Quilcene.
- **November 16**: "D. W." encountered a black biped while hunting outside Greenwater.
- In **December**, a Mukilteo resident spied Bigfoot as he drove through Pierce County while an undated sighting placed Sasquatch outside Camano, routing campers with its eerie cries.[96]

2003

Winter-Spring Sightings

- **February 8**: Four Thurston County youths saw "a large silhouette like human" pass their rural home.
- In **March**, a "very hairy" nine-foot creature visited Nespelem Elementary School.
- **April 24**: Motorist "K. P." saw a seven-foot biped cross Highway 4 on KM Mountain.
- **May 8**: Another driver suffered the same shock outside Port Townsend.
- **June 17**: Two hikers on the Quinault Rain Forest Nature Trail saw "something dark and large" moving through lake side reeds.
- **June 28**: Skamania County Sheriff logged a driver's Sasquatch sighting, while another motorist talked his way out of a speeding ticket in McCleary that same month by claiming Bigfoot had spooked him.[97]

Summertime Sightings

- In **July**, a "very large, hairy, upright 'thing'" was seen by three witnesses outside Van Zandt and "something large" ambling along the beach on Puget Island.

- **August 7**: The night watchman at a logging camp near Morton saw a creature eight or nine feet tall prowling the grounds.

- **August 15**: A six-foot biped approached a car parked near Moulton Falls.

- **September 3**: A weary driver parked somewhere in Snohomish County saw Bigfoot watching him from the treeline.

- **September 5**: A hunter met Bigfoot on a dirt road outside Naches.

- An **undated** summer sighting placed a nine-foot creature near Battle Ground.[98]

Autumn Sightings

- **October 12**: Two Tennessee tourists met Bigfoot while hiking in Mount Rainier National Park.

- **October 16**: A beast covered in "thick silver fur" disrupted a picnic at Sullivan Lake.

- **November 2**: An elk hunter had a sighting in Aberdeen.

- **November 4**: Another hunter claimed that Bigfoot stole part of his kill outside Dixie.

- **Undated** cases for 2003 include a sighting from Duvall and a second-hand report from Naselle.[99]

Bigfoot sightings persist in the twenty-first century. *Courtesy of William Rebsamen.*

2004

- **February 21**: Two sightings occurred this day, at a cabin north of Arlington and on Balch Road in Oakville.
- **June 15**: A bipedal "large animal" surfaced at Whatcom County's Baker Lake.
- **July 18**: A birdwatcher met a Sasquatch on Kettle Crest Trail, near Republic. Two weeks later, motorists logged a sighting near Lake Quinault Lodge.
- In **August**, another driver reported Bigfoot from Highway 2 near Leavenworth, strangely claiming the date as the 7th and 21st within a single brief report.
- **September 1**: There was another sighting from Highway 20 near Republic.
- **September 15**: Bigfoot was seen on U.S. 101 outside Humptulips.
- **October 16**: A hairy six-foot "living hunchback" startled drivers south of Forks.
- **November 28**: There was news of "a large dark object standing like a person" in Gifford Pinchot National Forest.
- **November 29**: Another driver glimpsed a Sasquatch at Eagle Cliffs.
- **December** produced a sighting from Klickitat County's Summit Creek, filed by an anonymous witness who claimed "seven or eight" encounters in the same vicinity.[100]

2005

- **February 4**: A hiker reported a sighting near Rockport.
- **June 17**: Bigfoot was seen visiting a home in Snoqualmie.
- **June 23**: Bigfoot also played Peeping Tom at Duvall.
- **June 25**: A Sasquatch spooked drivers near Port Angeles.
- **Late June**: An undated sighting placed a malodorous "very large human like creature" outside Sammamish.
- In **July**, a Sasquatch prowled around Cougar and woke drowsy campers at Pend Oreille County's Sullivan Lake.
- **August 21**: A hairy biped strolled the beach at Ocean Shores.
- **September 26**: A hulking intruder at Jarrel Cove, on Harstine Island, was reported.
- **November 15**: A driver saw Bigfoot near Poulsbo.
- **November 17**: A hiker filed a sighting from Silver Star Mountain.
- **Undated** reports came from Mossyrock and Camas (where a "family" of three creatures appeared).[101]

2006

- **January 19**: An Auburn resident saw Bigfoot passing his home with a "nonchalant stride."
- **June 28**: Two hunters near Omak glimpsed a "large and hairy" beast that "moved like a mother."
- In **July**, a hiker followed large footprints and overtook their maker outside Aberdeen.
- **October 26**: A Sasquatch frightened a motorist outside Deception Pass State Park.[102]

2007

- **February 8**: An unnamed witness claimed that Bigfoot touched him in a cave that "smelled distinctly of apes," location undisclosed.
- In **May**, a suspicious report was placed by the SIS near "Highway E" between the nonexistent towns of "Gaul" and "Harris."
- **July 28**: Skeet shooters logged a highway sighting between Ashford and Elbe.
- **August 18**: BFRO investigator Bart Cutino reported a personal encounter from Chinook Pass.
- **August 23**: A passenger aboard the cruise boat *Lady of the Lake* snapped photos of a supposed Sasquatch on Lake Chelan's shore.
- **October 6**: A ten-foot biped was sighted near Toppenish.
- **October 23**: A driver saw Bigfoot on Old Olympic Highway, outside Kamilche.
- **November 16**: A motorist took five blurry cell phone photos of a Sasquatch near Union.[103]

2008

- **April 5**: "D. I." and "E. P." described a biped crossing Highway 8 between Elma and McCleary.
- **April 12**: A young camper met Bigfoot near Naselle while another April sighting, from Odessa, depicts a "large shaggy form" crossing a roadway in four strides.
- **July 1**: A motorist saw a Sasquatch "running real fast" outside of Indianola.

- **July 14**: Another highway sighting occurred on North Shore Road outside Quinault.
- **August 27**: A mountain biker met an eight-foot creature at some undisclosed location northwest of Chelan.[104]

2009

- Sometime in **January**, the SIS logged a hunter's meeting with a "very large w[h]ite hairy creature," but withheld the location.
- **March 23**: Three campers saw a seven-foot yellow-eyed beast somewhere between Port Angeles and Sequim.
- **April 9**: A "hairy, black, and tall animal" allegedly chased an unnamed hiker, somewhere "100 miles from civilization" in King County.[105]

Odds and Ends

Our survey of Washington Bigfoot sightings includes thirty-nine reports lacking any reference to dates. Those with witnesses fully identified include (alphabetically):

- Damon Anderberg's glimpse of a "tall hominid male" on Ingalls Creek.
- Fred Bradshaw's report that a Sasquatch charged him along the North River.
- William Clark's complaint that a hairy biped rocked his car on the Colville Reservation.
- Alissa Donkel's meeting with a ten-foot specimen near Carson.
- Grace Gensman's report of Sasquatch drinking from a stream and biting cattle near Randle.
- Fisherman Jay Morgan's two sightings of a "saltwater Sasquatch" know as the "Sea Man" in offshore waters.
- Jim Packwood's observation of Bigfoot urinating on State Road 12, near Packwood.
- Datus Perry's assertion that a female creature wearing "a cape of deer skin" near Lava Butte seemed physically attracted to him.
- Jim and Pat Stepp's claim that a Sasquatch peered into their boat, near Yale.
- George Stoican's meeting with an eight-foot creature on a ferry dock at Sequim.[106]

Partial witness names are known for six more reports:

- "Mildred" saw five or six bipedal creatures gathered on a hillside near her home, at Moses Lake.
- Berry-picker "Tom A." saw two at Elephant Rock.
- "Greg" and a friend reported "a big hairy thing" trailing their car near Lake Dorothy.
- Hoaxer Ray Wallace delivered "Mr. Coleman's" report of two creatures holding hands and "crying" along the Lewis River.
- Members of the Hoyt family saw Bigfoot raid their porch freezer at Onalaska.
- "Jeff H." and two companions met a seven-footer on Mount St. Helens.[107]

These undated reports are relatively mundane:

- A young mother living somewhere in the south-central Cascades saw Bigfoot pass her home and measured its eighteen-inch tracks.
- A smelly Sasquatch peered at loggers outside White Swan.
- Highway sightings occurred at Mount Adams, Prospect, Raymond, and Yacolt.
- Witnesses ducked stones hurled by a Sasquatch at Collins Hot Springs and Swift Reservoir.
- In Kittitas County, vague sightings emerged from Milk Lake and Halfway Flat Campground.
- A hiker at untraceable "Black Pass" reported a beast making sounds "like a radio playing and an opera singer warming up," and then decided that "it could have been a bear."[108]

More unusual — some might say "incredible" — sightings include:

- An elderly man's report of Bigfoot "romping with a dog" on the beach at Oysterville.
- Another senior citizen's description of a Sasquatch clubbing salmon on the White River.
- A hairy biped's futile pursuit of a woman and her sons near Forks.
- Another beast that stoned and chased loggers near McKenna.
- A hunter's claim that a Sasquatch stole his kill near Bonneville.
- A report that Lewis County's sheriff fired on Bigfoot near Winlock (denied by the sheriff's office in October 2009).
- The story of a Powers family that sheltered a crippled Sasquatch; and the tale of a "Bigfoot family surrounding soldiers" on Mount Rainier.[109]

The most bizarre stories begin with Ray Wallace's claim that an unnamed hunter had shot a Bigfoot near Amboy, offering its corpse for sale with a $100,000 price tag, and two reports of hairy bipeds killed by cars came from Snoqulamie Pass and Yale (where a Forest Service helicopter carried the body away).[110] Without supporting evidence, none of those tales seem credible.

Chapter Eight

The Crypto Zoo

Even now, the Pacific Northwest's strange menagerie is not exhausted. Many unknown creatures still remain, fitting none of the broad categories already examined. Some are known today only from ancient folklore, while others have been sighted in the twenty-first century. Some strain credulity, while others may be scientifically explained.

Many muntjacs have both tusks and antlers. *Courtesy of the U.S. National Oceanic and Atmospheric Association.*

Monsters of Legend

Folklore provides us with glimpses of two cryptic beasts, lacking specific modern sightings. One, the Black Tamanous, was a man-eating monster or demon feared by various northwestern tribes, regrettably neglected when their "transformer" deity purged Earth of its evil predators. Some sources suggest that the Tamanous name was borrowed by members of a secret sect within the Kwakiutl tribe, whose members also practiced cannibalism.[1]

Our second legendary cryptid is an elk supposed to sport a set of large tusks in its upper jaw. Irish author Ronan Coghlan describes the elusive ungulate as "bigger and sturdier" than a common elk or wapiti (Cervus canadensis), but his alleged source is an Internet website devoted to study of unknown hominids in Great Britain, containing no reference to North American cryptids. Another website does refer in passing to the tusked elk, offering a rather simple explanation.[2]

Plainly stated, some deer do have tusks of a sort. Asia's water deer (Hydropotes inermis) — native to China and Korea, introduced to Britain and Europe in the nineteenth century — lacks antlers but has enlarged upper canine teeth. Another Asian breed, the muntjacs (genus Muntia-cus), have both tusks and small antlers. Naturally ranging from India and Sri Lanka through Indonesia, China, Taiwan and Japan, muntjacs have also been transplanted to England, where they now breed in the wild.[3]

Nor are elk themselves excluded from the list of deer with tusks. In fact, their "ivory" was commonly collected by Native American hunters and worn as decorative items, later prized by members of a fraternal lodge, the Benveolent & Protective Order of Elks. An article from *The New York Times*, published in June 1900, reported the sale of four hundred elk tusks in Spokane, Washington, for $1,000. Scarcity had inflated the price, with the article noting that an head dress decorated with eight hundred elk teeth sold for $80 in 1886, while a similar head dress bearing 280 tusks went for $200 in 1899.[4] It would be no great shock, therefore, if modern hunters claimed a tusked-elk sighting — and they might exaggerate that feature on "the one that got away."

Marsupial Madness

On December 24, 1900, *The Daily Review* of Roseburg, Oregon, published a startling cryptid report under the headline "A Kangaroo Man." It read:

> The Sixes mining district in Curry county has for the past thirty years gloried in the exclusive possession of a "kangaroo man." Recently while Wm. Page and Johnnie McCulloch, who are mining there, went out hunting McCulloch saw the strange animal-man come down to a stream to drink. In calling Page's attention to the strange being it became frightened, and with cat-like agility, which has always been a leading characteristic, with a few bounds was out of sight.

> The appearance of this animal is almost enough to terrorize the rugged mountain sides themselves. He is described as having the appearance of a man — a very good looking man — is nine feet in height with low forehead, hair hanging down near his eyes, and his body covered with a prolific growth of hair which nature has provided for his protection. Its hands reach almost to the ground and when its tracks were pursued its feet were found to be 18 inches in length with five well formed toes. Whether this is a devil, some strange animal or a wild man is what Messrs. Page and McCulloch would like to know, says the Myrtle Point Enterprise.[5]

Nothing stated in the article supports comparison of the tall, shaggy "man" with a kangaroo, and many researchers lump this report together with Oregon's sightings of Bigfoot, discussed in *Chapter Six*.

A possibly related case involves the sighting of a "giant rabbit" by three unnamed hunters in Klickitat County, Washington. Sadly, we have no date for the event beyond a reference to March, and credibility is not enhanced by reference to giant birds and "tiny horses."[6]

Little People

Most cultures have legends of diminutive races, variously known as brownies, elves, fairies, gnomes, leprechauns, pixies, wee folk, and by other names too numerous for listing here. Native tribes of the Pacific Northwest knew them as Atnan, Chiniath, Ninimbe, Squolk-ty-mish, Tsiak, and Ya-ai, describing humanoid figures ranging from several inches to three feet tall, commonly dressed in clothing and equipped with simple tools.[7] Those tales might be dismissed as superstitious fantasy, if "little people" did not keep appearing during modern times.

The first published reference to little people in the Pacific Northwest comes to us from members of the Lewis and Clark expedition, in 1804. William Clark himself introduced the subject, in a journal entry dated August 24. He wrote:

> In a northerly direction from the mouth of this creek, in an immense plain, a high hill is situated, and appears of a conic form, and by the different nations of Indians in this quarter, is supposed to be the residence of devils: that they are in human form with remarkable large heads, and about 18 inches high, that they are very watchful, and are armed with sharp arrows with which they can kill at a great distance. They are said to kill all persons who are so hardy as to attempt to approach the hill. They state that tradition informs them that many Indians have suffered by these little people, and, among others, three Maha men fell a sacrafice [sic] to their merciless fury not many years since. So much do the Maha, Sioux, Otos, and other neighboring nations, believe this fable, that no consideration is sufficient to induce them to approach the hill.[8]

Expedition members explored the hill, described by Clark in a journal entry of August 25.

> A cloudy morning. Captain Lewis and myself concluded to go and see the mound which was viewed with such terror by all the different nations in this

quarter. We selected Shields, J. Fields, W. Bratton, Sergeant Ordway, J. Colter, Carr, and Corporal Warfington and Frazer, also G. Drouilliard, and dropped down to the mouth of Whitestone River, where we left the pirogue with two men; and, at two hundred yards, we ascended a rising ground of about sixty feet. From the top of this high land, the country is level and open as far as can be seen, except some few rises at a great distance, and the mound which the Indians call "Mountain of little people, or spirits." This mound appears of a conic form, and is N. 20° W. from the mouth of the creek. We left the river at 8 o'clock. At four miles, we crossed the creek, twenty-three yards wide, in an extensive valley, and continued on two miles further....

This mound is situated on an elevated plain in a level and extensive prairie, bearing N. 20° W. from the mouth of Whitestone Creek nine miles. The base of the mound is a regular parallelogram, the long side of which is about three hundred yards in length, the shorter sixty or seventy yards. From the longer side of the base, it rises from the north and south, with a steep ascent to the height of sixty-five or seventy feet, leaving a level plain on the top twelve feet in width and ninety in length. The north and south parts of this mound are joined by two regular rises, each in oval forms of half its height, forming three regular rises from the plain. The ascent of each elevated part is as sudden as the principal mound at the narrower sides of its base.

The regular form of this hill would in some measure justify a belief that it owed its origin to the hand of man; but as the earth and loose pebbles and other substances of which it was composed bore an exact resemblance to the steep ground which borders on the creek, in its neighborhood, we concluded it was most probably the production of nature.

The only remarkable characteristic of this hill, admitting it to be a natural production, is that it is insulated or separated a considerable distance from any other, which is very unusual in the natural order or disposition of the hills....

One evidence which the Indians give for believing this place to be the residence of some unusual spirits is that they frequently discover a large assemblage of birds about this mound. This is, in my opinion, a sufficient proof to produce in the savage mind a confident belief of all the properties which they ascribe to it.[9]

Expedition member John Ordway, who participated in the search for tiny "devils," noted that his group "found none of the little people there but we Saw Several holes in the ground."[10]

Our first twentieth century witness is Ellen Jonerson of Canby, Oregon. One day in April 1950, while tending her lawn, she saw a tiny man on her next-door neighbor's property. He was eight or nine inches tall and walked with a waddling gait, passing underneath a 1937 Dodge sedan without stooping, then vanished into tall grass nearby. Jonerson said the man had dark skin, as if deeply tanned, with hair the same color. He wore a skullcap, a plaid shirt, and pants described in various accounts as resembling coveralls or "rompers." Jonerson experienced no sense of fear, assuming that the little passer-by had business elseswhere and meant her no harm.[11]

Two years later, in September 1952, another sighting occurred at Central Point, Oregon, 195 miles south of Canby. Motorist L. L. Zamrzla was turning from Old Stage Road onto Scenic Avenue, accompanied by his wife and their twelve-year-old daughter, when his headlights framed "three white, odd shaped forms" crossing the road. Zamrzla estimated their height between three and four feet, noting that they seemed to glide across the pavement. Later, he compared them to the "shmoos" drawn by cartoonist Al Capp in his syndicated Li'l Abner comic strip. Zamrzla saw no limbs or facial features, but reported that the figures' heads and necks were "about half the length of the body itself."[12]

At 7 a.m. on August 13, 1965, a man named Ryerson delivered his two teenage daughters to a beanfield outside Renton, Washington, where they were scheduled to work for the day. As the girls — Ellen and Laura — approached the field, they were accosted by two strange figures. The first was a "little, gray wrinkled elf-like being" or "gnome," dressed in a gray shirt and pants, wearing a "funny little hat." It danced and cackled in front of a larger gray-faced companion, some five feet tall, whose skull featured a pulsating "bulbous extension with veins showing through it" in back. The taller figure watched the girls with bulging eyes like a frog's, whistling through a small pipe held in its mouth. Its one-piece outfit was purple and shiny, like satin, with deep pockets hiding its hands. As the Ryerson sisters turned to flee, both figures vanished without a trace.[13]

Three decades passed before the next reported sighting, near Bend, Oregon, in August 1999. The witness was a child, playing beside a woodland creek when he observed two dark-skinned "people" watching him. They stood no more than eighteen inches tall, and both wore garments fashioned from some kind of animal skin. After watching the boy for ten to fifteen seconds, the entities retreated and vanished among the trees. The boy fetched his parents, who reportedly found tiny footprints but did not pursue their trail.[14]

Our most recent "little people" sighting is sadly lacking in details. Six teenagers allegedly were riding all-terrain vehicles somewhere in Washington, specific date unknown, when one of their four-wheelers bogged down in mud. While they were trying to free it, "an elf like person" emerged from the woods to watch them. The figure wore a peaked hat above pointed ears, and was armed with a bow and arrow. No other information on the sighting was available at press time for this book.[15]

A Jumbo Shrimp

In 1990 the editors of Strange Magazine found a peculiar message on their telephone answering machine. The caller, one Virginia Staples, introduced herself as a former resident of Bremerton, Washington, then sobbed her way through an account of a strange event dating back to 1948. As she described it, the laundry room of her apartment house was located in the building's "gigantically huge basement," where "huge holes" yawned in the walls. The building's manager spread rumors that "there was a passage to the water" from the basement, presumably referring to nearby Puget Sound.[16]

On the day in question, Staples had finished her wash and was hanging her clothes up to dry, when she experienced "a creepy feeling" of being observed. Turning toward the basement's rear wall, she saw a nightmarish creature watching her from one of the wall's gaping holes. It was equal in height to her own five feet, and "had a bright orange colored body and little spidery thin legs and antennae on its head that kept moving back and in and out." When the monster moved in her direction, Staples bolted back to her apartment, packed her things, and left immediately for a relative's home in Seattle. Later, visiting a local aquarium, she saw shrimp that resembled the creature exactly, except for its size. By the time she got up nerve enough to revisit Bremerton, in the late 1980s, the apartment building had been razed to accommodate the expanded Puget Sound Navy Yard. Staples ended her call on a plaintive note: "Nobody would really believe this, but as God is my witness it really happened."[17]

Giants Among Us

Four years after the giant shrimp's visit to Bremerton, in October 1952, a humanoid giant appeared in northwestern Oregon. Witness Opal Church was driving with her nephew, somewhere between Corvallis and Salem, when she passed a startling figure on the roadside. The heavyset figure appeared to be male, with a pallid face and round eyes three inches in diameter, with reticulations "resembling the filaments in old electric light bulbs." His garb was equally unusual, topped by "headgear similar to an Arab's," with an off-white uniform resembling "fluorescent heavy satin, or perhaps fine metallic mesh." The outfit included gloves and boots of the same material, and a ribbed belt. The figure walked swiftly, but with "fluid movements."[18]

After passing the strange pedestrian at a distance of some fifteen feet, Church made a hasty U-turn to afford herself another look. Strangely, although the countryside was clear and flat, the giant had vanished.[19]

Another king-sized encounter occurred in March 1976, as members of an unnamed family were returning from some outing, to their farm outside Yakima, Washington. Crossing the Toppenish-Zillah Bridge, they were surprised to see several very tall men chasing cattle along the highway. The figures all had long hair framing extremely pale faces, and stood at least seven feet tall. All wore "black outfits with white trapezoid emblems on the chest area," otherwise undescribed. The gaping witnesses passed by and never saw the strange giants again, but UFO researcher Albert Rosales asserts that "similar beings" were seen in the same vicinity, three months earlier.[20]

Home Invaders

Strange beings are not always glimpsed in passing, during chance encounters. Sometimes they call on witnesses at home. Our first case, from spring 1967, involves a witness sleeping at his parents' home in Pullman, Washington, suddenly roused from sleep by some unknown stimulus to find himself in a strange circular room with a red velvet floor. Nearby, an entity resembling "a fetus" sat watching him from a chair. The unnamed witness recalled nothing more, and it is easy to dismiss his experience as a nightmare, but he is not alone.[21]

Days later, in Des Moines, Washington, a seven-year-old witness woke in the middle of the night to find a naked child-sized figure smiling at his bedside. The intruder had sharp teeth and "burnt like cracked skin" with visible open sores. Despite the thing's disturbing appearance, the child soon went back to sleep, perhaps suggesting another nightmare.[22]

Our next recipient of an unwelcome wake-up call was an adult female resident of Yelm, Washington. One night during October 1989, the unnamed woman woke to find a tall, thin figure with "a bulb-shaped head" leaning over her bed. The stranger pressed a "silver pencil-shaped object" against her arthritic shoulder, producing "a floating sensation" followed by unconsciousness. When the women woke the next morning, her shoulder was seemingly healed.[23]

At 9 a.m., August 13, 1992, an unnamed resident of Salem, Oregon, was eating breakfast at the dining table in her home, when she glimpsed "something" outside the window set into her kitchen door. Before she could investigate, a "short hairless greenish-gray figure" entered the kitchen without invitation, moving to stand beside a pantry cabinet. The intruder had "an elongated head and what appeared to be large 'eyelids' drawn over the eyes." It vanished suddenly, after the witness "attempted to communicate telepathically."[24]

Despite her shock — and the peculiar lack of reaction displayed by her dog, which was lying nearby — the woman searched her home for lingering intruders and found none. Twenty minutes later, as she sat down to the remnants of her meal, a "greenish three-fingered hand" reached out from behind her, lightly touching her wrist and imparting the painful sensation of an electric shock. The prowler then vanished once more, leaving only a circular burn on the woman's wrist, which appeared two days later. UFO researcher Albert Rosales considers the incident an extraterrestrial encounter, although no unidentified flying objects were seen.[25]

Three years later, shortly before noon on November 8, 1995, a male resident of Manson, Washington, was startled by the appearance of two humanoid figures in his apartment. Both wore "scuba type suits" and "wrap around glasses." One aimed an unknown "flashing object" at the witness, with no apparent effect, then both turned and walked through a wall, disappearing from sight.[26]

Late in the evening of February 27, 1996, a Seattle resident reported "a very short dwarf-like creature" in her bedroom, disappearing after several seconds. Albert Rosales reports that the unnamed witness was "involved in other encounters," but offers no details.[27]

At 2 a.m., September 6, 1998, a resident of Bothell, Washington, woke to find his bedroom bathed in white light surrounding two curious figures. The taller of the pair was roughly three feet six inches tall, and both had "large dark round eyes" in faces marred by "rough scaly skin." The man screamed and flailed at the intruders with his only available weapon — a pillow — which woke his wife. As she sat up in bed, the dwarf figures "stepped back and vanished."[28]

Around 9:30 p.m. on April 4, 1999, an unidentified resident of Bainbridge Island, Washington, woke to find three figures standing in his bedroom, speaking among themselves in muffled tones. He "felt they were men," but was not sure. Paralyzed with fright, the man could not defend himself as one of the home invaders touched his throat, producing an odd tingling sensation in his torso. He was rescued when the bedside telephone rang, and his tormentors "apparently vanished." Albert Rosales writes that a subsequent medical examination diagnosed the witness with hyperthyroidism, but he offers no opinion on its link the reported incident.[29]

Five years passed before the next reported home-invasion incident, on February 16, 2004. Another unnamed witness woke from sleep at 3 a.m., roused by a sound at his window. Strangely unable to move, he struggled for breath and then lost consciousness as a "shadowy figure shaped somewhat like a human but all black like a shadow" loomed over his bed. He woke again at 5 o'clock with vague alleged memories of an IV needle piercing his arm and a voice saying "send him back."[30]

On the night of January 2, 2008, an unnamed married couple in Seattle, Washington, fell asleep while watching television in their living room. The husband woke at 2:41 a.m. on January 3, to "an odd buzzing noise and a strange light pattern on the ceiling" above him. Next came scuffling sounds from the nearby kitchen, but before he could rise to investigate, "three distinct figures with huge heads and small bodies 'glided' into the room." Tight-fitting coveralls revealed their slender, four-foot-tall forms, and they wore masks with holes revealing "huge black eyes." Despite the room's darkness, the man "could plainly see they were not human." Like other witnesses to similar events, the man was paralyzed and unable to speak. Despite various "mechanical sounds" and a noise suggesting that the intruders were "breathing through ventilators," the man's wife slept on while he rose a foot off the couch, "as if by magic." Silent prayers allegedly compelled the three creatures to flee, leaving the witness convinced that he was rescued by divine intervention.[31]

Three months later, on March 29, 2008, another home invader surfaced in Port Angeles, Washington. An unnamed female witness woke to chilling cold, sometime after midnight, and found her fiancé standing near their open bathroom door. As she asked what he was doing, the woman saw a long-haired figure of indeterminate sex standing between her fiancé and the doorway. When her fiancé turned on a lamp, the intruder was gone.[32]

Our last home invasion incident occurred late one night in the summer of 2008. The witnesses were staying with friends in Kennewick, Washington, with the woman sleeping in a guest room and her boyfriend on the living room sofa. The woman woke to find a tall, lean "alien" standing between the foot of her bed and the bedroom's open door. The figure was bald, with a head "too small and disproportionate to the body, "but its arms and legs seemed normal. Illuminated by a night light in the outer hallway, the stranger appeared to be "slightly floating." Despite her surprise, the woman rolled over and went back to sleep. The next morning, her boyfriend described a "weird dream" involving the same strange intruder.[33]

While Albert Rosales and other researchers treat such incidents as "close encounters" with extraterrestrial visitors, science offers a more prosaic explanation in the form of night terrors and sleep paralysis, recognized medical conditions advanced as explanations for many hauntings and alleged alien abductions.[34]

A Three-Legged Mystery

One afternoon in mid-October 1964, twelve-year-old Kathy Danzer took her dog for a walk along Skyline Road, north of Portland, Oregon. At the intersection of Cornelius Pass Road, she paused to examine a large tree felled by gale-force winds on Columbus Day. While thus engaged, she heard her dog begin to growl and turned in time to see a dark "thing" dart between two trees, some 150 feet distant. As she described the object three decades later, "The solid-black thing was rectangular, had three legs, and was huge and low-slung like a cow." She guessed that it was eight feet long and five feet tall, noting that none of its three legs appeared to move. Passing a tree, "it sort of disappeared, like there might have been a 'portal' or something, as it was obviously too large to hide behind the tree."[35]

Terrified, Danzer fled for home with her dog close behind. Thirty-two years later she reported the encounter to Ray Crowe, founder of the International Bigfoot Society, although the apparition she had seen bore no resemblance to Sasquatch. Crowe asked if the object "could be some sort of 'manned' craft," but Danzer — now Kathy Danzer-James — declined to speculate.[36]

Stumpy Dumpty

During August 1965 residents of Nisqually, Washington, reported multiple encounters with a creature unlike any known to science. Dates and details are sparse, the witnesses unnamed, but their descriptions were consistent. All referred to a seven-foot-tall humanoid figure with a bald "egg-shaped" head, pink glowing eyes, a small nose and ears, and a mouth without visible lips. Despite its height, the being's lower body was described as "stumpy." Several witnesses recalled a white jacket resembling a doctor's lab coat, from the sleeves of which protruded massive "ham-sized" hands. One teenaged witness allegedly shot the strange being with a .22-caliber rifle from twenty-five feet, knocking it down, before it sprang erect and fled. Perhaps discouraged by that rude reception, the prowler left Nisqually for parts unknown.[37]

Walking "Tree Stumps"

In 1966, sixteen-year-old Kathy Reeves lived with her parents on Pioneer Mountain, a 794-foot peak in Lincoln County, Oregon, located almost four miles from Toledo. Founded by former residents of Toledo, Ohio, in 1866, the town became Lincoln County's seat in 1905 and retained that designation until 1954, when the administrative center moved to Newport. Toledo's primary employer was a sawmill owned by the Pacific Spruce Corporation, which sparked racist violence by importing Japanese labor in the 1920s.[38]

That ugly episode was largely forgotten by April 1966, when Kathy Reeves and a friend saw an airborne dome-shaped object "as high as a room," glowing and expelling smoke from its underside. A few days later, Reeves was walking alone in a meadow near her home, when she saw three objects she described as little "tree stumps," displaying shades of blue, orange, yellow, white, and watermelon-pink. Stranger still, the so-called stumps were walking silently across the field, finally disappearing from sight.[39]

Kathy Reeves was not the only local witness to encounter the ambling "stumps." By mid-October, five other persons reported seeing the same entities at two different locations east of Toledo. Meanwhile, the Reeves household suffered an outbreak of apparent poltergeist activity, while a pair of elderly neighbors reported visits from "a group of cyclopean like beings." Finally, as autumn waned, the rash of eerie incidents subsided.[40]

The Beast of Bald Mountain

Bald Mountain is a 1,634-foot peak in the heart of the Cascade Range, located in Washington's Klickitat County. In early November 1974, an unknown "fiery object" fell to Earth some five miles from the mountain. Its identity and precise point of impact remain officially unknown, since the National Aeronautics and Space Administration allegedly conducted the only investigation and failed to announce its findings.[41]

Within a week of that incident, deer hunter Paul Smith was scanning the slopes of Bald Mountain with binoculars, in search of prey, when he beheld an unexpected creature. Author Carole Marsh writes that the beast "was horse-sized, covered with scales and standing on four rubbery legs with suckers like octopus tentacles. Its head was football shaped with an antenna sticking up and its body gave off a green, iridescent light." Although armed with a high-powered rifle, Smith retreated in fear, without firing a shot.[42]

Bald Mountain, scene of a unique creature sighting in 1974. *Courtesy of U.S. Dept. of Fish & Wildlife.*

Nor was that the last seen of the creature. Marsh reports that several anonymous witnesses subsequently glimpsed the beast "and thought it was some kind of neon sign until they came closer." No further details are provided for those sightings.[43]

Portland's "Mole Man"

Sometime in 1978, a pair of students at Oregon's Portland State College were strolling near campus at dusk, when they heard strange scrabbling noises from an old sewer or storm drain nearby. Pausing to investigate, they saw a creature which they described as a "mole man" emerge from the tunnel. According to the unnamed witnesses, it "was not hairy, had big eyes, fangs, a long snout, three claws for the feet, but these were circular, and appeared not to be worn out." Despite a shared sense that the creature "psychically knew them, and that it was conscious," the students pelted it with stones until it retreated and vanished in darkness. Presumably insulted by that brief encounter, the thing has not appeared to any other witnesses.[44]

Species Unknown

On the afternoon of December 1, 1979, an unidentified bow hunter was stalking deer on the outskirts of Saddle Mountain State Park, in Oregon's Clatsop County, when he had an unusual experience. Skulking through heavy timber, he suddenly saw three "black objects" standing in a patch of Oregon grape, some eighty yards distant. The witness described them as roughly five feet six inches tall, heavily built, and "just standing around." When he knocked on a tree stump, the figures "ran off." No further details were forthcoming, and this sighting may involve Bigfoot-type creatures, or something entirely different.[45]

El Chupacabra

The cryptid known as El Chupacabra ("the goat sucker," in Spanish) earned its name by draining blood from Puerto Rican livestock in the mid-1990s. Two decades earlier, in spring of 1975, another unidentified predator known as the "Moca Vampire" had staged a series of similar raids.[46] Today, Chupacabra attacks are reported worldwide, but few researchers have noted an Oregon incident that preceded coinage of the famous nickname by nearly two years.

It may (or may not) be significant that Oregon's first Chupacabra witness was Hispanic farmer Jesse Navarro, residing at Forest Grove. At 12:30 a.m. on November 13, 1993, Navarro was herding his goats and chickens into his barn, when he heard a "strange noise" in some nearby bushes. Going to investigate, Navarro found one of his goats lying dead, and glimpsed a "short hairy creature" fleeing into the adjacent forest. Subsequent examination revealed that the goat bore "strange puncture wounds and its internal organs [were] apparently sucked out."[47]

Forty months elapsed without another incident, when El Chupacabra returned with a vengeance in April 1997. At 11 p.m. on April 4, a farmer identified only as "John" went searching for two missing cows, three or four miles north of Vernonia, on the west side of the Northern Oregon Coast Range. He found one of the animals dead and mutilated, with its eyes removed and "fang marks" on its neck. The searchlights on

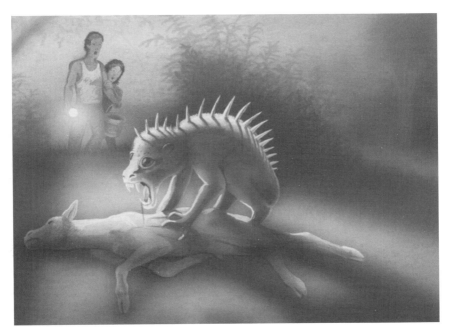

First reported from Puerto Rico, the Chupacabra has also been seen in Oregon. Courtesy of William Rebsamen.

John's pickup truck revealed a "gargoyle like green creature" standing twenty-five to thirty feet from the bovine carcass, hissing and glaring with "reptilian looking eyes" that reflected no light. The animal stood about four feet tall, and seemed to have a pair of wings folded on its back. Nonetheless, when it fled after ten to fifteen seconds the thing ran, instead of flying. Farmer John reported that the cow he found was drained of blood.[48]

On April 25, 1997, witnesses "John and Marcia" were driving north of Portland, Oregon, at the same intersection of Cornelius Pass and Skyline Roads where Kathy Danzer saw a three-legged rectangular thing flitting between trees in October 1964. A very different creature ran across the road in front of their car, described as three feet tall and green, with long spines sprouting from its back. The beast had "a triangle shaped head with multi-faceted eyes."[49]

Seven weeks later, Bigfoot researcher Nathan Peak visited April witness "John" at his farm near Vernonia, to obtain more details of his Chupacabra sighting. As luck would have it, John had lost another cow that day, and Peak joined him to search for it at 8 p.m. They found the cow unharmed, and also saw the "gargoyle" creature, described by Peak as four feet tall, weighing approximately ninety pounds, with wings five to six feet long. Peak called Ray Crowe with an excited report of the meeting, and while Crowe continued citing Peak as a source on his IBS website, he rated the incident's credibility at zero.[50] A final report from Peak, logged in early July 1997, described a Chupacabra sighting at Klamath Falls, Oregon. An unnamed farmer heard his cat shrieking and grabbed his .30-30 rifle, rushing from his house to find the cat under attack by a three-foot-tall creature with red glowing eyes. The Chupacabra was yellow, with a row of long spines down its back. The farmer fired one shot from a range of ten feet, whereupon the Chupacabra screamed and fled, leaving no trace of blood in the yard. Ray Crowe logged Peak's report, with another "zero" credibility rating.[51]

Whether the predator was hurt or merely frightened off, that shooting seemed to do the trick. No further sightings of the Chupacabra have been logged from Oregon since 1997.

From Thin Air

Peculiar entities sometimes appear as if by magic, prompting some authors to speculate on the existence of time warps, alternate realities, and "windows" or "wormholes" to other dimensions. One such case occurred in September 1969, when a witness identified only as "Susan" heard her dogs barking in the fenced yard of her Yakima, Washington home. Stepping outside, she saw a clean-cut boy of apparent Hispanic or Native American race, with dark skin and black hair, walking along the street. He wore a royal blue shirt and denim jeans, the very picture of normality. However, when he passed behind a tree and failed to reappear, Susan's dogs began to whine, as if in fear. She waited several moments, then crossed the street to seek the vanished boy, but found no trace of him.[52]

Researcher Albert Rosales logged another incident, from Portland, in June 1995. The muddled tale begins with "two main witnesses" — apparently a married couple — meeting "a peculiar stranger" at a party, then returning home without incident. The next morning, while their son was playing in the family's backyard, he saw "a tall, large man, with muscles in his face, wearing shiny black clothes" materialize in a next-door neighbor's yard, apparently out of thin air. The stranger approached a gate in an intervening fence, shook it several times, then glared at the boy for several moments before retreating. As the child watched, the man "once again disappeared in plain sight." Rosales treats both incidents as UFO-related, although no aircraft were seen in either case.[53]

At 11 a.m., May 18, 2005, an unnamed resident of Newberg, Oregon, was approaching his car in a public parking lot, when a "semi-short" figure "appeared out of nowhere," standing beside his vehicle. According to Albert Rosales, the witness "was not sure what color it was but it stood like a human, but with hook-like legs at the knees. The face looked like it had been severely burned." Mistaking the figure for a homeless person, the witness called out, "Hey, buddy, what are you doing down there by my car?" The figure then made "a kind of gurgling sound" and leaped over the car's hood, scratching its paint in the process. The frightened witness watched it disappear once more, then hurried home.[54]

Panic in Moonshine Park

Our next strange encounter comes from eighteen-acre Moonshine Park, located on the Upper Siletz River in Lincoln County, Oregon. The park features fishing and swimming holes, plus multiple camping sites with fireplaces and picnic tables.[55]

On July 4, 1995, one of those camp sites was occupied by a married couple who remain unidentified today. The husband, signing himself "Paul A.," posted his version of the incident to a website on paranormal phenomena in August 2003. An identical account signed "Rain," told once again from the husband's perspective, was posted to the same website ten months later. According to those carbon-copy tales, strange sounds drew the couple to a cliff overlooking the river around 9 p.m.

Moonshine Park, scene of a monstrous encounter in 1995. *Courtesy of U.S. Dept. of Fish & Wildlife.*

Their flashlight beams revealed "a thing that was shaped like a person: two arms, two legs, but it had claws with three fingers on each claw [sic]. It was floating in the river on the rocks. It was at the shore moving away from us very slowly." When the figure turned to look at them, Paul/Rain "could see its eyes. They covered about half its head, which was shaped like a bullet — tapered up to a point in the back. Its eyes reflected back the light from the flashlight like a cat's eyes would." The creature's body was "covered in short brown hair, with wisps of hair on the top of the head." Fleeing in terror, the couple returned the next morning, to find no trace of the monster.[56]

Blurry Beasts

Some cryptids are apparently so strange that witnesses cannot describe them adequately, but the beast that showed itself to witness Evan Canoose on February 10, 1995, took confusion to a new level. Canoose and two unnamed friends were camped near the Larch Mountain Honor Camp, a minimum-security prison located at Yacolt, Washington, now known as Larch Corrections Center. At 6:30 a.m. on the day in question, Canoose rose before his companions and saw a strange creature he described as "blurry" and "out of focus," standing thirty to forty feet distant. Despite its fuzzy appearance, he later described the thing as six feet four inches tall, with a wide torso, reddish-orange in color like an orangutan, with a black face and "black chest markings." After a staredown lasting some forty-five seconds, Canoose retreated and did not observe the animal's departure.[57]

Two unnamed witnesses in Spokane, Washington, met another nondescript creature on the night of April 29, 1995. Although drawn to unexplained bright lights along a local riverbank, which surrounded and illuminated the beast in question, neither witness could describe it coherently.[58]

A Cryptid Kidnapped?

One afternoon in October 1996, Dr. Jonathan Reed was hiking with his golden retriever near Snoqualmie Pass, in Washington, when his dog raced ahead, barking frantically. Reed caught up and found the dog clinging to the left arm of a humanoid figure. At Reed's shouted order, the dog disengaged and retreated, but the unknown thing extended "a fleshy pseudo pod" that struck the retriever's muzzle and left a deep wound. Instantly, like something from a horror film, the dog's tissues

Snoqualmie Pass, site of Dr. Jonathan Reed's strange report in October 1996. *Courtesy of U.S. Dept. of Fish & Wildlife.*

"seemed to 'flow' into this wound. She was consumed in a matter of seconds," leaving only "a fine white powder on the ground." Enraged, Reed grabbed a fallen tree limb and clubbed the monster with it, apparently killing it. That done, Reed "finally remembered" the video camera in his backpack and taped the creature's corpse.[59]

The tale, already strange enough, soon became even more bizarre. Noting a "strange, low frequency vibration" in the air around him, Reed saw "a black craft like device" floating inches off the ground, nearby. Approaching it, he touched the object and found it so cold that his fingers were burned. Though feeling "very sick," Reed spent "several hours" videotaping the hovering shape, then decided to carry the dead monster home. Wrapping it in a convenient blanket, he drove it to his Seattle residence and placed it in his freezer.[60]

Examining the monstrosity at leisure, Reed determined that it was four feet tall, with light-colored "large bloated eyes." Four days after placing the thing in cold storage, Reed allegedly heard sounds emanating from his freezer and opened it to find the thing revived. Slamming the lid, Reed telephoned a friend, who joined him in futile efforts to communicate with the creature over several days. The thing rejected food but guzzled water, subsisting on a liquid diet until "apparently unknown government agents broke into the house and removed the creature." Presumably, they took Reed's tapes as well, since none have surfaced to this day.[61]

Send in the Trolls

Around 1 p.m., May 6, 1997, while driving near Enterprise, Oregon, motorist "Ann Lisa L." saw a strange creature cross the highway in front of her car. In a subsequent telephone call to a radio station in Idaho Falls, Idaho, she described the animal as "five feet [tall], no body hair, two arms and legs, head like a conehead, a light orange color, couldn't see its mouth or nose, it moved funny — bent arms and knees, and bent its back — very skinny, three fingers on a hand, glowing yellow eyes like a goblin or troll, long fingernails, and it didn't make any noise." Stopping her car to watch the creature pass, Ann Lisa thought it "looked disoriented, hesitated several times, didn't seem to know where it was going, but like it was looking for something." After covering some twenty feet with halting strides, the figure vanished in the roadside forest.[62]

Reptoid Nightmares

Humanoid creatures of reptilian appearance have been reported worldwide throughout recorded history. Various theories, offered by those who take the sightings seriously, range from alleged descriptions of a subterranean "reptoid" empire to speculation on intergalactic travel by members of advanced reptilian species.[63] The 1990s brought two peculiar sightings of such creatures from the Pacific Northwest.

"Reptoid" creatures have been seen in Washington and Oregon. *Courtesy of William Rebsamen.*

Around 10 p.m., January 30, 1995, an unnamed child reported seeing several "reptilian or lizard type humanoids with bright red eyes" standing outside her home in Olympia, Washington. She called her father to investigate, but he found nothing to support the story.[64]

Fewer details are available for a nocturnal incident reported in July 1998. The female witness is anonymous, no date is furnished, and we know only that the alleged event occurred somewhere in Oregon. Ms. X reports that after lying down to rest, she "suddenly found herself transported to an underground kingdom" ruled by a huge reptoid who introduced himself as "King Leo." Before magically returning the witness to her home, King Leo explained that his race had evolved from dinosaurs.[65]

Down in the Dumps

In 2006 crypto-researcher Chad Arment was contacted by a resident of Lebanon, Oregon, who related a strange encounter from summer 1999. While scavenging for antique glass and other treasures at a rural dumping site, outside an unidentified small town, the woman (unnamed by Arment, but identified as "Paula" on an Internet website) noted "tunneling-like holes...of a peculiar size" in the soil. Intrigued, she started excavating one, and soon uncovered a remarkable creature — or, rather, part of one.[66]

As described by the witness, the visible bit was five inches long and two inches in diameter, covered in "soft dusty skin" resembling a human's, with erratic patches of thin "peach-like fuzz." No other features were visible at first, until "two big beautiful crystal blue eyes" suddenly opened to stare at the woman. Although the witness denied seeing any eyelids, she described the creature blinking slowly, like a turtle. After four or five minutes, the presumed head and neck withdrew into subterranean darkness. Arment reported that the witness planned to seek the creature out again and photograph it, but no further reports were forthcoming.[67]

Speculation on the creature's possible identity is fruitless without further details. "Peach fuzz" seemingly rules out reptiles and amphibians, but no mammalian species known to modern science matches the description offered by Arment's correspondent. It was not, however, the only strange cryptid reported from Oregon dumping grounds.

After reading Paula's story online, witness "Kent P." submitted his own alleged encounter with a cryptid to the same website. According to that tale, Kent was a resident of Helix, Oregon. While celebrating his high-school graduation with friends in June 2001, he drove past a rural dump outside the nearby town of Athena, and saw a weird creature rise from a roadside ditch, proceeding slowly into an adjacent field. According to Kent, "The creature walked on two legs, like a human, but had a shell, protective back, like a turtle, or a porcupine. It had claws that were easily visible, even in the darkness of the night, and it still gives me the creeps." And as if this were not strange enough, Kent also reports local sightings of "a half-cow/half-man, or a half-horse/half-man" in the same vicinity.[68]

Hellhounds

In 1999, while riding in a friend's Jeep near Glenwood, Autumn Williams saw a quadrupedal creature running in a roadside field. She describes the beast as resembling "a cross between a dog and a man," with a huge head and "very ugly, terrible and horrifying" face. Its rippling muscles reminded Williams of a body-builder's, underneath a coat of blue-black hair like that of a Labrador retriever. The driver doubled back, but Williams found no tracks in the freshly-plowed field.[69]

Williams dubbed the creature a "hellhound" and tried to forget it, until an acquaintance mentioned his sighting of a similar beast near Eugene's Autzen Stadium, several years later. Intrigued, Williams continued her research and soon unearthed the report of an unnamed Washington resident who logged two sightings of a nearly-identical beast near the Cowlitz River, sometime in the late 1980s. That witness claimed two encounters, in July and December. Noting that it sometimes walked bi-pedally, the witness sketched a creature combining canine and ursine features, "but human-like, too."[70]

A final sighting, also anonymous, comes from a couple who met the beast at an undisclosed location in Oregon. It stood upright, revealing pointed ears, long arms, and "a snout kind of like a wolf." On three other visits to the same site, the couple heard rumbling snarls "like a four-stroke engine" and promptly departed.[71]

Mystery Maulers

In April 2004, Internet researcher Kimba D'Michi reported her husband's encounter with an unknown creature while camping along the North Fork of Washington's Snoqualmie River. The beast was approximately five feet tall, with glowing eyes, a full coat of dark hair, "and a huge bushy upright tail." The witness compared it to "a giant squirrel or something, with squat back legs," and was astounded when it leaped fifteen feet into a nearby tree, scrambling out of sight in the foliage.[72]

The next morning, D'Michi's husband had a flat tire near the campsite, and was offered a ride by a fifty-something stranger who heard the strange

Cat mutilations frightened residents of Oak Harbor in 2005. *Courtesy of U.S. Dept. of Fish & Wildlife.*

tale and replied that he had been "researching these creatures for years." The motorist claimed that "they are slowly moving north and are related to the Chupacabra," that "they travel in regimes or family clans and that they hunt in the twilight and kill in the dark, they stalk their prey and are carnivorous." Try as she might, D'Michi was unable to locate the mysterious stranger for more detailed interviews.[73]

A year later, during June and July 2005, the Whidbey Island community of Oak Harbor, Washington, suffered a rash of cat mutilations that alarmed local residents and animal control officers. While police blamed the deaths on coyotes, skeptics accused predatory cryptids or alien vivisectionists transported to the scene by UFOs. One Oak Harbor resident described her cat's corpse as being hollowed out like "a child's hand puppet." Linda Moulton Howe, an Emmy-winning telejournalist residing in New Mexico, investigated the case and quoted a deceased U.S. Army officer, Lieutenant Colonel Philip Corso, as claiming that "highly classified documents about the unusual deaths of animals around the world attributed to extraterrestrial biological entities. No blood, no tracks." Dismissing official explanations, Howe told the *Tacoma Daily Index*, "They always say it's [a] predator, disease or [a] Satanic cult. All of these are easily eliminated by field investigation. Perhaps the current rash of half-cats in Oak Harbor and the Seattle region are the work of real coyotes. But coyotes would not explain the hundreds of bloodless half-cats found over the past decades from England to Canada throughout the United States."[74]

A Snake with Legs

In early May 2005, an unnamed resident of Richland, Washington, reportedly killed a snake in her garden. The reptile was allegedly unique for having "little leg buds coming off its hips." Upon closer examination, however, the "legs" proved to be hemipenes possessed by many male snakes and lizards, undoubtedly extruded when the hapless creature was bludgeoned to death.[75]

A Horny Troll

Irish author Ronan Coghlan contributes our final report, allegedly logged from the "Horny Chessman camping grounds" near Seaside,

Oregon. There, he claims, visitors and local residents have seen a seven-foot tall "hairy monster, referred to as a troll."[76]

Founded as a summer resort in the 1870s, by railroad magnate Benjamin Holladay, modern Seaside boasts many camping facilities, but none in the vicinity — or anywhere else in Oregon — are called "Horny Chessman" or known by any conceivable similar name. Making matters worse, Coghlan's source for the report is an untitled, now-defunct Internet website.[77]

Bigfoot's Pub 'n Grub, a popular restaurant in Seaside, Oregon.

Ironically, while no trace of a real-life monster can be found in Seaside, the town does boast a steakhouse called Bigfoot's Pub 'n Grub, located at 2427 South Roosevelt Drive, which rates high marks from its diners.[78] Unlike the other creatures described herein, this Bigfoot accepts reservations.

Endnotes

Note: Abbreviated citations refer to sources listed in the bibliography. Sources not listed there are cited with full details on their first appearance below.

INTRODUCTION

1. Newton, Encyclopedia, p. 3.
2. Ibid., p. 6; Laura Klappenbach, "How many species inhabit our planet?" http://animals.about.com/b/2007/08/13/how-many-species-on-earth.html.
3. "Spider as big as a plate among scores of new species found in Greater Mekong," *The Telegraph* (London), December 16, 2008; James Owen, "Grizzly bear-sized catfish caught in Thailand," *National Geographic News*, June 29, 2005; Scott Norris, "Three new lemurs discovered, add to Madagascar's diversity," *National Geographic News*, June 26, 2006; Nicolo Gnecchi, "Giant spitting cobra discovered," *New Zealand Herald*, December 10, 2007; Amazon Association for the Preservation of Nature, http://www.marcvanroosmalen.org/newspecies.html.
4. Newton, p. 5; Blake de Pastino, "'Lost' giant waterfall discovered in California," *National Geographic News*, August 15, 2005.
5. Newton, pp. 4-5.
6. Chad Arment. Cryptozoology: Science & Speculation. Landisville, Pennsylvania: Coachwhip, 2004, p. 16.

CHAPTER 1

1. Wikipedia. "History of Oregon" (http://en.wikipedia.org/wiki/History_of_Oregon) and "History of Washington" (http://en.wikipedia.org/wiki/History_of_Washington).
2. "History of Oregon"; "History of Washington."
3. "History of Oregon"; "History of Washington"; "George Vancouver," Wikipedia, http://en.wikipedia.org/wiki/George_Vancouver.
4. "Nootka Convention," Wikipedia, http://en.wikipedia.org/wiki/Nootka_Convention.
5. From "Lewis and Clark Expedition," Wikipedia, http://en.wikipedia.org/wiki/Lewis_and_Clark_Expedition.
6. "Discovering the Great Claw," Academy of Natural Sciences, www.ansp.org/museum/jefferson/megalonyx/history-01.php; Martin Brunswick, George Cuvier, Fossil Bones, and Geological Catastrophes. University of Chicago Press, 1997; p. 25-26.
7. "Discovering the Great Claw."
8. "Louisiana Purchase," Wikipedia, http://en.wikipedia.org/wiki/Louisiana_Purchase; "Lewis and Clark Expedition," Wikipedia, http://en.wikipedia.org/wiki/Lewis_and_Clark_Expedition.
9. "Lewis and Clark Expedition."
10. "Lewis and Clark Expedition."
11. "Meriwether Lewis," Wikipedia, http://en.wikipedia.org/wiki/Meriwether_Lewis.
12. Eric Penz. Cryptid. New York, New York: iUniverse, 2005.
13. "William Clark," Wikipedia, http://en.wikipedia.org/wiki/William_Clark_(explorer).
14. "Oregon Country," Wikipedia, http://en.wikipedia.org/wiki/Oregon_Country; "History of Oregon"; "History of Washington."
15. "Lewis and Clark Expedition"; "Oregon," Wikipedia, http://en.wikipedia.org/wiki/Oregon; "Washington," Wikipedia, http://en.wikipedia.org/wiki/Washington.
16. "Oregon"; "Washington."
17. "Oregon," www.statemaster.com/state/OR/oregon/geo-geography; Oregon Facts and Trivia, www.50states.com/facts/oregon.html; "Washington," www.statemaster.com/state/WA-washington/geogeography; Washington Facts and Trivia, www.50states.com/facts/washingt.html; State of Washington Trivia, www.ipdnet.com/trivia/stategeo.html; USDA Forest Service, www.fs.fed.us/recreation/map/state_list.shtml; "List of Oregon Mountain Ranges," Wikipedia, http://en.wikipedia.org/wiki/List_of_Oregon_mountain_ranges.
18. "Cartography," Wikipedia, http://en.wikipedia.org/wiki/Cartography.

CHAPTER 2

1. Carol Ostrom, "The Pacific Northwest's elusive mountain beaver," *Seattle Times*, February 9, 2009; Hystrichopsylla schefferi, http://everything2.com/title/Hystrichopsylla%2520schefferi; Flea News, Vol. 49, http://www.ent.iastate.edu/fleanews/fleanews49.html#numbers.
2. "Invertebrate," Wikipedia, http://en.wikipedia.org/wiki/Invertebrate; "Insect," Wikipedia, http://en.wikipedia.org/wiki/Insect.
3. Insects and Spiders of the Lowland Pacific Northwest, http://share3.esd105.wednet.edu/rsandelin/Fieldguide/Animalpages/Insects/Insectsintro.htm; Eugene Kozloff and Linda Price, Marine Invertebrates of the Pacific Northwest (Seattle University of Washington Press, 1996).
4. U.S. Geological Survey, "Nonindigenous Aquatic Species," http://nas.er.usgs.gov/queries/SpeciesList.asp?Group=&State=WA&Sortby=%5BGroup%5D,Genus,Species,SubSpecies&submit2=Submit.
5. Oregon Department of Fish & Wildlife (hereafter ODWF), "Oregon's Ten Most Unwanted Invaders," http://www.dfw.state.or.us/conservationstrategy/invasive_species/most_unwanted.asp.
6. Boersma, Reichard and Van Buren, pp. 126-8, 132-5, 138-9, 142-3.
7. "Fishes Found in Fresh Water in the Pacific Northwest," www.streamnet.org/pub-ed/ff/species/Index.html; Oregon Invasive Species Council,

www.oregon.gov/OISC/most_dangerous.shtml; U.S. Geological Survey, "Nonindigenous Aquatic Species."

8. U.S. Geological Survey, "Nonindigenous Aquatic Species."

9. Ibid.; ODFW, "Oregon's Ten Most Unwanted Invaders"; "Northern snakehead," Wikipedia, http://en.wikipedia.org/wiki/Northern_snakehead; Internet Movie Database, http://www.imdb.com.

10. Reptiles and Amphibians of the Pacific Northwest, www.californiaherps.com/northwest.html; Amphibians and Reptiles of Oregon, www.uoregon.edu/~titus/herp/herp.html; Reptiles of Washington, www.washington.edu/burkemuseum/collections/herpetology/reptile.php; U.S. Geological Survey, "Nonindigenous Asiatic Species."

11. Boersma, Reichard and Van Buren, p. 146-7; ODFW, "Oregon's Ten Most Unwanted Invaders."

12. Reptiles and Amphibians of the Pacific Northwest; Amphibians and Reptiles of Oregon; Reptiles of Washington.

13. Reptiles and Amphibians of the Pacific Northwest; ODFW, "Oregon's Ten Most Unwanted Invaders"; Boersma, Reichard and Van Buren, p. 166-7.

14. "Nile monitor," http://en.wikipedia.org/wiki/Nile_monitor; U.S. Geological Survey, "Nonindigenous Asiatic Species."

15. DeFranceschi; Lisi.

16. "Crocodilia," http://en.wikipedia.org/wiki/Crocodilia.

17. Bord, Unexplained, p. 389.

18. Ibid.; Longoria.

19. Miller, "The Mystery of Willamina's gator."

20. "Oregon police look for escaped alligator."

21. "Strange lizard found in Oregon."

22. "Alligator-like creature spotted"; WDFW Enforcement Program 2005 Report, p. 19, http://wdfw.wa.gov/enforcement/annual_reports/2005_enf_annual_report.pdf.

23. "Complete Checklist of Oregon's Birds," http://home.teleport.com/~skipr/birds/obrclist.html; Washington Ornithological Society; "Checklist of Washington Birds," http://www.wos.org/WAlist01.html.

24. Oregon Invasive Species Council (hereafter OISC), "100 most dangerous invaders to keep out," http://www.oregon.gov/OISC/most_dangerous.shtml; "Mute Swan," http://en.wikipedia.org/wiki/Mute_swan.

25. "Mammals of Oregon," http://www.mammalsociety.org/statelists/ormammals.html; "Mammals of Washington," http://www.washington.edu/burkemuseum/collections/mammalogy/mamwash.

26. "Mammals of Oregon"; "Mammals of Washington."

27. National Feral Swine Mapping System, http://128.192.20.53/nfsms; Oregon Invasive Species Council; Coblenz and Bouska; Morris; WDFW News Release, June 22, 2001.

28. "Wild Boar," http://en.wikipedia.org/wiki/Boar; "Hogzilla," http://en.wikipedia.org/wiki/Hogzilla.

29. Bord, Unexplained, p. 389; Coleman, Mysterious America, p. 160-87; "Kangaroo," http://en.wikipedia.org/wiki/Kangaroo; "Wallaby," http://en.wikipedia.org/wiki/Wallaby; "Wallabies warm to Britain," The Independent (London), May 5, 1997.

30. Coleman, Mysterious America, pp. 136-7, 155-6; Shuker, p. 168; Eberhart, p. 314.

31. Bord, Unexplained, p. 389; "Black panther," http://en.wikipedia.org/wiki/Black_panther; Coleman, Mysterious America, pp. 150-4, 292-6; "American Lion," http://en.wikipedia.org/wiki/American_Lion.

32. "Coelacanth," http://en.wikipedia.org/wiki/Coelacanth.

33. Mammals of Oregon; Mammals of Washington; Sandsberry.

34. Wiley; "Giant Palouse earthworm," http://en.wikipedia.org/wiki/Giant_Palouse_earthworm.

35. Wiley.

CHAPTER 3

1. Where Be "Here Be Dragons"? MapHist, http://www.maphist.nl/extra/herebedragons.html.

2. LeBlond and Bousfield, pp. 3-7.

3. Pacific, http://www.st.nmfs.noaa.gov/st5/publication/communities/Pacific_Summary_Communities.pdf.

4. Pugwis with Kingfisher Mask, http://www.artnatam.com/first-nations/troy-roberts/gallery/pugwis-kingfisher-mask.html; Coastal Treasures, http://www.coastaltreasures.org/AlfredPugwisTotemPole.html; Guiley, p. 135.

5. Pugwis with Kingfisher Mask; Pugwis Mask with Cormorant, http://www.artnatam.com/first-nations/troy-roberts/gallery/pugwis-mask-cormorant.html; U'mista Cultural Society, http://www.umista.org/giftshop/item.php?item=841; Pugwis with Frog, http://www.justart.ca/pugwis-with-frog-stanc-hunt-802-pictures.html; Coastal Treasures.

6. Coleman, Mothman, pp. 90-1.

7. LeBlond and Bousfield, p. 94.

8. "An electric monster," Tacoma Daily Ledger, July 3, 1893.

9. Ibid.

10. "Washington Place Names database," Tacoma Public Library, http://search.tpl.lib.wa.us/wanames/wpnv2.asp.

11. LeBlond and Bousfield, p. 94.

12. "Hood Canal," http://en.wikipedia.org/wiki/Hood_Canal.

13. "The sea serpent of the Pacific."

14. Ibid.

15. "Oarfish," http://en.wikipedia.org/wiki/Oarfish.

16. Museum of Hoaxes, http://www.museumofhoaxes.com/hoax/photo_database/image/pacific_sea_monster; Damon Agnos, "The return of the supposedly mythical sea serpent," Seattle Weekly, March 25, 2009.

17. "Graveyard of the Pacific," http://en.wikipedia.org/wiki/Graveyard_of_the_Pacific.

18. Ciams.

19. Ibid.

20. Head, Neck and Whiskers, http://www.cornes1.fsnet.co.uk/head,%20neck%20and%20whiskers.html; De Wire, pp. 296-7.

21. Ciams; Dark Destinations, http://www.thecabinet.com/darkdestinations/location.php?sub_id=dark_destinations&letter=m&location_id=mouth_of_the_columbia_river&start=0&limit=5&d_order=ASC.

22. Bragg, p. 15.

23. Ibid., pp. 15-16.

24. Ciams; Adams.

25. LeBlond and Bousfield, p. 104; "Jake the Alligator Man," http://en.wikipedia.org/wiki/Jake_the_Alligator_Man.

26. "Devils Lake" (Lincoln County, Oregon), http://en.wikipedia.org/wiki/Devils_Lake_(Lincoln_County,_Oregon); Ciams.

27. Ciams; Adams; Gregory Bangs, "Have you seen your serpent?" http://cnc.virtuelle.ca/ogopogo/press/press4.html.

28. Ciams; "Elasmobranchii," http://en.wikipedia.org/wiki/Elasmobranchii.

29. Heuvelmans, p. 507.

30. LeBlond and Sibert, p. 27.

31. Ciams; Adams.

32. LeBlond and Bousfield, pp. 49-50.

33. Ciams.

34. LeBlond and Bousfield, pp. 114-15.

35. Dark Destinations, http://www.thecabinet.com/darkdestinations/location.php?sub_id=dark_destinations&letter=m&location_id=mouth_of_the_columbia_river&start=0&limit=5&d_order=ASC.

36. Michael Cenedella, "20th & 21st Century Dinosaurs—Sea Serpent? Plesiosaur?", http://s8int.com/dino28.html; Loren Coleman, "Mystery Photos: Sea Serpent or Plesiosaur? Name That Carcass!", http://www.cryptomundo.com/bigfoot-report/sea-serpent-or-plesiosaur.

37. LeBlond and Bousfield, p. 59.

38. Eberhart, pp. 484-7.

39. Loren Coleman, "'Sea serpent' beached," http://www.cryptomundo.com/cryptozoo-news/trachipterus; "In Search of the Mysterious Sea Serpent," http://current.com/items/89558010_in-search-of-the-mysterious-sea-serpent.htm; Russell Jenkins, "Woman angler lands legendary sea monster," The Times (London), February 21, 2003.

40. "List of giant squid specimens and sightings," http://en.wikipedia.org/wiki/List_of_giant_squid_specimens_and_sightings; "List of colossal squid specimens and sightings," http://en.wikipedia.org/wiki/List_of_Colossal_Squid_specimens_and_sightings; Adams.

41. Loren Coleman, "Ahoy, thar be sea monsters, arr, otters!", http://www.cryptomundo.com/cryptozoo-news/ahoy-otters.

42. "Sea otter," http://en.wikipedia.org/wiki/Sea_otter.

43. Newport, Oregon—Yaquina Bay Sea Monster, http://www.roadsideamerica.com/tip/18624; "Kronosaurus," http://en.wikipedia.org/wiki/Kronosaurus.

44. "Random samples," Science 315 (March 20, 2007): 1773; Victoria Jaggard, "Photo in the news: Jurassic 'crocodile' found in Oregon," National Geographic, http://news.nationalgeographic.com/news/2007/03/070322-crocodile.html.

45. Anthonie Oudemans, The Great Sea Serpent: An Historical and Critical Treatise. Leiden: E.J. Brill, 1892.

46. "Rupert Gould," http://en.wikipedia.org/wiki/Rupert_Gould; Heuvelmans, p. 441.

47. Heuvelmans, pp. 546-65.

48. LeBlond and Sibert.

49. Gary Mangiacopra, "The great unknowns of the 19th century," Of Sea and Shore 7 (Winter 1976-77): 201-5, 228; 8 (Spring 1977)): 17-24, 58; (Summer 1977): 95-104; (Fall 1977): 175-8; "The great unknowns into the 20th century," Of Sea and Shore 11 (Spring 1980): 13-20; (Summer 1980): 123-7; (Fall 1980) 175-8; (Winter 1980-81): 259-61.

50. Bruce Champagne, "A preliminary evaluation of a study of the morphology, behavior, autoecology, and habitat of large, unidentified marine animals, based on recorded field observations." Crypto Dracontology Special No. 1 (November 2001): 93-112.

51. Coleman and Huyghe, Field Guide to Lake Monsters, pp. 40-5; Cheryl-Samantha Owen, "New manta ray species discovered," The Telegraph (London), July 25, 2008.

52. LeBlond and Bousfield, pp. 14-25.

53. Ibid., pp. 93-121.

54. Ibid., p. 71.

55. Ibid., pp. 57-8, 71, 78-9, 101-2.

56. Ibid., pp. 50-56.

57. Ibid., pp. 46-8, 56-7.

58. Karl Shuker, The Unexplained (North Deighton, Massachusetts: JG Press, 1996), p. 150.

CHAPTER 4

1. Coleman and Huyghe, Field Guide to Lake Monsters, p. 306; Eberhart, p. 655.

2. US Cities & State Gazetteer, http://hometownlocator.com; USA Place Names, http://www.placenames.com/us; StateMaster, http://www.statemaster.com.

3. Loren Coleman, Mysterious America (Boston, Massachusetts: Faber and Faber, 1983), p. 278; Coleman, Mysterious America (Revised edition, 2001), pp. 310-11; Coleman and Huyghe, Field Guide to Lake Monsters, pp. 318-19; Kirk, pp. 297-8; Eberhart, pp. 686-7.

4. "Crater Lake," http://en.wikipedia.org/wiki/Crater_Lake.

5. Rose, p. 362.

6. Skinner, Vol. 2, pp. 302-3.

7. Internet Movie Database; DVD Drive-in, http://www.dvddrive-in.com/reviews/a-d/craterlakemonster.html.

8. Herndon.

9. "I saw the Crater Lake monster."

10. Ibid.

11. "Crescent Lake (Oregon)," http://en.wikipedia.org/wiki/Crescent_Lake_(Oregon).

12. Garner, p. 119; "Klamath County, Oregon," http://en.wikipedia.org/wiki/Klamath_County,_Oregon.

13. Ciams.

14. Skinner, Vol. 2, p. 303.

15. Eberhart, p. 17; USA Place Names; Dragons of Fame, http://www.blackdrago.com/fame_a.htm.

16. Rose, pp. 15, 21, 30.

17. "Lake Chelan," http://en.wikipedia.org/wiki/Lake_Chelan.

18. Burns; Clark, Indian Legends, pp. 70-2.

19. Eberhart, p. 687; Clark, Indian Legends, p. 70.

20. "Lake Quinault," http://en.wikipedia.org/wiki/Lake_Quinault.

21. Clark, Indian Legends, pp. 64-5.

22. "Lake Steilacoom," http://en.wikipedia.org/wiki/Lake_Steilacoom.

23. James Wickersham, "Nusqually mythology, studies of the Washington Indians," Overland Monthly XXXII (July-December 1898): 345-351; Hauck, p. 445.

24. "Lake Steilacoom."

25. "Lake Union," http://en.wikipedia.org/wiki/Lake_Union.

26. Sandi Doughton, "In Lake Union, a slippery star is born," Seattle Times, October 11, 2005; Willatuk, http://www.willatuk.com/willatuk/home.asp.

27. "Lake Washington," http://en.wikipedia.org/wiki/Lake_Washington.

28. Burns.

29. Dorpat; Garner, pp. 117-18.

30. Dorpat.

31. Ibid.

32. Ibid.; "The Madrona Sea-Monster"; Garner, p. 117.

33. "Lake Washington."

34. Garner, p. 118.

35. "Dead sturgeon puts an end to monster tales in Washington State," New York Times, November 7, 1987; "White sturgeon," http://en.wikipedia.org/wiki/White_sturgeon.

36. McBee; "Common snapping turtle," http://en.wikipedia.org/wiki/Chelydra; "Alligator snapping turtle," http://en.wikipedia.org/wiki/Alligator_Snapping_Turtle;

37. Holt.

38. Ibid.

39. Longoria; Born Free USA, http://www.bornfreeusa.org/b4a2_exotic_animals_state.php?s=wa.

40. Kamb.

41. Doughton, "In Lake Union"; "Willatuk," http://en.wikipedia.org/wiki/Willatuk.

42. "Moses Lake, Washington," http://en.wikipedia.org/wiki/Moses_Lake,_Washington.

43. Burns; Kirk, p. 164.

44. "Metolius River," http://en.wikipedia.org/wiki/Metolius_River; "The Cove Palisades State Park," http://en.wikipedia.org/wiki/The_Cove_Palisades_State_Park.

45. Mangiacopra and Wright, p. 80.

46. Ibid., pp. 80-1.

47. Ibid., p. 82.

48. "Omak Lake," http://en.wikipedia.org/wiki/Omak_Lake.

49. Colville Indian Reservation, http://en.wikipedia.org/wiki/Colville_Indian_Reservation; Walter Cline, "Religion and World View," in Leslie Spier (ed.), The Sinkaietk or Southern Okanagon of Washington (Menasha, Wisconsin: George Banta, 1938), pp. 131, 171.

50. LaFountaine, pp. 2, 45; iUniverse website, http://www.iuniverse.com/Bookstore/BookDetail.aspx?BookId=SKU-000028745.

51. "Pend Oreille River," http://en.wikipedia.org/wiki/Pend_Oreille_River.

52. Kirk, p. 298; "Pend d'Oreilles (tribe)," http://en.wikipedia.org/wiki/Pend_d'Oreilles_(tribe).

53. Turtle Island Storytellers Network, http://www.turtleislandstorytellers.net/tis_montana/transcript_k_camel.html; Kirk, pp. 164-7.

54. USA Place Names.

55. Skinner, Vol. 2, p. 303.

56. Spokane Outdoors, http://www.spokaneoutdoors.com/rocklake.html.

57. Ibid.

58. "Catostomidae," http://en.wikipedia.org/wiki/Sucker_(fish).

59. Kirk, p. 162; Spokane Outdoors.

60. "Spirit Lake (Washington)," http://en.wikipedia.org/wiki/Spirit_Lake_(Washington).

61. "Spirit Lake (Washington)"; Clark, Indian Legends, pp. 63-4.

62. "Upper Klamath Lake," http://en.wikipedia.org/wiki/Upper_Klamath_Lake.

63. Skinner, Vol. 2, p. 304.

64. "Wallowa Lake," http://en.wikipedia.org/wiki/Wallowa_Lake.

65. Wallowa Lake Monster, http://www.americanmonsters.com/monsters/lakemonsters/index.php?detail=article&idarticle=176; Wallowa Lake Monster, http://www.unknownexplorers.com/wallowalakemonster.php.

66. Lake Monsters, http://www.geocities.com/Area51/Dungeon/8511/lake.html.

67. "Monster of Wallowa Lake Spotted in 1885." http://www.oregongenealogy.com/wallowa/reavis/wallowa_lake_monster.htm.

68. "Steller's Sea Cow," http://en.wikipedia.org/wiki/Steller%27s_sea_cow.

69. Wallowa Lake Monster, http://www.americanmonsters.com/monsters/lakemonsters/index.php?detail=article&idarticle=176; Wallowa Lake Monster, http://www.unknownexplorers.com/wallowalakemonster.php; Lake Monsters.

70. Monica Olson, "Gems in the wilderness," Home & Away (February 1, 2009), http://www.homeandawaymagazine.com/content.cfm?a=1025&pgn=2; Wallowa Lake Monster, http://www.unknownexplorers.com/wallowalakemonster.php.

71. Douglas Larson, "Where's Wally, now that he's needed?" http://www.bigfootforums.com/index.php?showtopic=4353&mode=threaded&pid=86482

72. Kirk, p. 158.

73. Ibid.

74. Ibid., p. 159.

75. Ibid.; Eberhart, p. 51.

76. Kirk, pp. 158-9.
77. Larson.
78. Miller, "Fourth of July outing ends with mysterious catch."
79. Ibid.
80. All Catfish Species Inventory, http://silurus. acnatsci.org; "Catfish," http://en.wikipedia.org/wiki/Catfish.
81. "Willamette River," http://en.wikipedia.org/wiki/Willamette_River; ODFW, "Attention Sturgeon Anglers," http://www.dfw.state.or.us/resources/fishing/docs/sturgeon_angler_notice_flyer.pdf; "Sturgeon Fishing on the Willamette River," http://www.chrisbrooks.org/2005/09/12/Sturgeon-FishingOnTheWillametteRiver.aspx.
82. Rose, p. 396; "Wishpoosh," http://www.answers.com/topic/wishpoosh.
83. Wish Poosh Campground, Washington, http://www.publiclands.org/explore/site.php?search=YES&back=Search%20Results&id=4936; "Cle Elum Lake," http://en.wikipedia.org/wiki/Cle_Elum_Lake.
84. Coleman and Huyghe, *Field Guide to Lake Monsters*, pp. 192-201; "Giant Beaver," http://en.wikipedia.org/wiki/Giant_Beaver.

CHAPTER 5

1. Hall, pp. 66-7.
2. Gladdie Bills, "Bird Like UFO's," *Fate* 7 (December 1954), pp. 128-9.
3. "Andean Condor," http://en.wikipedia.org/wiki/Andean_Condor; "California Condor," http://en.wikipedia.org/wiki/California_Condor.
4. "Golden Eagle," http://en.wikipedia.org/wiki/Golden_Eagle; "Bald Eagle," http://en.wikipedia.org/wiki/Bald_Eagle.
5. "Teratornithidae," http://en.wikipedia.org/wiki/Teratornithidae.
6. "Argentavis," http://en.wikipedia.org/wiki/Argentavis.
7. "Teratornithidae"; "Aiolornis," http://en.wikipedia.org/wiki/Aiolornis.
8. "Teratornis," http://en.wikipedia.org/wiki/Teratornis.
9. "Teratornithidae."
10. Hall, pp. 11-12.
11. "Pterosaur," http://en.wikipedia.org/wiki/Pterosaur.
12. Quoted in Garner, pp. 48-9.
13. "An amphibious monster," *Daily Picayune*, December 4, 1892.
14. Schleif.
15. Coleman, Mothman, p.p. 28-9.
16. Ibid.
17. 1948 Humanoid Reports, http://www.ufoinfo.com/humanoid/humanoid1948.shtml.
18. Ibid.
19. "Leonardo da Vinci: His Flying Machines," http://www.angelfire.com/electronic/awakening101/leonardo.html.
20. "Batsquatch," http://www.unknown-creatures.com/batsquatch.html; Roberts.
21. Roberts.
22. Ibid.
23. Ibid.; USA Place Names.
24. "Batsquatch," http://www.batsquatch.com/batsquatch/batsquatch.html; "Unknown Explorers," http://www.unknownexplorers.com/batsquatch.php.
25. "Batsquatch," http://www.batsquatch.com/batsquatch/batsquatch.html.
26. Ibid.
27. Frame 352, http://paranormalbigfoot.blogspot.com/2009/05/demons-in-my-neighborhood-beware.html.
28. Arnold, pp. 91-2; *Unexplained Mysteries*, http://www.unexplained-mysteries.com/forum/index.php?showtopic=79382; Mount Pilchuck, http://en.wikipedia.org/wiki/Mount_Pilchuck.
29. Arnold, pp. 91-2; *Unexplained Mysteries*.
30. Arnold, pp. 91-2; *Unexplained Mysteries*.
31. 1996 Humanoid Reports, http://www.ufoinfo.com/humanoid/humanoid1996.shtml.
32. Ibid.

CHAPTER 6

1. Sasquatch Information Society, http://www.bigfoot-info.org/data.
2. Bord, *Bigfoot*, pp. 220-310.
3. Green, *Sasquatch*, pp. 6, 93.
4. Murphy, p. 8.
5. BFRO, http://www.bfro.net/GDB/state_listing.asp?state=or.
6. Oregon Bigfoot (hereafter OBF), http://www.oregon-bigfoot.com/state_results.php?state=OR.
7. IBS website, no longer accessible.
8. Native American Sasquatch Names, http://www.geocities.com/Yosemite/Forest/3080/names.html.
9. Newton, Encyclopedia, pp. 60, 412.
10. "John McLoughlin," http://en.wikipedia.org/wiki/John_McLoughlin; IBS.
11. Terry, "Bigfoot legend lives large in Northwest lore, locales."
12. Ibid.
13. Washington State University Libraries, http://www.wsulibs.wsu.edu/masc/walkerdescription.html; Terry, "Bigfoot legend lives large in Northwest lore, locales."
14. Bigfoot Encounters, http://www.bigfootencounters.com; "Curry County, Oregon," http://en.wikipedia.org/wiki/Curry_County,_Oregon.
15. Sidney Warren, p. 159.
16. Quoted ibid., pp. 159-62.
17. IBS.
18. "Hunting a wild man," *Daily Free Press* (Winnipeg, Mantoba), December 31, 1885.
19. Sanderson, *Abominable Snowmen*, pp. 115-16.
20. Ibid., p. 116.
21. Bigfoot Encounters, http://www.bigfootencounters.com.
22. Green, *Sasquatch File*, p. 5.
23. IBS.
24. Arment, Historical, p. 267; Bord, *Bigfoot*, pp. 26, 222.
25. "Sixes wild man again," Lane County Leader, April 7, 1904.
26. IBS.
27. Green, *Sasquatch File*, p. 15.
28. Ibid.; Arment, Historical, pp. 268-9; IBS #1367, 2021.

29. IBS.
30. Bord, *Bigfoot*, p. 229.
31. Green, *Sasquatch*, pp. 412-15.
32. IBS.
33. Ibid.
34. BFRO; IBS.
35. IBS.
36. Bord, *Bigfoot*, p. 231; USA Place Names.
37. IBS.
38. Ibid.
39. BFRO.
40. IBS.
41. Bord, *Bigfoot*, pp. 66, 233.
42. IBS.
43. Bord, *Bigfoot*, pp. 66, 234; IBS #3988.
44. IBS.
45. IBS; 1959 Humanoid Reports, http://www.ufoinfo. com/humanoid/humanoid1959.shtml.
46. IBS; OBF; Hammers.
47. SIS.
48. IBS; Regan Lee, "The Ghost in Conser Lake," http://paranormalbigfoot.blogspot.com/2009/02/ ghost-in-conser-lake.html; Long; Sanderson, Abominable Snowmen, pp. 140-1.
49. Bord, *Bigfoot*, p. 236; Long.
50. Bord, *Bigfoot*, p. 235.
51. IBS; OBF.
52. Bord, *Bigfoot*, pp. 71, 237; ODFW Hunting Resources, http://www.dfw.state.or.us/resources/ hunting/big_game/regulations/seasons.asp.
53. IBS.
54. IBS; Bord, *Bigfoot*, p. 240.
55. Bord, *Bigfoot*, pp. 240, 242; IBS.
56. IBS.
57. IBS; Bord, *Bigfoot*, p. 246.
58. IBS; Bord, *Bigfoot*, pp. 89, 102-3, 247-8.
59. IBS; Bord, *Bigfoot*, pp. 104, 249.
60. IBS; BFRO; Bord, *Bigfoot*, pp. 249-50.
61. Bord, *Bigfoot*, pp. 105-6, 251.
62. IBS; BFRO.
63. BFRO; Bord, *Bigfoot*, p. 252.
65. Bord, *Bigfoot*, pp. 253-4; BFRO.
66. IBS; Bord, *Bigfoot*, p. 256.
67. IBS; BFRO; OBF; GCBRO; Bord, *Bigfoot*, pp. 118-20, 260; IBS.
68. IBS; BFRO; Bord, *Bigfoot*, p. 260.
69. BFRO; IBS; Bord, *Bigfoot*, p. 261; OBF.
70. IBS; Bord, *Bigfoot*, pp. 122, 124, 263; BFRO.
71. Bord, *Bigfoot*, p. 265; OBF; IBS.
72. IBS; Bord, *Bigfoot*, p. 266, 268; OBF; GCBRO.
73. Bord, *Bigfoot*, pp. 128-9.
74. Bord, *Bigfoot*, pp. 129, 269, 270; IBS.
75. Bord, *Bigfoot*, p. 271; OBF; IBS; BFRO.
76. Bord, *Bigfoot*, p. 274; BFRO; IBS.
77. OBF; IBS.
78. Bord, *Bigfoot*, p. 276; IBS.
79. IBS; Bord, *Bigfoot*, p. 277; BFRO.
80. IBS.
81. Bord, *Bigfoot*, p. 278; IBS; SIS; BFRO.
82. BFRO; GCBRO; IBS.
83. IBS; *Bigfoot Encounters*.
84. IBS; Bord, *Bigfoot*, p. 281.
85. BFRO; OBF; GCBRO; IBS; Bord, *Bigfoot*, p. 282.
86. BFRO; IBS; Bord, *Bigfoot*, p. 284.
87. IBS; *Bigfoot Encounters*.
88. Bord, *Bigfoot*, p. 285; IBS.
89. IBS; BFRO; OBF.
90. Bord, *Bigfoot*, p. 289.
91. Bord, *Bigfoot*, p. 290; IBS; OBF.
92. IBS.
93. Baker; "Ted Kulongoski," http://en.wikipedia.org/ wiki/Ted_Kulongoski.
94. IBS; Bord, *Bigfoot*, p. 291; BFRO.
95. BFRO; OBF.
96. BFCU; IBS.
97. IBS.
98. Bord, *Bigfoot*, pp. 299-300; IBS; GCBRO; IBS.
99. Bord, *Bigfoot*, p. 300; IBS; OBF; BFRO.
100. BFRO; IBS; OBF.
101. Bord, *Bigfoot*, p. 303; IBS; BFRO; OBF.
102. BFRO; IBS.
103. IBS; GCBRO; OBF.
104. IBS; Bord, *Bigfoot*, p. 305.
105. OBF; IBS; Bord, *Bigfoot*, p. 306; BFRO.
106. IBS; Bord, *Bigfoot*, p. 307; BFRO.
107. IBS; OBF.
108. IBS.
109. BFRO; IBS; Bord, *Bigfoot*, pp. 308-9; IBS; *Bigfoot Encounters*.
110. OBF; BFRO; IBS; Bord, *Bigfoot*, p. 309; *Bigfoot Encounters*; SIS.
111. IBS; OBF.
112. OBF; IBS; USA Place Names.
113. OBF; IBS; BFRO; Snyder.
114. IBS; SIS; BFRO.
115. IBS.
116. *Bigfoot Encounters*; BFRO; OBF; IBS.
117. IBS; BFRO.
118. GCBRO; BFRO; IBS.
119. IBS; BFRO; OBF.
120. Bord, *Bigfoot*, p. 181; IBS; BFRO; OBF; SIS.
121. IBS; BFRO; OBF; 1987 Humanoid Sighting Reports, http://www.ufoinfo.com/humanoid/ humanoid1987.shtml.
122. IBS; BFRO; *Bigfoot Encounters*; OBF.
123. IBS; OBF; BFRO.
124. IBS; BFRO; GCBRO; OBF.
125. IBS.
126. IBS; BFRO.
127. IBS; BFRO.
128. IBS; BFRO.
129. IBS; BFRO; OBF.
130. IBS; BFRO.
131. IBS; BFRO.
132. IBS; OBF.
133. IBS; BFRO.
134. IBS; BFRO; OBF.
135. BFRO; IBS.
136. IBS; BFRO; OBF.
137. IBS; BFRO; OBF.
138. BFRO; Hammers; IBS; OBF.
139. IBS; OBF; BFRO.
140. IBS; BFRO.
141. IBS; OBF.
142. IBS; BFRO.
143. IBS; *Bigfoot Encounters*; BFRO.
144. IBS; BFRO; *Bigfoot Encounters*.
145. IBS; Beck.

146. IBS.
147. IBS; BFRO.
148. BFRO; *Bigfoot Encounters*; IBS; OBF.
149. IBS; OBF; BFRO.
150. IBS; OBF; *Bigfoot Encounters*.
151. IBS; SIS, BFRO; OBF.
152. GCBRO; OBF.
153. SIS; IBS; BFRO, OBF.
154. BFRO; OBF, *Bigfoot Encounters*.
155. SIS; IBS; BFRO; OBF.
156. *Bigfoot Encounters*; BFRO; SIS; OBF; IBS.
157. OBF; Bord, *Bigfoot*, pp. 204-5; SIS; BFRO.
158. BFRO; *Bigfoot Encounters*; OBF; Freeman.
159. BFRO.
160. BFRO; SIS; OBS; *Bigfoot Encounters*.
161. OBF; BFRO.
162. OBF.
163. OBF; BFRO.
164. OBF; BFRO; SIS.
165. OBF; SIS.
166. OBF; GCBRO; SIS.
167. BFRO; OBF; SIS.
168. OBF.

CHAPTER 7

1. Green, *Sasquatch*, p. 6.
2. Murphy, p. 8.
3. IBS.
4. OBF; BFRO; SIS.
5. Native American Bigfoot Names; Arment, Historical, pp. 325-8.
6. Arment, Historical, p. 320; Green, *Sasquatch*, p. 29.
7. IBS; Norman, p. 89; Tim Banse, "Warren Smith: UFO Investigator or Hoaxer?" http://kevinrandle.blogspot.com/2007/05/warren-smith-ufo-investigator-or.html; USA Place Names.
8. IBS.
9. Ibid.
10. Bord, *Bigfoot*, pp. 32-3, 37-8.
11. BFRO.
12. Beck, *I Fought*; Green, *Sasquatch*, p. 90; "Logger says his big mouth is responsible for Bigfoot," *Associated Press*, April 4, 1982.
13. IBS.
14. Blair; IBS.
15. BFRO; Bord, *Bigfoot*, p. 229; IBS.
16. IBS; Bord, *Bigfoot*, p. 230; BFRO.
17. *Longview Daily News*, May 22-June 6, 1950; Don Hunter and René Dahinden, *Sasquatch* (New York, New York: Signet, 1973), pp. 2-6.
18. BFRO.
19. BFRO; IBS; Bord, *Bigfoot*, p. 232.
20. IBS.
21. IBS; Bord, *Bigfoot*, p. 234.
22. BFRO; OBF; IBS.
23. IBS; Bord, *Bigfoot*, p. 237.
24. IBS; Bord, *Bigfoot*, p. 238.
25. BFRO; Bord, *Bigfoot*, pp. 239-40; IBS.
26. Bord, *Bigfoot*, pp. 241-42.
27. BFRO; Bord, *Bigfoot*, p. 243; IBS.
28. BFRO; IBS; Bord, *Bigfoot*, pp. 88, 245.
29. BFRO; IBS; Bord, *Bigfoot*, p. 247.
30. Bord, *Bigfoot*, pp. 90, 248; BFRO; IBS.
31. Bord, *Bigfoot*, pp. 249, 251; BFRO; IBS; USA Place Names.
32. Bord, *Bigfoot*, pp. 177-8, 252; IBS; BFRO.
33. Bord, *Bigfoot*, pp. 252-3; IBS.
34. Bord, *Bigfoot*, pp. 254-5; "Sasquatch watch!" Ocean Shores (WA) *Ocean Observer*, August 17, 1969; IBS.
35. Bord, *Bigfoot*, pp. 113, 255-6; BFRO; IBS.
36. Bord, *Bigfoot*, pp. 236-7, 244; IBS; BRFO.
37. Bord, *Bigfoot*, pp. 257-9; SIS.
38. Bord, *Bigfoot*, pp. 116, 259-60.
39. BFRO; IBS.
40. Bord, *Bigfoot*, pp. 262-4; BFRO; IBS.
41. Bord, *Bigfoot*, p. 265; IBS; BFRO.
42. Bord, *Bigfoot*, pp. 264, 269; BFRO; IBS.
43. IBS; OBF; Bord, *Bigfoot*, pp. 265, 269.
44. BFRO; Bord, *Bigfoot*, pp. 272, 274, 276; IBS.
45. OBF; Bord, *Bigfoot*, pp. 276, 279; BFRO; IBS.
46. BFRO; IBS; Bord, *Bigfoot*, p. 143, 283-4; OBF.
47. IBS; BFRO; Bord, *Bigfoot*, pp. 289-90.
48. Bord, *Bigfoot*, p. 291, 294, 296; BFRO; OBF; IBS.
49. Sheppard-Wolford; OBF; IBS.
50. IBS; BFRO; Bord, *Bigfoot*, pp. 300, 304; OBF; 1978 Humanoid Reports.
51. BFRO; Bord, *Bigfoot*, pp. 305, 307; IBS; OBF.
52. IBS; BFRO.
53. BFRO.
54. "Mount St. Helens," http://en.wikipedia.org/wiki/Mount_St._Helens; BFRO; IBS.
55. Bord, *Bigfoot*, pp. 308-9; IBS; BFRO.
56. BFRO; OBF; Bord, *Bigfoot*, p. 310; IBS.
57. BFRO; GCBRO; IBS.
58. BFRO; Cockle; IBS.
59. IBS; GCBRO; BFRO.
60. IBS; BFRO; OBF; SIS.
61. IBS; BFRO.
62. SIS; BFRO.
63. BFRO; IBS.
64. OBF; IBS; BFRO; GCBRO; Bord, *Bigfoot*, p. 186.
65. IBS; BFRO; GCBRO.
66. IBS; BFRO.
67. SIS; OBF; BFRO; IBS; Cockle.
68. IBS; BFRO; OBF.
69. SIS; BFRO; Bord, *Bigfoot*, p. 190; IBS.
70. BFRO; IBS; SIS; OBF.
71. IBS; BFRO.
72. IBS; SIS; BFRO.
73. BFRO; IBS; OBF.
74. BFRO; IBS.
75. BFRO; IBS; Bord, *Bigfoot*, pp. 194-5.
76. IBS; BFRO.
77. IBS; BFRO.
78. BFRO; IBS; Bord, *Bigfoot*, p. 196.
79. IBS; BFRO; OBF.
80. IBS; BFRO.
81. IBS; BFRO; Bord, *Bigfoot*, p. 197; Blair.
82. IBS; GCBRO; BFRO.
83. IBS; BFRO; GCBRO; SIS.
84. IBS; BFRO.
85. SIS; IBS; BFRO; OBF.
86. IBS; BFRO; SIS.
87. IBS; BFRO.
88. BFRO; IBS; Bord, *Bigfoot*, p. 199; SIS.
89. IBS; OBF; GCBRO; Bord, *Bigfoot*, p. 200.

90. IBS; BFRO; SIS.
91. BFRO; IBS.
92. OBF; BFRO; IBS; GCBRO.
93. BFRO; Bord, *Bigfoot*, p. 204; OBF; Blair.
94. SIS; BFRO; GCBRO; OBF.
95. OBF; Bord, *Bigfoot*, p. 205; BFRO; SIS.
96. OBF; BFRO; Phil Stanford, "Sittin' in at Sweet Oregon Grill," *Portland Tribune*, October 4, 2002; IBS.
97. GCBRO; OBF; BFRO.
98. BFRO; OBF; SIS.
99. GCBRO; SIS; OBF; BFRO.
100. OBF; BFRO; SIS; GCBRO.
101. OBF; BFRO; SIS.
102. OBF; BFRP; SIS.
103. OBF; SIS; BFRO.
104. BFRO; SIS.
105. SIS; OBF.
106. IBS.
107. Ibid.
108. Ibid.; OBF.
109. IBS; Email to the author from Chief Criminal Deputy Gene Seiber, October 29, 2009; OBF.
110. IBS.

CHAPTER 8

1. Rose, p. 51; "Tamanous," http://wiki.dumpshock.com/index.php/Tamanous.
2. Coghlan, *Dictionary of Cryptozoology*, pp. 238. 270; British Hominid Research, http://www.britishhominidresearch.co.uk; Unknown Large Herbivores, http://www.angelfire.com/bc2/crypt-odominion/biggame.html.
3. "Water deer," http://en.wikipedia.org/wiki/Water_deer; "Muntjac," http://en.wikipedia.org/wiki/Muntjac.
4. Elk Ivory Teeth, http://www.elkusa.com/elk_ivory_teeth.htm; "General notes," *New York Times*, June 18, 1900.
5. Quoted in Green, *Sasquatch*, pp. 45-6.
6. IBS.
7. Eberhardt, pp. 23, 388, 518.
8. Journals of Lewis and Clark, http://xroads.virginia.edu/~HYPER/journals/LEWIS.html.
9. Ibid.
10. Gary Moulton, ed., *The Definitive Journals of Lewis and Clark, Vol. 9* (Lincoln, Nebraska: University of Nebraska Press, 2003), p. 44.
11. Janet Bord, *Fairies: Real Encounters with Little People* (New York: Dell, 1997), p. 96; 1950 Humanoid Reports, http://www.ufoinfo.com/humanoid/humanoid1950.shtml
12. 1952 Humanoid Reports, http://www.ufoinfo.com/humanoid/humanoid1952.shtml.
13. 1965 Humanoid Sighting Reports, http://www.ufoinfo.com/humanoid/humanoid1965.shtml.
14. Humanoid Contact Database, http://www.iraap.org/rosales/1999.htm.
15. 2000 Humanoid Reports, http://www.ufoinfo.com/humanoid/humanoid2000.shtml.
16. *Strange Magazine*, http://www.strangemag.com/firstperson.html#giantshrimp.
17. Ibid.
18. 1952 Humanoid Reports, http://www.ufoinfo.com/humanoid/humanoid1952.shtml.
19. Ibid.
20. 1976 Humanoid Sighting Reports, http://www.ufoinfo.com/humanoid/humanoid1976.shtml.
21. 1967 Humanoid Reports, http://www.ufoinfo.com/humanoid/humanoid1967.shtml.
22. 1967 Humanoid Reports.
23. 1989 Humanoid Reports, http://www.ufoinfo.com/humanoid/humanoid1989.shtml.
24. Humanoid Contact Database, http://www.iraap.org/rosales/1992.htm.
25. Ibid.
26. 1995 Humanoid Sighting Reports, http://www.ufoinfo.com/humanoid/humanoid1995.shtml.
27. 1996 Humanoid Reports, http://www.ufoinfo.com/humanoid/humanoid1996.shtml.
28. 1998 Humanoid Reports, http://www.ufoinfo.com/humanoid/humanoid1998.shtml.
29. 1999 Humanoid Reports, http://www.ufoinfo.com/humanoid/humanoid1999.shtml.
30. 2004 Humanoid Reports, http://www.ufoinfo.com/humanoid/humanoid2004.shtml.
31. 2008 Humanoid Reports, http://www.ufoinfo.com/humanoid/humanoid2008.shtml.
32. Ibid.
33. Ibid..
34. "Night terror," http://en.wikipedia.org/wiki/Night_terror; "Sleep paralysis," http://en.wikipedia.org/wiki/Sleep_paralysis.
35. IBS.
36. Ibid.
37. 1965 Humanoid Sighting Reports.
38. Coleman, *Mothman*, p. 10; "Toledo, Oregon,"http://en.wikipedia.org/wiki/Toledo,_Oregon; Ted Cox, "The Toledo Incident of 1925," http://www.old-worldpublications.com/index.htm.
39. Coleman, *Mothman*, p. 10; 1966 Humanoid Reports, http://www.ufoinfo.com/humanoid/humanoid1966.shtml.
40. 1966 Humanoid Reports.
41. Bald Mountain, WA, http://www.lat-long.com/Latitude-Longitude-1529131-Washington-Bald_Mountain.html; Marsh, p. 23.
42. 1974 Humanoid Sightings, http://www.ufoinfo.com/humanoid/humanoid1974.shtml; Marsh, p. 23.
43. Marsh, p. 23.
44. 1978 Humanoid Reports, http://www.ufoinfo.com/humanoid/humanoid1978.shtml.
45. 1979 Humanoid Reports, http://www.ufoinfo.com/humanoid/humanoid1979.shtml.
46. Nick Redfern, "Dark Visitors: Puerto Rico's Moca Vampire," http://www.ufomystic.com/the-redfern-files/moca-vampire1.
47. Humanoid Contact Database, http://www.iraap.org/rosales/1993.htm.
48. IBS.
49. Ibid.
50. Ibid.
51. Ibid.
52. 1969 Humanoid Reports, http://www.ufoinfo.com/humanoid/humanoid1969.shtml.
53. Humanoid Contact Database, http://www.iraap.org/rosales/1995.html.

54. Humanoid Contact Database, http://www.iraap.org/rosales/2005.html.
55. Moonshine Park, http://www.co.lincoln.or.us/lcparks/moonshine.html.
56. "Oregon Creature," http://paranormal.about.com/library/blstory_august03_27.htm; "The Mysterious Creature in Oregon," http://paranormal.about.com/library/blstory_june04_06.htm.
57. Larch Corrections Center, http://www.doc.wa.gov/facilities/prison/lcc; 1995 Humanoid Sighting Reports, http://www.ufoinfo.com/humanoid/humanoid1995.shtml.
58. 1995 Humanoid Sighting Reports.
59. 1996 Humanoid Reports, http://www.ufoinfo.com/humanoid/humanoid1996.shtml.
60. Ibid.
61. Ibid.
62. IBS.
63. "Reptilian humanoid," http://en.wikipedia.org/wiki/Reptilian_humanoid; "Lizard Men," http://www.americanmonsters.com/monsters/hyrbid/index.php?detail=article&idarticle=100.
64. 1995 Humanoid Sighting Reports.
65. Humanoid Contact Database, http://www.iraap.org/rosales/1998.html.
66. Arment, "A Western Oddity"; "The Creature of the Dump," http://paranormal.about.com/library/weekly/aa051401a.html.
67. Arment, "A Western Oddity."
68. "Strange Shelled Creature," http://paranormal.about.com/library/blstory_july01_11.html.
69. Autumn Williams, OBF Blog, http://www.oregonbigfoot.com/blog/bigfoot/dogmen-again-im-supposed-to-be-looking-for-bigfoot/?utm_source=feedburner&utm_medium=feed&utm_campaign=Feed%3A+OregonBigfootBlog+%28Oregon+Bigfoot+Blog%29.
70. Ibid.
71. Ibid.
72. Kimba D'Michi email, posted to the Chupacabra newsgroup (chupacabra@yahoogroups.com) on April 26, 2004.
73. Ibid.
74. Jessie Stensland, "Mutilated cats mystery draws worldwide attention," *Tacoma Daily Index*, July 23, 2005; "Linda Moulton Howe," http://en.wikipedia.org/wiki/Linda_Moulton_Howe.
75. Coghlan, Cryptosup, p. 33; Ellin Betz, Her-PET-POURRI, http://ebeltz.net/column/chs/2005colu.html.
76. Coghlan, Dictionary of Cryptozoology, p. 109.
77. "Seaside, Oregon," http://en.wikipedia.org/wiki/Seaside,_Oregon; Oregon Campgrounds, http://web.oregon.com/recreation/camping/camping_map.cfm; Oregon Parks and Recreation Department, http://www.oregon.gov/OPRD/PARKS/camping.shtml; RV Parks and Campgrounds, http://www.rv-clubs.us/oregon_rv_campgrounds.html#Coast; Coghlan, *Dictionary*, pp. 109, 271.
78. Bigfoot's Pub 'n Grub, http://www.yelp.com/biz/bigfoots-pub-n-grub-seaside.

Creature Index

Bibliography

"A Sasquatch alert in the Hoh Rain Forest." Seattle, Washington: *Seattle Post-Intelligencer*, July 1, 2000.

Adams, J.D. "Oregon Mysteries of the Sea." Accessed at http://www.travel-to-oregon-tips.com/mystery-sea.html.

"Alligator-like creature spotted in Puyallup pond." Seattle, Washington: KIRO-TV Channel 7, August 18, 2005.

Arment, Chad. *The Historical Bigfoot*. Landisville, Pennsylvania: Coachwhip Books, 2006.

Arnold, Neil. *Monster! The A-Z of Zooform Phenomena*. Bideford, North Devon, U.K.: CFZ Press, 2007.

"A Western Oddity." North American BioFortean Review 3 (May 2006): 73-5.

Baker, Mark. "Shadowing Bigfoot." Eugene, Oregon: Register-Guard, December 17, 2006.

Beck, Ellen. "Things we don't understand." Spokane, Washington: Spokesman-Review, May 29, 2003.

Beck, Ronald. *I Fought the Apemen of Mount St. Helens, Wa.* Kelso, Washington: self-published, 1967.

Bigfoot Central, http://www.angelfire.com/biz/bigfootcentral.

Bigfoot Encounters, http://www.bigfootencounters.com/sbs/ebbetts.htm.

Bigfoot Field Researchers Organization, http://www.bfro.net.

"Bigfoot leaves trail—161 steps." *Seattle Times*, October 16, 1974.

"Bigfoot prints examined." Lewiston, Idaho: *Lewiston Tribune*, January 29, 1976.

"Bigfoot reported." *The Columbian*, July 2, 2003.

"Bigfoot tracks." Centralia, Washington: *Daily Chronicle*, May 2, 1977.

Blair, Seabury. "Sasquatch not a mystery to some." *Kitsap Sun*, November 7, 2006.

Boersma, P. Dee, Sarah Reichard, and Amy Van Buren. *Invasive Species in the Pacific Northwest*. Seattle, Washington: University of Washington Press, 2006.

Bord, Janet, and Colin Bord. *Alien Animals*. Harrisburg, Pennsylvania: Stackpole, 1981.

 Bigfoot Casebook Updated. Enumclaw, Washington: Pine Winds Press, 2006.

 Unexplained Mysteries of the 20th Century. Chicago, Illinois: Contemporary Books, 1989.

Borgaard, Cheryll. "Most notorious — A legend or just elusive?" Longview, Washington: *Daily News*, April 30, 2006.

Bragg, Lynn. *Myths and Mysteries of Washington*. Guilford, Connecticut: Globe Pequot Press, 2005.

British Center for Bigfoot Research, http://british-bigfoot.tripod.com/britishbigfootresearch-center/id7.html.

Burns, Phyllis. "Lake spirits of Washington State." Accessed at http://www.bellaonline.com/articles/art22990.asp.

Chasan, Daniel. "If sturgeon could talk." Accessed at http://crosscut.com/2009/04/29/animals-wildlife/18962/?pagejump=1

Ciams, Peter. "Colossal Claude and Marvin the Monster." Portland, Oregon: *The Oregonian*, September 24, 1967.

Clark, Ella. *Indian Legends of the Pacific Northwest*. Berkeley, California: University of California Press, 2003.

Clark, Jerome. *Unnatural Phenomena*. Santa Barbara, California: ABC-CLIO, 2005.

Clark, Jerome, and Loren Coleman. *Creatures of the Outer Edge*. New York, New York: Warner, 1978.

Coblentz, Bruce, and Cassie Bouska. *Pest Risk Assessment for Feral Pigs in Oregon*. Corvallis, Oregon: Department of Fisheries and Wildlife, 2007.

Cockle, Richard. "Smitten Bigfooters keep making tracks into the Blue Mountains." Portland, Oregon: *The Oregonian*, March 20, 2005.

Coghlan, Ronan. *Cryptosup*. Bangor, North Ireland: Xiphos, 2005.

 A Dictionary of Cryptozoology. Bangor, North Ireland: Xiphos, 2004.

 Further Cryptozoology. Bangor, North Ireland: Xiphos, 2007.

Coleman, Loren. *Bigfoot!* New York, New York: Paraview, 2003.

 Mothman and Other Curious Encounters. New York, New York: Paraview, 2002.

 Mysterious America. New York, New York: Paraview, 2001.

Coleman, Loren, and Paul Huyghe. *The Field Guide to Bigfoot, Yeti, and Other Mystery Primates Worldwide*. New York, New York: Avon, 1999.

 The Field Guide to Lake Monsters, Sea Serpents, and Other Mystery Denizens of the Deep. New York, New York: Tarcher/Penguin, 2003.

"The Creature of the Dump." Paranormal Phenomena, http://paranormal.about.com/library/weekly/aa051401a.html.

DeFranceschi, Joe. "Nile monitor: Six-foot lizard caught by dad Ryan Nelson." *Associated Press*, September 9, 2008.

Desiano, Dionne. "Tracking Bigfoot." University of Washington, Seattle: *The Daily*, May 6, 2005.

DeWire, Elinor. *The Lightkeepers' Menagerie: Stories of Animals at Lighthouses*. Sarasota, Florida: Pineapple Press, 2007.

Dorpat, Paul. "Now or never: The Madrona sea monster." *Pacific Northwest Magazine* (Seattle Times), April 1, 2001.

"Eastern Oregon couple cashes in on 'Bigfoot kit.'" Portland, Oregon: KATU-TV, Channel 2, July 30, 2001.

Ellison, Bob. "Don't shoot that Bigfoot." Focus on Agriculture (American Farm Bureau Federation), July 28, 2000.

Fattig, Paul. "Bigfoot beware." Medford, Oregon: *Mail Tribune*, August 24, 2006.

"'I've always believed there is a Bigfoot.'" Medford, *Oregon: Mail Tribune*, September 3, 2006.

Fisher, David. "'Sasquatch cast' makes a big impression on anatomists, TV." Seattle, Washington: *Seattle Post-Intelligencer*, June 17, 2002.

"Footprints of 'Bigfoot' reported." Lewiston, Idaho: *Lewiston Tribune*, January 27, 1976.

Freeman, Mark. ""Johnson out to prove Bigfoot is not a myth." Medford, Oregon: *Mail Tribune*, April 3, 2003.

Garner, Betty. *Monster! Monster!* Blaine, Washington: Hancock House, 1995.

Gordon, David. *Field Guide to the Sasquatch*. Seattle, Washington: Sasquatch Books, 1992.

Green, John. *On the Track of the Sasquatch*. New York, New York: Ballantine, 1973.

    Sasquatch: The Apes Among Us. Blaine, Washington: Hancock House, 1978.

    The Sasquatch File. Victoria, British of Columbia: Cheam, 1978.

Guenette, Robert, and Frances Guenette. *The Mysterious Monsters*. Los Angeles, California: Schick Sun, 1975.

Guiley, Rosemary. *Atlas of the Mysterious in North America*. New York, New York: Facts on File, 1995.

Gulf Coast Bigfoot Research Organization, http://www.gcbro.com.

Hall, Mark. *Thunderbirds*. New York, New York: Paraview, 2004.

Hammers, Scott. "Domain of the hairy man?" Lake Oswego, Oregon: *Lake Oswego Review*, March 11, 2004.

Haney, Nick. "Is Bigfoot lurking on the Hoh?" Port Angeles, Washington: *Peninsula Daily News*, June 29, 2000.

Hannula, Don. "Many may scoff but...Deputy insists he watched Sasquatch." Seattle, Washington: *Seattle Times*, March 18, 1971.

"Secret's out: Sasquatch 'sighting' admitted.' Seattle, Washington: *Seattle Times*, June 16, 1970.

Hansen, Mary. "A big, hairy, wild idea." Eugene, Oregon: *Register-Guard*, April 25, 2005.

Hauck, Dennis. *Haunted Places*. New York, New York: Penguin, 1996.

Henriksen, Erik. "I hunt the giant man-ape." Portland, Oregon: *Portland Mercury*, September 11, 2003.

Herndon, Charles. "Georgia woman discovers the mystery of Crater Lake." Ft. Myers, Florida: *News-Press*, May 2, 2002.

Heuvelmans, Bernard. *In the Wake of the Sea Serpents*. New York, New York: Hill and Wang, 1968.

Hillhouse, Vicki. "Country music channel puts Bigfoot spotlight on Walla Walla." *Walla Walla Union-Bulletin*, May 26, 2005.

Holt, Gordy. "Is something lurking in Lake Washington?" Seattle, Washington: *Seattle Post-Intelligencer*, March 1, 2005.

"I saw the Crater Lake monster." Farshores, http://farshores.org:80/pytt11.html.

International Bigfoot Society, http://www.internationalbigfootsociety.com.

Jewett, Dave. "Native son tries hand at television writing." *The Columbian*, September 7, 1999.

Kamb, Lewis. "Big sturgeon a rare catch here." Seattle, Washington: *Seattle Post-Intelligencer*, June 10, 2005.

Kirk, John. *In the Domain of the Lake Monsters*. Toronto, Canada: Key Porter Books, 1998.

Krantz, Grover. *Bigfoot Sasquatch Evidence*. Blaine, Washington: Hancock House, 1999.

Kulongoski, Ted. "Bigfoot protector elected Oregon governor." *Washington Post*, November 7, 2002.

LaFountaine, Frank. *The Omak Lake Monster*. Lincoln, Nebraska: iUniverse, 2005.

LeBlond, Paul, and Edward Bousfield. *Cadborosaurus: Survivor from the Deep*. Victoria, British of Columbia: Horsdal & Schubart, 1995.

LeBlond, Paul, and John Sibert. "Observations of large unidentified marine animals in British Columbia and adjacent waters." Vancouver, Canada: Institute of Oceanography, University of British Columbia, 1973.

Lind, Carol. *Western Gothic*. Seattle, Washington: self-published, 1983.

Lisi, Therese. "Nile monitor lizard caught in Grant's Pass, Oregon." *Associated Press*, September 9, 2008.

Long, Greg. "The Monster of Conser Lake," http://www.geocities.com/Area51/Shadowlands/6583/cattle066.html.

Longoria, Ruth. "Lake Washington Loch Ness Monster?" *Mercer Island Reporter*, March 10, 2005.

"The Madrona Sea-Monster." *Western Folklore 6* (April 1947): 187.

"Man, beast or Sasquatch?" Aberdeen, Washington: *Aberdeen World*, April 21, 1982.

"Man offering $1 million for a baby Bigfoot." *FlashNews*, March 10, 1998, http://www.flashnews.com/news/9jtt8jt0.htm.

Mangiacopra, Gary, and Dwight Smith. Chad Arment (ed.). "Freshwater Cephalopods." *Cryptozoology and the Investigation of Lesser-Known Mystery Animals*. Landisville, Pennsylvania: Coachwhip, 2006.

Marsh, Carole. *Washington History! Surprising Stories About Our State's Founding Mothers, Fathers & Kids!* Peachtree City, Georgia: Gallopade International, 1996.

Marshall, John. "Surviving in Bigfoot's backyard." Fort Wayne, Indiana: *Ft. Wayne Journal Gazette*, June 16, 2006.

"Mass media fakers strike again." San Diego, California: KFMB-TV Channel 8, May 29, 2002.

McBee, Dave. "Menace on Lake Washington," http://www.getlostmagazine.com/mcbee/1999/9911monster/monster.html.

McGauley, Jennifer. "Is Sasquatch for real?" Grays Harbor, Washington: *Grays Harbor Chronicle*, June 13, 1984.

McGuire, Richard. "Brief to the Standing Policy Committee for Agriculture and Rural Development." Western Stock Grower, February 27, 1996.

Meldrum, Jeff. *Sasquatch: Legend Meets Science*. New York, New York: Forge, 2006.

Miletch, Steve. "Bigfoot follow-up: Expert tracker finds 8 possible prints along Willow Road." Bellevue, Washington: Journal American, January 10, 1978.

Miller, Henry. "Fourth of July outing ends with mysterious catch." Salem, Oregon: *Statesman Journal*, July 21, 2005.

"From bigfoot to pesky deer, readers have their stories." Salem, Oregon: *Statesman Journal*, October 6, 2005.

"The mystery of Willamina's gator." Salem, Oregon: *Statesman Journal*, May 15, 2003.

"Monster Time." *Fate 17* (August 1964): 18-20.

Morris, Scott. "Pigs run hog wild in the Olympics." *High Country News*, October 22, 2001; http://www.hcn.org/ issues/213/10799.

Munroe, Bill. "Organization is on Bigfoot's trail." Portland, Oregon: *The Oregonian*, June 12, 2006.

Murphy, Christopher. *Bigfoot Encounters in Ohio*. Blaine, Washington: Hancock House, 2006.

Murvosh, Marta. "Desperately seeking Sasquatch." *Skagit Valley Herald*, May 22, 2005.

Newton, Michael. *Encyclopedia of Cryptozoology*. Jefferson, North Carolina: McFarland, 2005.

"No forgetting the Sasquatch." Seattle, Washington: *Seattle Times*, October 17, 1974.

Norman, Eric. *The Abominable Snowmen*. New York, New York: Award, 1969.

"Olympic Peninsula man reports Bigfoot sighting." *Associated Press*, June 16, 2002.

Oppegard, Brett. "Bigfoot: Soul of a region." *The Columbian*, December 11, 2000.

OregonBigfoot.com, http://www.oregonbigfoot.com.

"Oregon police look for escaped alligator." Fort Wayne, Indiana: *Ft. Wayne News-Sentinel*, June 18, 2005.

Porto, Laura. "In search of Bigfoot with a PC." Northwest Digital IQ, April 15, 2001.

"Researchers disagree on Bigfoot reports." Seattle, Washington: *Seattle Post-Intelligencer*, July 6, 2000.

Roberts, C. R. "Mount Rainier-area youth has close encounter in the foothills." *Tacoma News Tribune*, April 24, 1994.

Rose, Carol. *Giants, Monsters & Dragons*. New York, New York: W.W. Norton, 2000.

Sanderson, Ivan. *Abominable Snowmen: Legend Come to Life*. Philadelphia, Pennsylvania: Chilton, 1961.

Sandsberry, Scott. "Tracking the ghost." *Yakima Herald-Republic*, February 23, 2006.

Sasquatch Information Society, http://www.bigfootinfo.org.

"Sasquatch watch!" Ocean Shores, Washington: *Ocean Observer*, August 17, 1969.

Sauls, Jane. "Southern Oregon Bigfoot lore." Jackson County, Oregon: *Jackson County News*, August 16, 2004.

Schleif, Rachel. "Man blames car wreck on prehistoric winged reptile." *Wenatchee World*, December 29, 2007.

"The Sea Serpent of the Pacific." New York, New York: *New York Times*, July 8, 1896.

"Searchers report huge footprints." *Tacoma News Tribune*, February 19, 1975.

Sheppard-Wolford, Sali. *Valley of the Skookum*. Enumclaw, Washington: Pine Winds Press, 2006.

Shuker, Karl. *Mystery Cats of the World*. London, England: Robert Hale, 1989.

Skinner, Charles. *Myths and Legends of Our Own Land*. Philadelphia, Pennsylvania: J.B. Lippincott, 1896.

Slate, Ann, and Alan Berry. *Bigfoot*. New York, New York: Bantam, 1976.

Snyder, Chad. "New book tells tall tale, but not necessarily a false one." *Curry Pilot*, August 12, 2009.

Stensland, Jessie. "Mutilated cats mystery draws worldwide interest." *Tacoma Daily Index*, July 23, 2005.

Stofflet, John. "Does Bigfoot walk the Northwest forests?" Seattle, Washington: KING-TV Channel 5, October 4, 2001.

"Strange lizard found in Oregon." Philadelphia, Pennsylvania: WPVI-TV Channel 6, June 28, 2005.

Terry, John. "Bigfoot legend lives large in Northwest lore, locales." Portland, Oregon: *The Oregonian*, June 5, 2005.

——. "A Bigfoot's infamous career leaves wide trail of mayhem." Portland, Oregon: *The Oregonian*, May 29, 2005.

Tetpon, John. "Sasquatch, real or imagined?" Portland, Oregon: *Seattle Courant*, April 4, 2009.

"Tracks of Sasquatch make near-believers of couple." Kirkland, Washington: *East Side Journal*, November 25, 1970.

Washington Bigfoot Sightings, www.spacepub.com/users/data/bigfoot/was/was.html.

Warren, Sidney. *Farthest Frontier: The Pacific Northwest*. New York, New York: Macmillan, 1949.

Washington Department of Fish and Wildlife, "Wildlife agency seeks information on wild pigs" (June 22, 2001), http://wdfw.wa.gov/do/newreal/release.php?id=jun2201a.

"Washington tracks." Montesano, Washington: *The Vidette*, April 29, 1982.

Wiley, John. "Giant earthworm resurfaces after nearly two decades." Seattle, Washington: *Seattle Post-Intelligencer*, May 27, 2006.

"You can search for Bigfoot near Applegate." Medford, Oregon: *Mail Tribune*, September 19, 2005.